THE CHARLES DICKENS COOKBOOK

Brenda Marshall

REED

Author's Note
The recipes in this book are intended for those who take pleasure both in food and in the writings of Charles Dickens. Nearly all the dishes described here, although they belonged to the nineteenth-century table, can be cooked and enjoyed today, although some of the recipes have been given for their idiosyncratic and informative value alone.

Sometimes ingredients and quantities have been changed, although the occasion for alteration rarely arose, in spite of the myth that recipes in the past have called for extraordinary feats on the parts of cooks and household economies. Those oddities that do appear usually do so because of the difference between then and today in what was readily available. I am extremely grateful to the cooks and writers of the last century who troubled to record their recipes, and on whose works I have drawn.

A H & A W REED PTY LTD
2 Aquatic Drive Frenchs Forest NSW 2086
68 Kingsford-Smith Street Wellington 3 NZ

First published 1979 as Mr Pickwick's Plentiful Portions 1980.
This edition 1982

© Brenda Marshall 1982

All rights reserved. No part of this publication may be
reproduced, stored in a retrieval system or transmitted
in any form or by any means electronic, mechanical,
photocopying, recording or otherwise, without the prior
written permission of the publishers.

National Library of Australia
Cataloguing-in-Publication Data
Marshall, Brenda, 1938—.
  The Charles Dickens Cookbook.
  Originally published as: Mr Pickwick's plentiful
  portions. Sydney: Reed, 1980.
  Includes index.
  ISBN 0 589 50379 0.
  1. Dickens, Charles 1812-1870. 2. Cookery. I. Title.
641'.5

Printed by Kyodo Shing Loong Printing Industries Pte Ltd, Singapore

Contents

Soups and invalid food 7
Fish 13
Lamb and mutton and their sauces 25
Veal and beef and their sauces 37
Pork and its sauces 53
Chicken and goose and their sauces 59
Savoury Pies 67
Variety meats and sausages 79
Potatoes and yorkshire pudding 105
Puddings and desserts 111
Biscuits, cakes, etc. 135
Drinks and beverages 153
Miscellaneous 167
Index 175

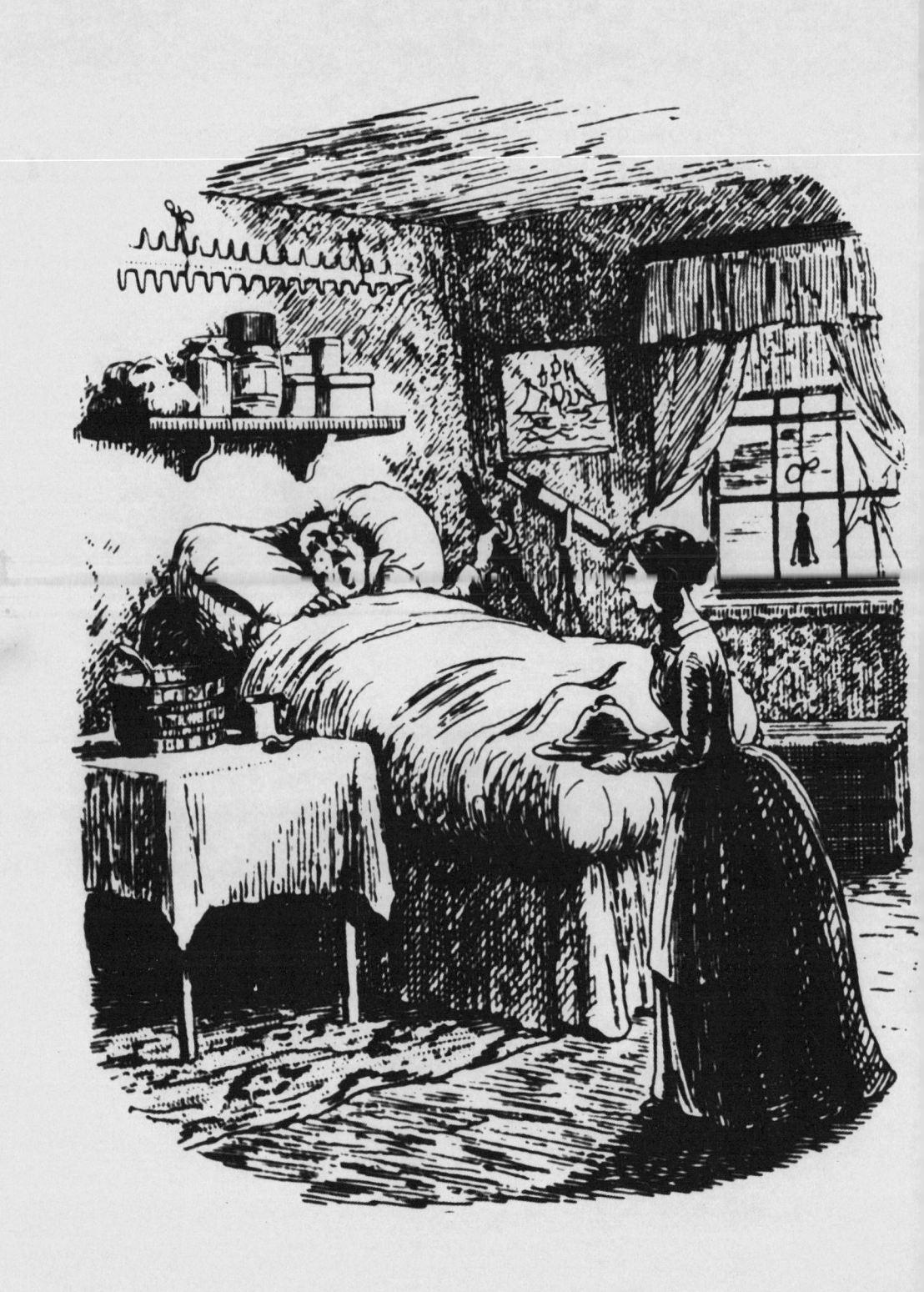

Old Bill Barley's grog is ready-mixed in a little tub on the table

Soups and Invalid Food

MUTTON BROTH WITH A CHOP

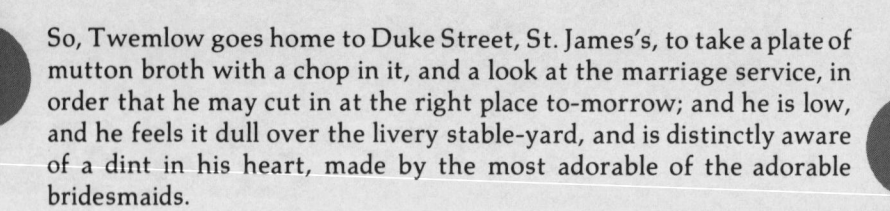

So, Twemlow goes home to Duke Street, St. James's, to take a plate of mutton broth with a chop in it, and a look at the marriage service, in order that he may cut in at the right place to-morrow; and he is low, and he feels it dull over the livery stable-yard, and is distinctly aware of a dint in his heart, made by the most adorable of the adorable bridesmaids.

Our Mutual Friend Ch X

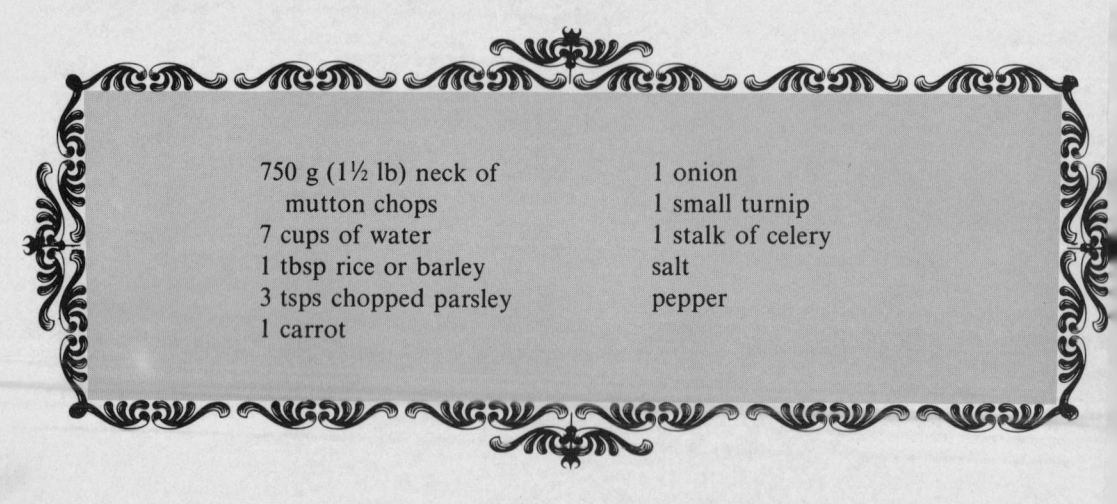

750 g (1½ lb) neck of mutton chops
7 cups of water
1 tbsp rice or barley
3 tsps chopped parsley
1 carrot
1 onion
1 small turnip
1 stalk of celery
salt
pepper

Trim away any surplus fat from the meat. Cut the vegetables into small pieces. Put the meat into a saucepan with the cold water, and bring to the boil. Skim well, add the rice or barley, salt and pepper, and the vegetables. Simmer for 2 hours, or until the meat is tender. Remove any grease from the top, taste for seasoning, and add the parsley. Serve in wide soup bowls. If preferred, the dish can be divided into a broth and a main course. In that case, use more vegetables in the cooking, and cut them into larger pieces, serving them as a garnish to the meat. To serve the broth, first have the liquid strained. Beat an egg in a soup tureen, then slowly pour the hot broth over it, stirring all the time.

A JUDICIOUS GRAVY SOUP

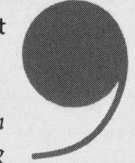

'... I fear the gravy soup for lunch was injudicious. We lost a great many passengers almost immediately afterwards.'

Report of the Second Meeting of the Mudfog Association for the Advancement of Everything

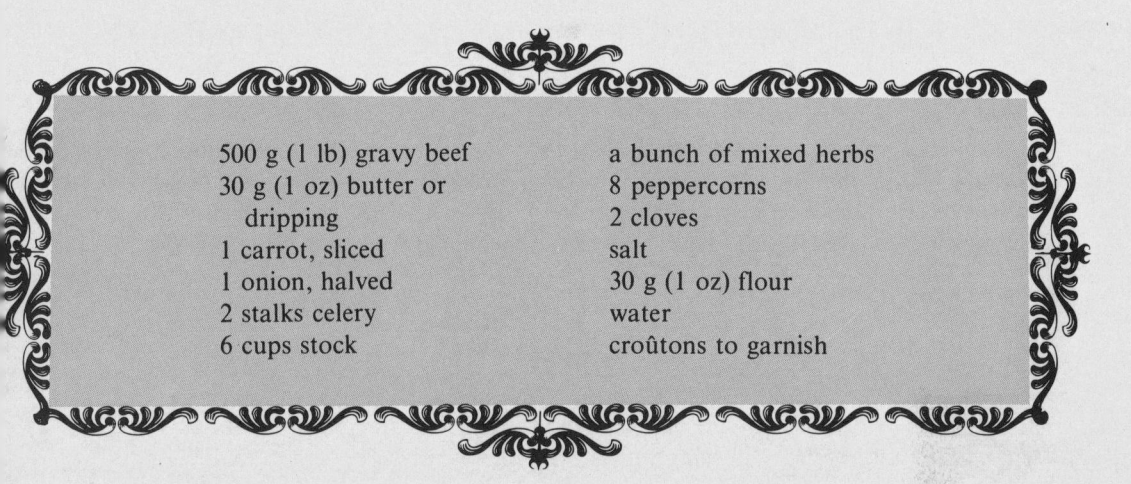

500 g (1 lb) gravy beef
30 g (1 oz) butter or dripping
1 carrot, sliced
1 onion, halved
2 stalks celery
6 cups stock
a bunch of mixed herbs
8 peppercorns
2 cloves
salt
30 g (1 oz) flour
water
croûtons to garnish

Chop the meat into small pieces. Melt the butter or dripping in a saucepan, and add the meat, carrot, onion, and celery. Sauté until brown. Add the stock, mixed herbs, peppercorns, and cloves, and season with salt. Bring to the boil and simmer for 2½ hours. Strain, and return the liquid to the saucepan. Blend the flour with a little cold water, and stir it into the soup. Simmer for 5 minutes, test for seasoning, and serve with croûtons.

A BASIN OF BEEF-TEA

> Refreshment then arrived in the form of chops and strong ale for the ladies, and a basin of beef-tea for the patient ...
>
> *Martin Chuzzlewit* Ch XXIX

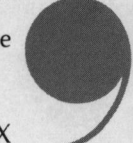

'When one pound of lean beef, free from fat, and separated from the bones, in a finely chopped state in which it is used for sausages or mince-meat, is uniformly mixed with its own weight in cold water, then slowly heated to boiling, and the liquid, after boiling briskly for a minute or two, is strained through a sieve, from the coagulated albumen and the fibrin, which are then become hard and horny, we obtain an equal weight of the most aromatic soup, of such strength as can be had even by boiling for hours from a piece of flesh; also when mixed with salt, and other additions by which soup is usually seasoned, and tinged somewhat darker by means of roasted onions, or burnt sugar, it forms the very best soup that can be prepared from a piece of flesh.'

CAUDLE

> 'And quite a family it is to make tea for,' said Mrs. Gamp; 'and wot a happiness to do it! My good young 'ooman'—to the servant-girl—'p'raps somebody would like to try a new-laid egg or two, not biled too hard. Likeways, a few rounds o' buttered toast, first cuttin' off the crust, in consequence of tender teeth, and not too many of 'em; which Gamp himself, Mrs. Chuzzlewit, at one blow, being in liquor, struck out four, two single and two double, as was took by Mrs. Harris for a keepsake, and is carried in her pocket at this present hour, along with two cramp-bones, a bit o' ginger, and a grater like a blessed infant's shoe, in tin, with a little heel to put the nutmeg in: as many times I've seen and said, and used for caudle when required, within the month.'
>
> *Martin Chuzzlewit* Ch XLVI

Caudle was one of the many efficacious, or otherwise, drinks like gruel, cheese whey, sago posset, vinegar whey, imitation asses' milk, and mustard whey, which filled the columns of that essential part of every housewife's *Guide:* 'Cooking for the Sick':

'Beat up 1 egg to a froth; add 1 wineglass of sherry and ½ pint of gruel; flavour with lemon peel and nutmeg, and sweeten to taste.'

Note: Ale can be substituted for the sherry.

WATER GRUEL AND BARLEY WATER

By dint of powerful medicine, low diet, and bleeding, the symptoms in the course of three days perceptibly decreased. A rigid perseverance in the same course of treatment for only one week, accompanied with small doses of water-gruel, weak broth, and barley-water, led to their entire disappearance.

Report of the First Meeting of the Mudfog Association for the Advancement of Everything

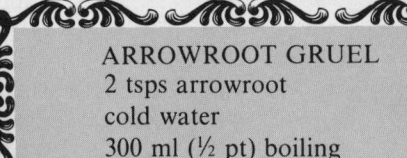

ARROWROOT GRUEL
2 tsps arrowroot
cold water
300 ml (½ pt) boiling water
1 tsp sherry
a pinch of grated nutmeg or lemon peel
sugar to taste

OATMEAL GRUEL
2 tbsps oatmeal
cold water
2½ cups boiling water
a pinch of salt
sugar to taste
cream

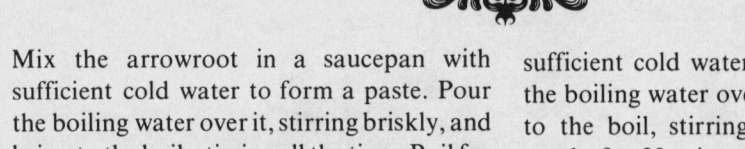

Mix the arrowroot in a saucepan with sufficient cold water to form a paste. Pour the boiling water over it, stirring briskly, and bring to the boil, stirring all the time. Boil for 2 minutes, remove from the heat, add the sherry and the nutmeg or lemon peel, and sugar to taste.

Mix the oatmeal in a saucepan with sufficient cold water to form a paste. Pour the boiling water over it, stirring well. Bring to the boil, stirring all the time. Simmer gently for 30 minutes, then strain. To each cup, add a little sugar and cream, 'when it will be fit for a king'. Alternatively, it can be turned on to toasted bread that has been cut into small pieces.

BARLEY WATER

30 g (1 oz) pearl barley
water
a pinch of salt
red-currant jelly (optional)

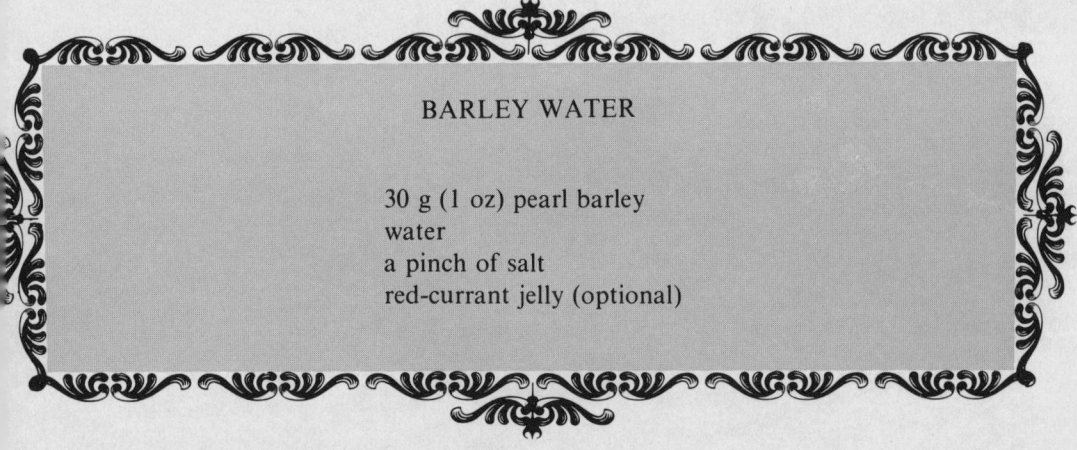

Wash the barley, then place it in a saucepan with 5 cups of water. Bring to the boil, simmer for 4 minutes, then strain, reserving the barley. Place the barley in a saucepan with 10 cups of water, and simmer with the lid off until the liquid is reduced by one half. Stir in a pinch of salt. Strain. The liquid can be flavoured with red-currant jelly if preferred.

Polly Poodle confronts the Dombey household

Fish

LOBSTER SALAD

> At dinner, too, Mr. Leaver *would* steal Mrs. Leaver's tongue, and Mrs. Leaver *would* retaliate upon Mr. Leaver's fowl; and when Mrs. Leaver was going to take some lobster salad, Mr. Leaver wouldn't let her have any, saying that it made her ill, and she was always sorry for it afterwards, which afforded Mrs. Leaver an opportunity for pretending to be cross, and showing many other prettinesses.
>
> *Sketches of Young Couples*

> All the servants in the meantime, have been breakfasting below. Champagne has grown too common among them to be mentioned, and roast fowls, raised pies, and lobster-salad, have become mere drugs.
>
> *Dombey and Son* Ch XXXI

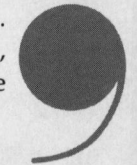

It will be a rare occasion—unfortunately it is not one grown 'too common'—when lobster is had for breakfast, or is experimented with rashly. Unless prepared with care by a chef, it is best to enjoy the sweetness and succulence of the flesh with no more than a garnish of lemon, or a very good mayonnaise. However, Dickens did, obviously, give a nod to lobster salad, it being made from a creature then in plentiful supply. The salad itself is one that supports the view that lobster should be treated simply—the meat is merely cooked and served with salad greens and a well-flavoured cold sauce. So, to provide a salad such as the skills of Mr Dombey's cook might have produced:

Remove the meat from a cooked hen lobster, reserving the coral. Take some lettuce, endive, and any other salad greens in season, then wash and dry them. Have ready for decorative garnish some chopped cooked beetroot, sliced cucumber, and 2 hard-boiled eggs. Make a sauce by blending to a perfectly smooth mixture 4 tablespoons of oil, 2 tablespoons of vinegar (lemon juice is an alternative), 1 teaspoon of made mustard, and the yolks of 2 eggs. A proper consistency will best be produced by blending the egg-yolks and mustard, then gradually adding, drop by drop, the oil, stirring well all the time. Finally blend in the vinegar or lemon juice; add some salt and pepper; then add just a quarter of a teaspoon of anchovy sauce. To prepare the finished dish, mix well together, but lightly, the salad greens, then toss half of the broken lobster meat among these. Separate the whites from the yolks of the hard-boiled eggs. Chop the whites finely; pass the yolks through a sieve; pass the lobster coral through a sieve. Arrange the salad greens and tossed lobster meat on a glass dish and garnish: 'first with a row of sliced cucumber, then with the [remaining] pieces of lobster, the yolks and whites of the eggs, coral, and beetroot placed alternately, and arrange in small separate bunches, so that the colours contrast nicely'.

WHITEBAIT AT GREENWICH

'What a dinner! Specimens of all the fishes that swim in the sea, surely had swum their way to it, and if samples of the fishes of divers colours that made a speech in the Arabian Nights (quite a ministerial explanation in respect of cloudiness), and then jumped out of the frying-pan, were not to be recognised, it was only because they had all become of one hue by being cooked in batter among the whitebait. And the dishes being seasoned with Bliss—an article which they are sometimes out of, at Greenwich—were of perfect flavour, and the golden drinks had been bottled in the golden age and hoarding up their sparkles ever since.'

Our Mutual Friend Bk 4 Ch IV

Spread out the whitebait, and pick over the fish, removing any that are broken. Have ready 1 tablespoon of flour, seasoned with pepper and salt, in a plastic or paper bag. Add approximately 125 g (4 oz) of the whitebait to the bag, and gently coat the fish with the flour. Carefully tip the fish into a strainer, and shake off any surplus flour. Repeat the process until all the fish are coated. Place sufficient whitebait in a frying basket to cover the bottom of it, and lower it into fat that has been heated to just below hazing point. Keep moving the basket while the fish are frying. When they are a golden brown turn them on to absorbent paper. Repeat until all the fish are cooked. Season to taste with cayenne, salt and pepper. 'Dish up on a folded napkin or lace paper, and send the fish to table accompanied with quarters of lemon and thin slices of brown bread and butter.'

PENNYWINKLES FOR TEA

'Oh well, Miss Floy! And won't your Pa be angry neither!' cried a quick voice at the door, proceeding from a short, brown, womanly girl of fourteen, with a snub nose, and black eyes like jet beads. 'When it was 'tickerlerly given out that you wasn't to go and worrit the wet nurse.' 'She don't worry me,' was the surprised rejoinder of Polly. 'I am very fond of children.'

'Oh! but begging your pardon, Mrs. Richards, that don't matter, you know,' returned the black-eyed girl, who was so desperately sharp and biting that she seemed to make one's eyes water. 'I may be very fond of pennywinkles, Mrs. Richards, but it don't follow that I'm to have 'em for tea.'

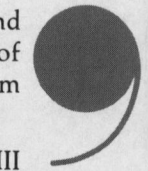

Dombey and Son Ch III

Periwinkles: 'although considered a poor man's luxury, they may be enjoyed by anybody'. It is suggested that they be boiled, and eaten directly while hot, with the addition of pepper and vinegar, to make 'a very nutritious and digestible meal'. The use of vinegar is positively taste-dependent; a small bowl of hot melted butter flavoured with lemon juice and a little garlic, for dipping, might well be an alternative.

OYSTERS, STEWED AND PICKLED

The poultry, which may perhaps be considered to have formed the staple of the entertainment—for there was a turkey at the top, a pair of ducks at the bottom, and two fowls in the middle—disappeared as rapidly as if every bird had the use of its wings, and had flown in desperation down a human throat. The oysters, stewed and pickled, leaped from their capacious reservoirs, and slid by scores into the mouths of the assembly. The sharpest pickles vanished, whole cucumbers at once, like sugar-plums, and no man winked an eye.

Martin Chuzzlewit Ch XVI

What was all this though—even all this—to the extraordinary dissipation that ensued, when Kit, walking into an oyster-shop as bold as if he lived there, and not so much as looking at the counter or the man behind it, led his party into a box—a private box, fitted up with red curtains, white table-cloth and cruet-stand complete—and ordered a fierce gentleman with whiskers, and called him—him, Christopher Nubbles—'sir' to bring three dozen of his largest-sized oysters, and to look sharp about it! Yes, Kit told this gentleman to look sharp; and he not only said he would look sharp, but he actually did, and presently came running back with the newest loaves, and the freshest butter, and the largest oysters, ever seen ... [With a pot of beer] they fell to work upon the supper in earnest; and there was Barbara, that foolish Barbara, declaring that she couldn't eat more than two, and wanting more pressing than you would believe before she would eat four; though her mother and Kit's mother made up for it pretty well, and ate, and laughed, and enjoyed themselves so thoroughly that it did Kit good to see them, and made him laugh and eat likewise from strong sympathy. But the greatest miracle of the night was little Jacob, who ate oysters as if he had been born and bred to the business—sprinkled the pepper and the vinegar with a discretion beyond his years—and afterwards built a grotto on the table with the shells.

The Old Curiosity Shop Ch XXXXIX

Oysters—pickled, stewed, baked, fried and scalloped; oysters made into soups, patties and puddings; oysters with condiments and oysters without; oysters with French rolls or buttered sliced bread—they were the food for all classes. As Sam Weller said, 'the poorer a place is, the greater call there seems to be for oysters. Look here, sir; here's a oyster-stall to every half-dozen houses. The street's lined vith 'em. Blessed if I don't think that ven a man's wery poor, he rushes out of his lodgings, and eats oysters in reg'lar desparation'.

STEWED OYSTERS

'Put a pint of oysters into a stewpan with their own liquor; [scald them, take them out, and strain the liquor]; add to the liquor a quarter of a pint of cream or milk, some mace and cayenne, and a little salt; when it boils stir in an ounce of butter mixed smoothly with some flour, then put in the oysters, bearded, or not, as you choose. A few moment's simmering is sufficient, and when ready to serve add a little lemon-juice.'

PICKLED OYSTERS

Take 100 oysters, and to each half-pint of vinegar take 1 blade of pounded mace, 1 strip of lemon-peel, and 12 black peppercorns. 'Get the oysters in good condition, open them, place them in a saucepan, and let them simmer in their own liquor for about 10 minutes very gently; then take them out one by one, and place them in a jar, and cover them, when cold, with a pickle made as follows:—Measure the oyster-liquor; add to it the same quantity of vinegar, with mace, lemon-peel, and pepper in the above proportion, and boil it for 5 minutes; when cold, pour over the oysters, and tie them down very closely, as contact with the air spoils them ... Put this pickle away in small jars; because, directly one is opened, its contents should immediately be eaten, as they soon spoil. The pickle should not be kept more than 2 or 3 months.'

COD-FISH AND NATIVE OYSTERS

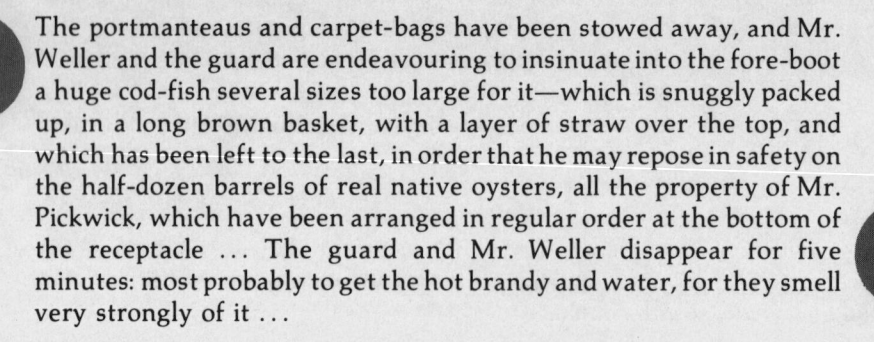

The portmanteaus and carpet-bags have been stowed away, and Mr. Weller and the guard are endeavouring to insinuate into the fore-boot a huge cod-fish several sizes too large for it—which is snuggly packed up, in a long brown basket, with a layer of straw over the top, and which has been left to the last, in order that he may repose in safety on the half-dozen barrels of real native oysters, all the property of Mr. Pickwick, which have been arranged in regular order at the bottom of the receptacle ... The guard and Mr. Weller disappear for five minutes: most probably to get the hot brandy and water, for they smell very strongly of it ...

The Pickwick Papers Ch XXVIII

Such a large cod would probably have been divided into several portions to be cooked, the head and shoulders being gently poached, then sent to the table on a napkin, garnished with lemon and horseradish, to be served with oyster sauce and plain melted butter. The gelatinous parts about the head and neck were much prized. Other slices might have been poached, ready to serve as a cold-table dish, others fried in butter and doused in cream for the last part of the cooking, while yet another portion, combined with such an excess of oysters, might well have gone into the making of a cod and oyster pie. The cod sound (the swimming bladder) was considered a delicacy. The sounds, after being simmered in milk, were rolled around a forcemeat based on oysters, anchovies, breadcrumbs and egg, then cooked gently before the fire in a Dutch oven.

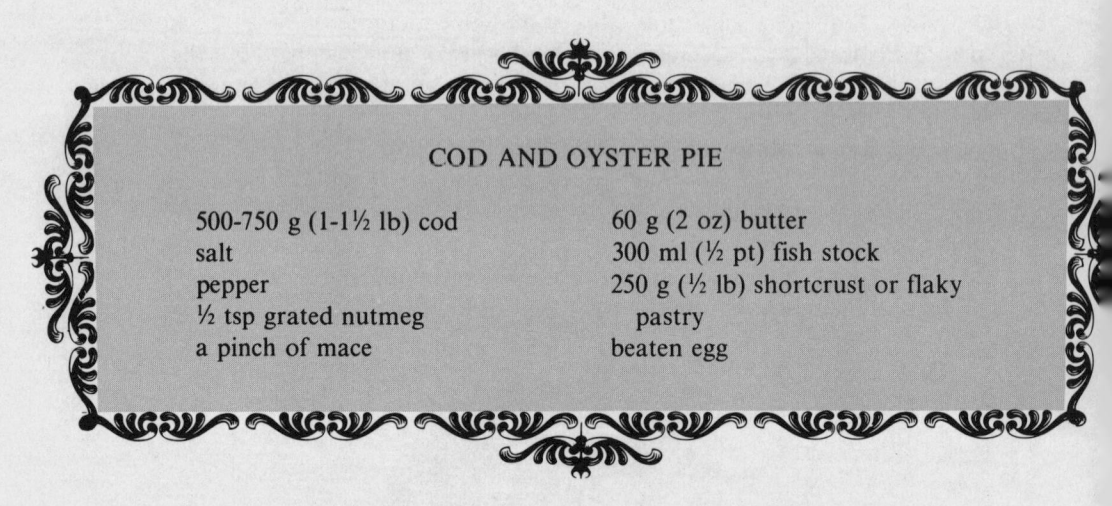

COD AND OYSTER PIE

500-750 g (1-1½ lb) cod
salt
pepper
½ tsp grated nutmeg
a pinch of mace
60 g (2 oz) butter
300 ml (½ pt) fish stock
250 g (½ lb) shortcrust or flaky pastry
beaten egg

Place the cod slices in a pie dish, and season with nutmeg, mace, salt and pepper. Add the butter and stock. Roll out the pastry on a floured board, and cut a strip to be placed around the dampened edge of the pie dish. Dampen the strip, then cover the dish with pastry, pressing the edges well to seal them. Make a hole in the centre of the pastry, and glaze the top with beaten egg. Bake at 220°C (425°F) for 15 minutes, then lower the heat to 180°C (350°F) and bake for a further 30 minutes. During the last stages of cooking, protect the pastry with greaseproof paper if it seems in danger of becoming too brown.

The Sauce:

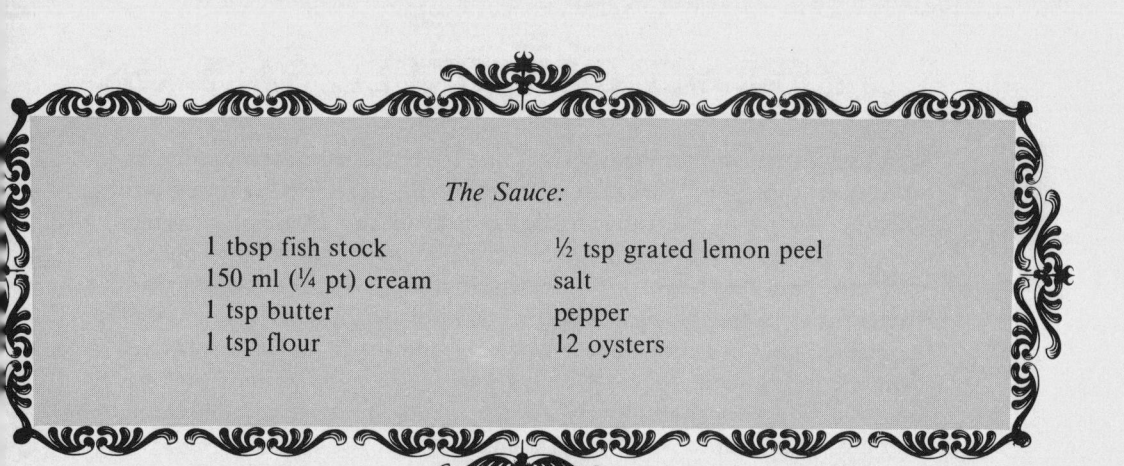

1 tbsp fish stock
150 ml (¼ pt) cream
1 tsp butter
1 tsp flour
½ tsp grated lemon peel
salt
pepper
12 oysters

To make the sauce: Heat together the stock and the cream. Blend together the butter and flour, and add the mixture in small pieces to the liquid, stirring well. Season with salt and pepper, and add the lemon peel and the oysters. Bring to the boil, then immediately remove the pan from the heat. As the sauce is to be poured into the pie, the hole at the top of the cooked pie may have to be enlarged to allow for the addition of the oysters. Pour the sauce into the pie, and serve.

A LITTLE BIT OF PICKLED SALMON

'I think, young woman,' said Mrs. Gamp to the assistant chambermaid, in a tone expressive of weakness, 'that I could pick a little bit of pickled salmon, with a nice little sprig of fennel, and a sprinkling of white pepper. I takes new bread, my dear, with just a little pat of fresh butter, and a mossel of cheese. In case there should be such a thing as a cowcumber in the 'ouse, will you be so kind as bring it, for I'm rather partial to 'em, and they does a world of good in a sick room. If they draws the Brighton Old Tipper here, I takes *that* ale at night, my love; it bein' considered wakeful by the doctors. And whatever you do, young woman, don't bring more than a shilling's-worth of gin and water-warm when I rings the bell a second time; for that is always my allowance, and I never takes a drop beyond!' ...

A tray was brought with everything upon it, even to the cucumber; and Mrs. Gamp accordingly sat down to eat and drink in high good humour. The extent to which she availed herself of the vinegar, and supped up that refreshing fluid with the blade of her knife, can scarcely be expressed in narrative.

Martin Chuzzlewit Ch XXV

This recipe was primarily used as a way in which to help keep the remainder of a whole fish after it had been presented to the table. It can be adapted to irregular quantities and various types of fish, as its basic flavour is one of vinegar:

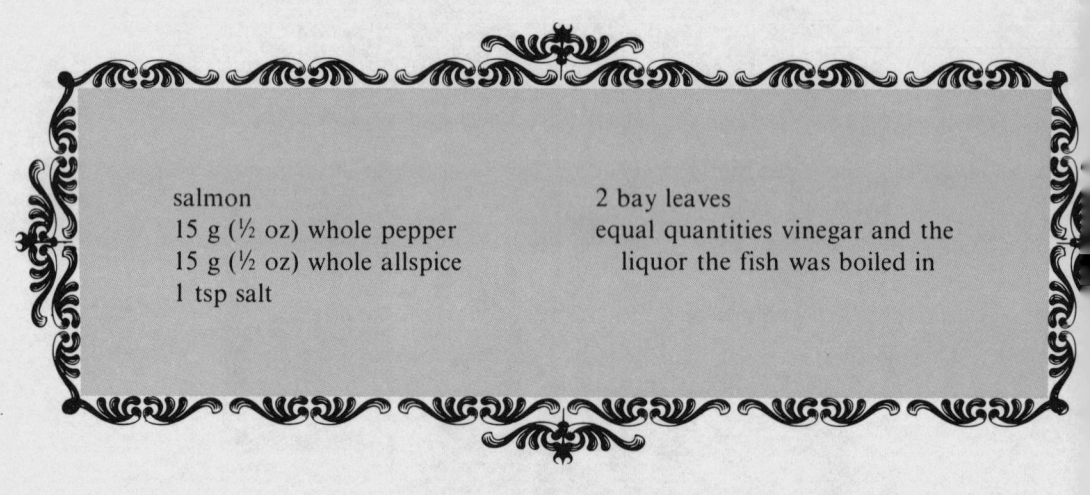

salmon
15 g (½ oz) whole pepper
15 g (½ oz) whole allspice
1 tsp salt
2 bay leaves
equal quantities vinegar and the liquor the fish was boiled in

'After the fish comes from table, lay it in a nice dish with a cover to it, as it should be excluded from the air, and take away the bone; boil the liquor and the vinegar with the other ingredients for 10 minutes, and let it stand to get cold; pour it over the salmon, and in 12 hours this will be fit for the table.'

A SAVOURY MEAL OF YARMOUTH BLOATERS

>Being roused in the morning at the appointed time, and roused with difficulty, after his late fatigues, Quilp instructed Tom Scott to make a fire in the yard of sundry pieces of old timber, and to prepare some coffee for breakfast; for the better furnishings of which repast he entrusted him with certain small moneys, to be expended in the purchase of hot rolls, sugar, Yarmouth bloaters, and other articles of housekeeping; so that in a few minutes a savoury meal was smoking on the board.
>
> *The Old Curiosity Shop* Ch L

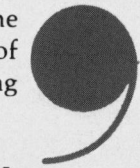

Split the bloaters open and remove the backbone and the roes, if any. Fold back into shape, or place two together with their insides facing. Rub the outsides with some dripping or butter. Grill for approximately 10 minutes, turning them two or three times. Do not allow the fish to become too dry in the cooking. The roe is cooked separately, either fried in a little butter, or brushed with dripping or butter and grilled.

BOILED TURBOT—A NOBLE DISH OF FISH

>It was a noble dish of fish that the housekeeper had put on the table, and we had a joint of equally choice mutton afterwards, and then an equally choice bird. Sauces, wines, all the accessories we wanted, and all of the best, were given out by our host from his dumb-waiter; and when they had made the circuit of the table, he always put them back again. Similarly he dealt us clean plates and knives for each course, and dropped those just disused into two baskets on the ground by his chair. No other attendant than the housekeeper appeared. She set on every dish; and I always saw in her face, a face rising out of the cauldron.
>
> *Great Expectations* Ch XXVI

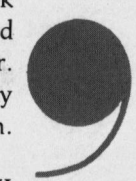

Prepare the turbot, trim the fins but do not cut them off, as the gelatinous parts near them are much prized. Make an incision along the back to prevent the skin cracking. Rub the white side with lemon juice. To cook the fish, it is preferable if a turbot kettle can be used rather than a standard fish kettle, as the former is shaped to suit the fish. If a kettle is not available, wrap the fish in muslin and place it on a plate in a suitable-sized saucepan, to facilitate removal of the fish without breaking it. Cover the fish with hot salted water, and raise the temperature to simmering. Simmer for 15-20 minutes. Serve with shrimp sauce (see later in this section) and a boat of plain melted butter. Garnish with lemon and parsley.

To Serve Turbot:

'First run the fish-slice down the thickest part of the fish lengthwise, quite through to the bone, and then cut handsome and regular slices across the fish until all the meat on the upper side is helped. When the carver has removed all the meat from the upper side of the fish, the backbone should be raised, put on one side of the fish, and the under side helped as the upper.'

A PAIR OF SOLES

I have my doubts, too, founded on the acute experience acquired at this period of my life, whether a sound enjoyment of animal food can develop itself freely in any human subject who is always in torment from tight boots. I think the extremities require to be at peace before the stomach will conduct itself with vigour.
On the occasion of this domestic little party, I did not repeat my former extensive preparations. I merely provided a pair of soles, a small leg of mutton, and a pigeon-pie. Mrs. Crupp broke out into rebellion on my first bashful hint in reference to the cooking of the fish and joint, and said, with a dignified sense of injury, 'No! No, sir! You will not ask me sich a thing; for you are better acquainted with me than to suppose me capable of doing what I cannot do with ampial satisfaction to my own feelings!' But, in the end, a compromise was effected; and Mrs. Crupp consented to achieve this feat, on condition that I dined from home for a fortnight afterwards.

David Copperfield Ch XXVIII

Punctual to five o'clock came the stranger, and shortly afterwards the dinner ...
'What's that?' he inquired, as the waiter removed one of the covers.
'Soles, sir.'
'Soles—ah!—capital fish—all come from London—stagecoach proprietors get up political dinners—carriage of soles—dozens of baskets—cunning fellows. Glass of wine, sir.'

The Pickwick Papers Ch II

'Cleanse and wash the fish carefully, cut off the fins, but do not skin it. Lay it in a fish kettle, with sufficient hot water to cover it, salted ... Let it gradually come to a boil, and keep it simmering for a few minutes, according to the size of the fish. Dish it on a hot napkin after well draining it, and garnish with parsley and cut lemon. Shrimp, or lobster sauce, and plain melted butter, are usually sent to table with this dish ...

'The usual way of helping this fish is to cut it right through, bone and all, distributing it in nice and not too large pieces. A moderately-sized sole will be sufficient for three slices; namely, the head, middle, and tail. The guests should be asked which of these they prefer. A small one will only give two slices. If the sole is very large, the upper side may be raised from the bone, and then divided into pieces; and the underside afterwards served in the same way.'
For Shrimp Sauce, see next recipe.

SHRIMP SAUCE TO PROMOTE QUIET DIGESTION

The neatly-served and well-cooked dinner (for everything about the Patriarchal household promoted quiet digestion) began with some soup, some fried soles, a butter-boat of shrimp sauce, and a dish of potatoes ...
There was mutton, a steak, and an apple-pie—nothing in the remotest way connected with ganders—and the dinner went on like a disenchanted feast, as it truly was.

Little Dorrit Ch XIII

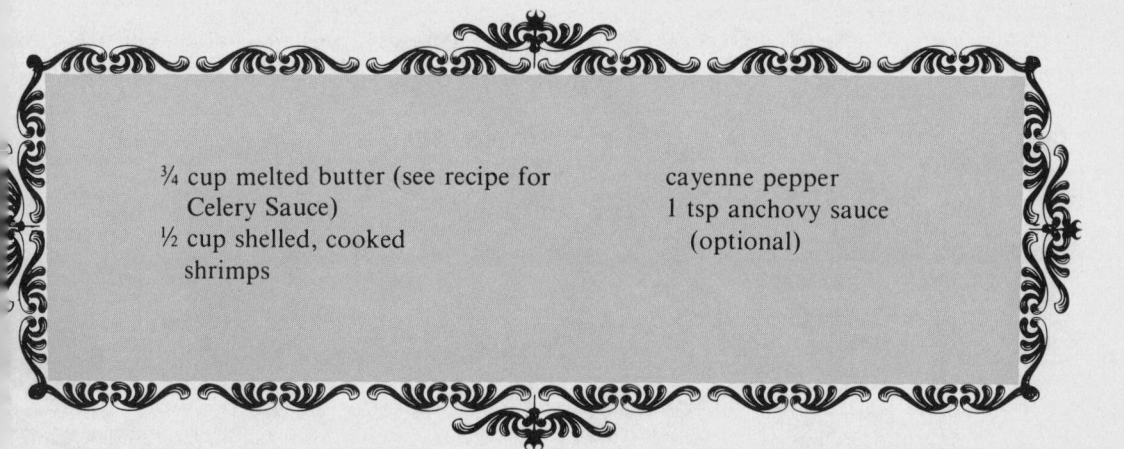

¾ cup melted butter (see recipe for Celery Sauce)
½ cup shelled, cooked shrimps

cayenne pepper
1 tsp anchovy sauce (optional)

Place the sauce and the shrimps in a saucepan. Season with cayenne pepper to taste; anchovy sauce can be added if liked. Allow the sauce to simmer—not to boil—for 1 minute. Serve with fish.

The kitchen's undying declaration

Lamb and Mutton and their Sauces

BOILED LEG OF MUTTON WITH CAPER SAUCE

'Did anybody ever find boiled mutton and caper-sauce growing in a cocoa-nut?'

Little Dorrit Ch XXXII

The greengrocer and his wife then arranged upon the table a boiled leg of mutton, hot, with caper sauce, turnips, and potatoes.

The Pickwick Papers Ch XXXVII

Boiled leg of mutton was standard fare in Dickens's time; it crops up as a food with horrifying frequency throughout his works. Given our accustomed use of roast leg of lamb, its appeal is much slighter, and, in fact, mutton is a fairly scarce meat. A pleasant and homely meal it must have been. It must have varied much in quality, for it seems to have been given that wary eye which we reserve for a dubious steak; one nineteenth-century cookery book offered the following seven requirements for the dish to be served to perfection:

'1st. The mutton must be *good*.
2nd. Must have kept a *good* time.
3rd. Must be boiled by a *good* fire.
4th. By a *good* cook.
5th. Who must be in a *good* temper.
6th. The mashed turnips must be *good*; and
7th. The eater must have a *good* appetite.'

1 leg of mutton
water
salt

'Cut off the shank bone, trim the knuckle, and wash and wipe it very clean; plunge it into sufficient boiling water to cover it; let it boil up, then draw the saucepan to the side of the fire, where it should remain until the finger can be borne in the water. Then place it sufficiently near the fire, that the water may gently simmer, and be very careful that it does not boil fast, or the meat will be hard. Skim well, add a little salt, and in about 2¼ hours after the water begins to simmer, a moderate-sized leg of mutton will be done.'

This is a very simple sauce, based on melted butter. Pickled nasturtium seeds, which have a flavour very similar to capers, were often used as a substitute—a practice which should still be current today.

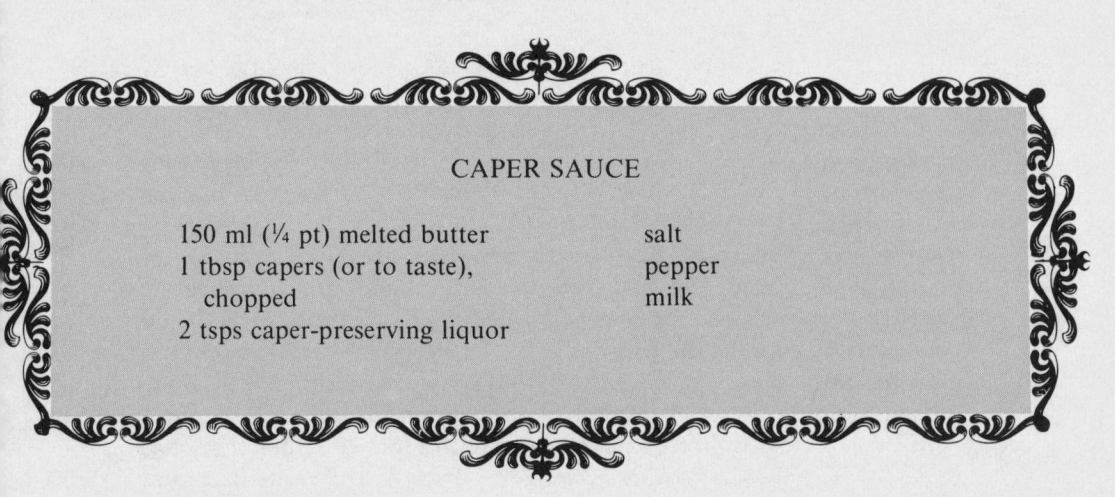

CAPER SAUCE

150 ml (¼ pt) melted butter
1 tbsp capers (or to taste), chopped
2 tsps caper-preserving liquor
salt
pepper
milk

Place the butter, capers, and preserving liquor in a saucepan, and season with salt and pepper. Heat, but do not boil. Stir in just enough milk to make the liquid smooth; heat through again, but do not boil. Serve with boiled mutton.

MUSHROOM KETCHUP AND MR MICAWBER'S DEVILLED MUTTON

'My dear friend Copperfield... If you will allow me to take the liberty of remarking that there are few comestibles better, in their way, than a Devil, and that I believe, with a little division of labour, we could accomplish a good one if the young person in attendance could produce a gridiron, I would put it to you, that this little misfortune may be easily repaired.'

There was a gridiron in the pantry, on which my morning rasher of bacon was cooked. We had it in, in a twinkling, and immediately applied ourselves to carrying Mr. Micawber's idea into effect. The division of labour to which he had referred was this:— Traddles cut the mutton into slices; Mr. Micawber (who could do anything of this sort to perfection) covered them with pepper, mustard, salt, and cayenne; I put them on the gridiron, turning them with a fork, and took them off, under Mr. Micawber's direction; and Mrs. Micawber heated, and continually stirred, some mushroom ketchup in a little saucepan. When we had slices enough done to begin upon, we fell-to, with our sleeves still tucked up at the wrist, more slices spluttering and blazing on the fire, and our attention divided between the mutton on our plates, and the mutton then preparing.

David Copperfield Ch XXVIII

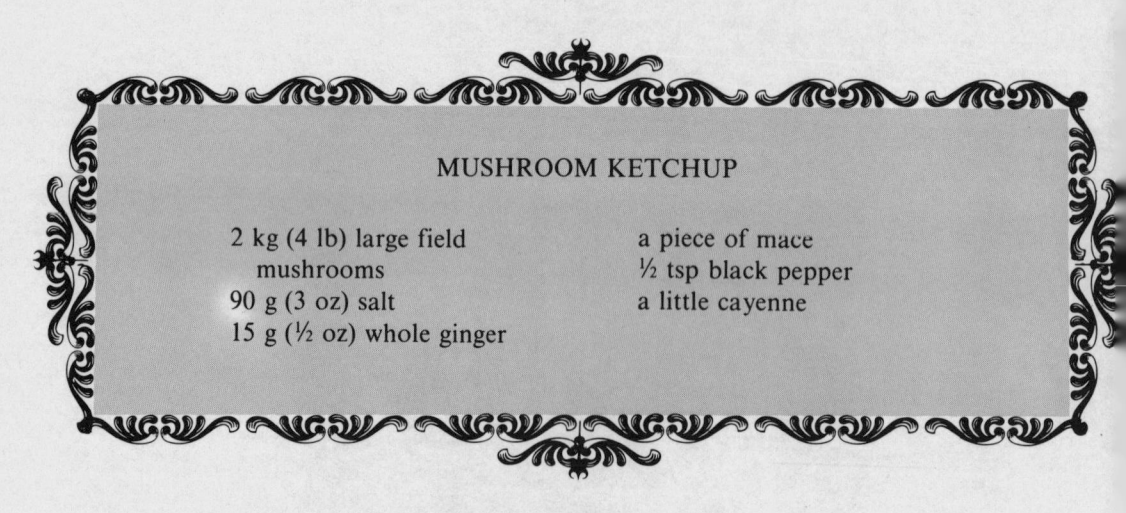

MUSHROOM KETCHUP

2 kg (4 lb) large field mushrooms
90 g (3 oz) salt
15 g (½ oz) whole ginger
a piece of mace
½ tsp black pepper
a little cayenne

Ketchup should be made only from fresh mushrooms gathered during dry weather. Remove any decayed, dirty, or worm-eaten pieces from the mushrooms, and slice about 13 mm (½ in.) from the stalk end. Wash the mushrooms very gently in a colander under a running tap. Leave to drain well. Break the mushrooms into small pieces, and place them in an earthenware casserole, with all layers sprinkled generously with salt. Cover the casserole, then stand it in a *cool* oven or a warm place. The mushrooms should be warm, but on no account should be allowed to cook. Leave for 24 hours, stirring occasionally. Strain off the liquor through a cloth, pressing the mushrooms gently to extract all the moisture. Place the liquid in a saucepan, add the spices tied in a muslin bag, and simmer gently until the liquid is reduced by approximately a half. Remove the spices, pour the liquid into a bowl, and leave to cool. When it is cold, strain into small bottles, and seal tightly. Keep in a cool, dry place.

Note: Mushroom ketchup was frequently made at home, to be used particularly in the flavouring of soups, sauces and stews. Apparently, it was preferable to make one's own, rather than buy it, for one writer stated that 'the majority of the ketchups retailed is a bad compound of liver and fish-roes, seasoned with pepper and drugs, not of the most healthful kind'.

MR MICAWBER'S DEVILLED MUTTON

While David Copperfield is inexplicit with regard to Mr Micawber's Devil, anyone should be able to experiment with it. Use warm or cold slices of roast meat (the moister the better), season with pepper, mustard, salt, and cayenne, and dribble a little melted butter over them while they grill. Alternatively, the pieces can first be brushed with melted butter before seasoning.

HASHED MUTTON

❝Nor did Mr. Pecksniff alone indulge in the creature comforts during this sad time. Mrs. Gamp proved to be very choice in her eating, and repudiated hashed mutton with scorn. In her drinking too, she was very punctual and particular, requiring a pint of mild porter at lunch, a pint at dinner, half-a-pint as a species of stay or holdfast between dinner and tea, and a pint of the celebrated staggering ale, or Real Old Brighton Tipper, at supper; besides the bottle on the chimney-piece, and such casual invitations to refresh herself with wine as the good breeding of her employers might prompt them to offer.❞

Martin Chuzzlewit Ch XIX

A leg of lamb or mutton was invariably followed the next day by that great nineteenth century standby for dealing with cold meat—the hash. It was a dish of which Dickens himself was much in favour. An insight into this proclivity is seen in a letter which he wrote to five-year-old William Hasting Hughes. William had been following the serialisation of *Nicholas Nickleby*, and had been upset because, after the routing of Squeers by Nicholas and the boys of Dotheby Hall, none of the heroes had been rewarded for their efforts towards proper justice. Could the author please amend this oversight? Dickens replied:

'I have carefully done what you told me in your letter about the lamb and the two 'sheeps' for the little boys. They have also had some good ale and porter, and some wine. I am sorry you didn't say *what* wine you would like them to have. I gave them some sherry which they liked very much, except one boy, who was a little sick and choked a good deal. He was rather greedy, and that's the truth, and I believe it went the wrong way, which I say served him right, and I hope you will say so, too. Nicholas had his roast lamb as you said he was to, but he could not eat it all, and says if you do not mind his doing so he should like to have the rest hashed tomorrow with some greens, which he is very fond of, and so am I. He said he did not like to have his porter hot, for he thought it spoilt the flavour, so I let him have it cold.'

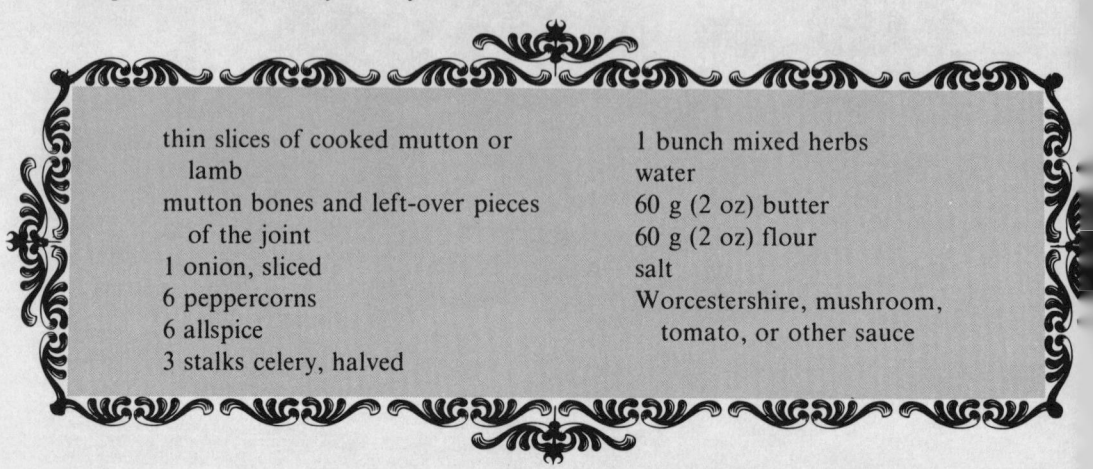

---

thin slices of cooked mutton or lamb
mutton bones and left-over pieces of the joint
1 onion, sliced
6 peppercorns
6 allspice
3 stalks celery, halved
1 bunch mixed herbs
water
60 g (2 oz) butter
60 g (2 oz) flour
salt
Worcestershire, mushroom, tomato, or other sauce

Chop the mutton bones and other scraps from the meat into pieces, and place them in a saucepan with the onion, peppercorns, allspice, celery, and mixed herbs. Cover with water, and simmer for 1¼ hours to make a stock. Strain, and return the liquid to the saucepan. Blend together the butter and flour, and add the mixture in small pieces to the hot liquid, stirring all the time. The quantity required to thicken the stock to make a gravy will depend upon the amount of liquid used. Bring to the boil, and simmer for 3 minutes. (In the nineteenth century, stock would have been readily available in the kitchen, so that making a hashed mutton would not have been such a lengthy several-stage process as it is when gravy is not so readily available in its proper form.) Flavour the gravy with salt and a sauce selected to suit. Place the meat slices in the gravy and heat them through gradually. Do not boil or the meat will harden. To serve, remove the meat slices, place them on a serving dish, and pour the gravy over.

BREADED LAMB CHOPS AND WARM ALE

Mrs. Micawber was quite as elastic. I have known her to be thrown into fainting fits by the king's taxes at three o'clock, and to eat lamb-chops breaded, and drink warm ale (paid for with two tea-spoons that had gone to the pawn-broker's) at four. On one occasion, when an execution had just been put in, coming home through some chance as early as six o'clock, I saw her lying (of course with a twin) under the grate in a swoon, with her hair all torn about her face; but I never knew her more cheerful than she was, that very same night, over a veal-cutlet before the kitchen fire, telling me stories about her papa and mama, and the company they used to keep.

David Copperfield Ch XI

Mrs. Varden ... could no more have reproached John Willet among those household gods, the kegs and bottles, lemons, pipes, and cheese, than she could have stabbed him with his own bright carving-knife. The order for dinner too—it might have soothed a savage. 'A bit of fish,' said John to the cook, 'and some lamb chops (breaded, with plenty of ketchup), and a good salad, and a roast spring chicken, with a dish of sausages and mashed potatoes, or something of that sort.' Something of that sort! The resources of these inns! To talk carelessly about dishes, which in themselves were a first-rate holiday kind of dinner, suitable to one's wedding-day, as something of that sort: meaning: if you can't get a spring chicken, any other trifle in the way of poultry will do—such as a peacock, perhaps!

Barnaby Rudge Ch XIX

One nineteenth-century manner of dealing with crumbed chops can readily be followed today:

Trim the chops, then dip them in a beaten egg, then in breadcrumbs. Season with salt and pepper. Place a tablespoon of dripping into a baking dish, and heat the fat in a moderate oven. Remove the baking dish from the oven, and increase the oven's temperature to 200°C (400°F). Place the chops in the baking dish, basting the top of them with fat. Cook for ¾-1½ hours, until the chops are tender, turning once during cooking.

Another way:

'Lamb.—Fry slices or chops of lamb in butter until they are slightly browned. Serve them on a *purée* of cucumbers, or on a dish of spinach; or dip the slices in bread-crumbs, chopped parsley, and yolk of an egg; some grated lemon and a little nutmeg may be added. Fry them, and pour a little nice gravy over them when served.'

MUTTON CHOPS, HOT AND HOT— GRILLED, AND HOT POT

At one o'clock there was a dinner, chiefly of the farinaceous and vegetable kind, when Miss Pankey (a mild little blue-eyed morsel of a child, who was shampoo'd every morning, and seemed in danger of being rubbed away altogether) was led in from captivity by the ogress herself, and instructed that nobody who sniffed before visitors ever went to heaven. When this great truth had been thoroughly impressed upon her, she was regaled with rice ... Mrs. Pipchin's niece, Berinthia, took cold pork. Mrs. Pipchin, whose constitution required warm nourishment, made a special repast of mutton-chops, which were brought in hot and hot, between two plates and smelt very nice ... For tea there was plenty of milk and water, and bread and butter, with a little black tea-pot for Mrs. Pipchin and Berry, and buttered toast unlimited for Mrs. Pipchin, which was brought in, hot and hot, like the chops.

Dombey and Son Ch VIII

GRILLED MUTTON CHOPS

'Cut the chops from a well-hung tender loin of mutton, remove a portion of the fat, and trim them into a nice shape; slightly beat and level them; place the gridiron over a bright clear fire, rub the bars with a little fat, and lay on the chops [*place the chops under a hot grill*]. Whilst broiling [*grilling*] frequently turn them, and in about 8 minutes they will be well done. Season with pepper and salt, dish them on a very hot dish, rub a small piece of butter on each chop and serve very hot and expeditiously.'

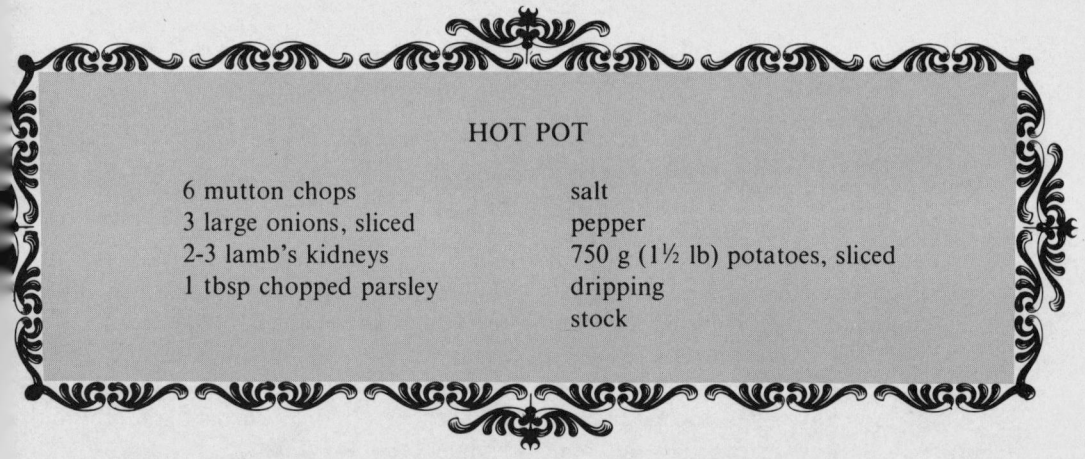

HOT POT

6 mutton chops
3 large onions, sliced
2-3 lamb's kidneys
1 tbsp chopped parsley
salt
pepper
750 g (1½ lb) potatoes, sliced
dripping
stock

Rub a casserole dish with dripping, trim the chops, and core and slice the kidneys. Place half the sliced potatoes on the bottom of the casserole, then add half the onions. Season well, then sprinkle with parsley and the sliced kidneys. Add the chops, the rest of the onion, and the remaining potatoes. Season well. Place a few small pieces of dripping on the top, and pour in 1½-2 cups of stock. Cover tightly, and cook at 180°C (350°F) for 30 minutes, then lower the heat to 160°C (325°F), and cook for a further 1½ hours. Remove the lid near the end of cooking time to allow the top potatoes to brown. Check during cooking to make sure that the liquid has not too greatly evaporated, adding more stock if necessary.

MR BARLEY'S LAMB AND SPLIT PEA STEW

'Look here, said Herbert, showing me the basket, with a compassionate and tender smile after we had talked a little; 'here's poor Clara's supper, served out every night. Here's her allowance of bread, and here's her slice of cheese, and here's her rum—which I drink. This is Mr. Barley's breakfast for tomorrow, served out to be cooked. Two mutton chops, three potatoes, some split peas, a little flour, two ounces of butter, a pinch of salt, and all this black pepper. It's stewed up together, and taken hot, and it's a nice thing for the gout, I should think!'

Great Expectations Ch XLVI

As a breakfast, split peas and mutton might be rather indisposing, but as a simple and economical evening meal it is to be applauded. Mr Barley's own recipe can be followed directly, or the following, improved variation can be used:

---

1 kg (2 lb) middle neck of lamb, or 750 g boneless mutton
30 g (1 oz) butter
1 tbsp oil
125 g (4 oz) bacon pieces (optional)
2 onions, sliced

3 cups stock or water
1 tsp freshly chopped mint
salt
pepper
1 cup dried split peas
mint for garnish

If using chops, cut and trim them, taking out any superfluous bone. If using boneless mutton, cut the meat into pieces of a convenient size for serving. Heat the butter and oil in a frying pan, and add the meat to it, proceeding slowly, so that the temperature of the pan is not too quickly lowered. Brown the meat on both sides, then remove it to a plate. Add the onions and bacon (if used) to the pan and brown. Place the meat, bacon, onions and split peas in a saucepan. (The split peas can be soaked overnight, but in this dish it is unnecessary, as there is a long cooking time.) Add some of the stock or water to the frying pan, and scrape it around to obtain as much of the brownings as possible. Add the contents of the frying pan and the rest of the stock to the saucepan. Add the mint, and season with salt and pepper. Gradually bring to the boil, and simmer for approximately 1½ hours, or until the meat is tender, stirring occasionally to prevent the peas from burning. Add more stock or water if the mixture seems too thick. Serve with potatoes boiled in their jackets, or, if you wish to emulate Mr Barley, add some quartered potatoes to the stew 30-40 minutes before the end of cooking time. Garnish with small sprigs of mint, or a little *freshly* chopped mint.

A NICE IRISH STEW

So, when I once asked Dora, with an eye to the cookery-book, what she would do, if we were married, and I were to say I should like a nice Irish stew, she replied that she would tell the servant to make it; and then clapped her little hands together across my arm, and laughed in such a charming manner that she was more delightful than ever.
Consequently, the principal use to which the cookery-book was devoted, was being put down in the corner for Jip to stand upon. But Dora was so pleased, when she had trained him to stand upon it without offering to come off, and at the same time to hold the pencil-case in his mouth, that I was very glad I had bought it.

David Copperfield Ch XLI

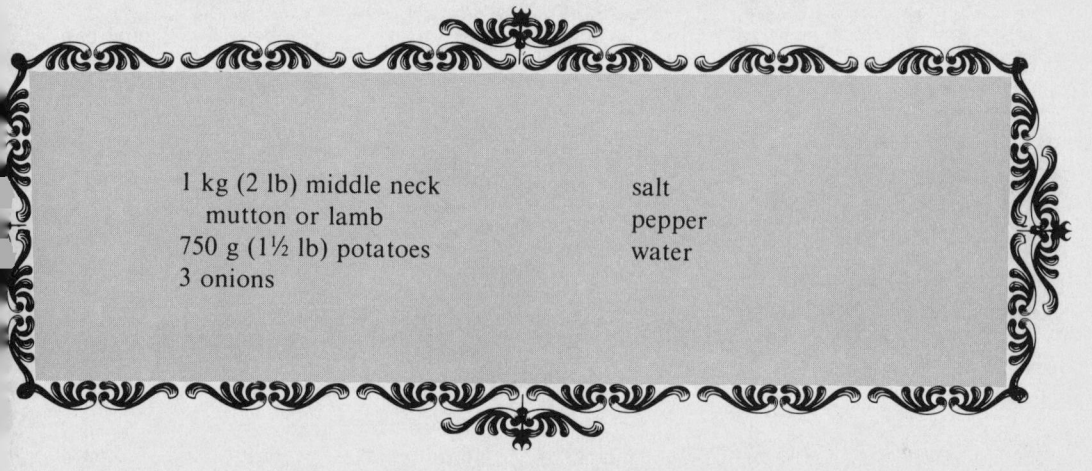

1 kg (2 lb) middle neck mutton or lamb
750 g (1½ lb) potatoes
3 onions
salt
pepper
water

Wipe the meat, trim it if necessary, and cut it into a number of joints of even sizes. Slice the potatoes and onions, or cut the potatoes into chunks. Put alternate layers of vegetable and meat in a casserole dish, seasoning with salt and pepper well between each layer, finishing with a layer of potatoes. Add sufficient water to half cover. Cover tightly with a lid and cook at 160°C (325°F) for 2 hours, or simmer gently on top of the stove.

MRS CRUMMLES'S ONION SAUCE

'We have but a shoulder of mutton with onion sauce,' said Mrs. Crummles, in the same charnel-house voice; 'but such that our dinner is, we beg you to partake of it.'

Nicholas Nickleby Ch XXIII

'Take two dozen onions and peel them, put them in salt and water for an hour, and then boil them until tender; drain them, and chop them up. Put them in a clean saucepan, with some butter and flour, half a tea-spoon of salt, and about half a pint of milk (cream would be richer), and simmer till done.'

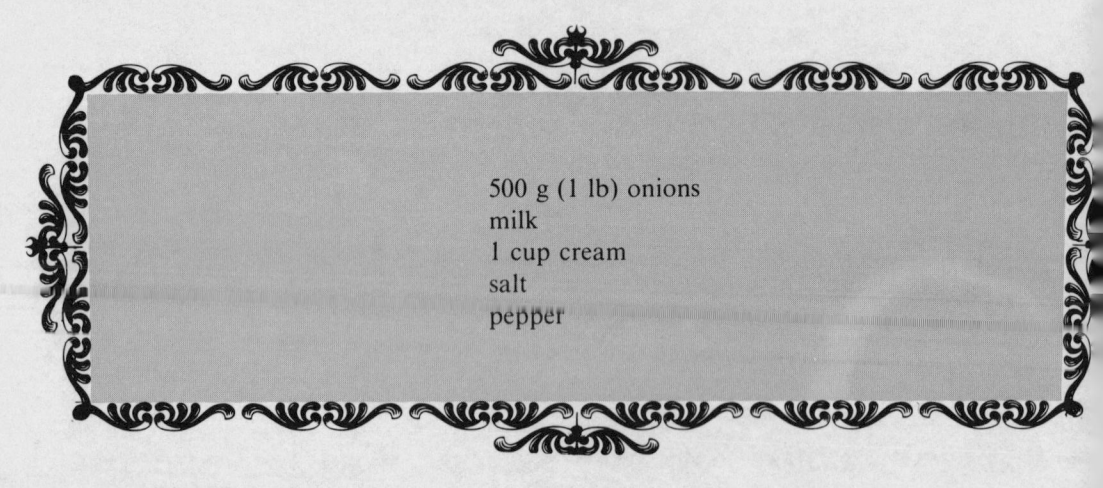

500 g (1 lb) onions
milk
1 cup cream
salt
pepper

Thinly slice the onions, place them in a saucepan, and just cover with milk. When they are cooked, place them in a blender and puree, or rub through a sieve. Simmer the remaining milk to reduce it to 150 ml (¼ pint). Add the onion puree and cream, and season with salt and pepper to taste. Reheat, but do not boil.

Veal and Beef and their Sauces

THE CHRISTENING BREAKFAST—STUFFED FILLET OF VEAL, MEAT PATTIES AND CALF'S HEAD PIE

The register signed ... they got into the carriage again, and drove home in the same bleak fellowship.

There they found Mr. Pitt turning up his nose at a cold collation, set forth in a cold pomp of glass and silver, and looking more like a dead dinner lying in state than a social refreshment. On their arrival Miss Tox produced a mug for her godson, and Mr. Chick a knife and fork and spoon in a case. Mr. Dombey also produced a bracelet for Miss Tox; and, on the receipt of this token, Miss Tox was tenderly affected. 'Mr. John,' said Mr. Dombey, 'will you take the bottom of the table, if you please? What have you got there, Mr. John?'

'I have got a cold fillet of veal here, Sir,' replied Mr. Chick, rubbing his numbed hands together. 'What have *you* got there, Sir?'

'This,' returned Mr. Dombey, 'is some cold preparation of calf's head, I think. I see cold fowls—ham—patties—salad—lobster. Miss Tox will do me the honour of taking some wine? Champagne to Miss Tox.'

There was a toothache in everything. The wine was so bitter cold that it forced a little scream from Miss Tox, which she had great difficulty in turning into a 'Hem!' The veal had come from such an airy pantry, that the first taste of it had struck a sensation as of cold lead to Mr. Chick's extremities. Mr. Dombey alone remained unmoved. He might have been hung up for sale at a Russian fair as a specimen of a frozen gentleman.

Dombey and Son Ch V

STUFFED FILLET OF VEAL

a fillet of veal (or boned shoulder)
60 g (2 oz) butter
1 cup breadcrumbs
1 tbsp chopped parsley
1 tbsp sultanas
1 tbsp chopped dates
½ tsp dried thyme
grated rind of half a lemon
salt
pepper
30 g (1 oz) butter
1 small onion, chopped
1 egg, beaten

Prepare the stuffing by first mixing together the breadcrumbs, parsley, sultanas, dates, thyme, lemon rind, salt and pepper. Melt the 30 g (1 oz) of butter in a saucepan, and in it sauté the chopped onion gently for 5 minutes. Add the butter and onion to the breadcrumb mixture, along with the beaten egg, mixing well. Add a little milk if the mixture seems too dry. Stuff the meat with the mixture, and secure with skewers or sew.

Spread the meat with the 60 g (2 oz) of butter, and wrap it in foil. Bake at 200°C (400°F), allowing 25 minutes per half-kilo (1 lb), and 25 minutes over. Remove the foil for the last half-hour of cooking time to allow the meat to brown, turning the meat at the same time, and basting well. Serve with gravy or a suitable sauce (gooseberry sauce, in season, is excellent) and 'never omit to send a cut lemon to table with roast veal'. Alternatively, the dish can be allowed to cool, and served as part of the cold table.

MEAT PATTIES

'Take any cold meat, game, or poultry (if underdone, all the better), mince it fine, with a little fat bacon or ham, or an anchovy; season it with pepper and salt; mix well, and make it into small cakes three inches long, an inch and a half wide, and half an inch thick: fry these a light brown, and serve them with a good gravy, or put into a mould, and boil or bake it.

N.B.—Bread-crumbs, hard yolks of eggs, onions, sweet herbs, savoury spices, zest, or curry-powder, or any of the forcemeats [can be added].'

Note: These are usually served hot, but they can be served, *à la* Dombey, cold.

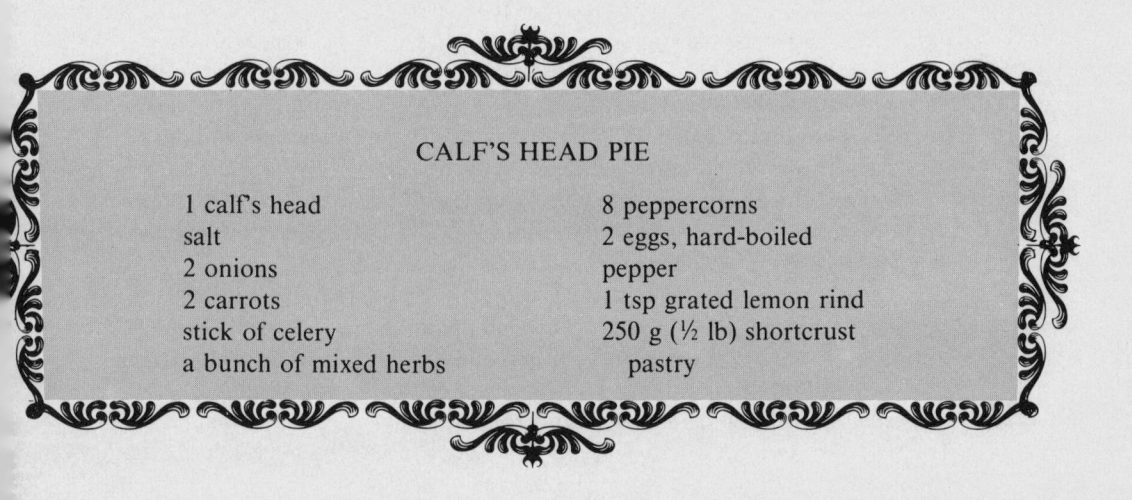

CALF'S HEAD PIE

1 calf's head
salt
2 onions
2 carrots
stick of celery
a bunch of mixed herbs
8 peppercorns
2 eggs, hard-boiled
pepper
1 tsp grated lemon rind
250 g (½ lb) shortcrust pastry

Clean the head and soak it overnight in salted water. Drain. Place the head in a large saucepan and cover with cold water. Slowly bring to the boil, simmer for 3 minutes, then drain. Cover again with cold water, add salt, onions, carrots, celery, the bunch of mixed herbs, and peppercorns. Slowly bring to the boil and simmer until cooked—approximately 3-4 hours. Some of the meat can be served hot with a parsley sauce; reserve the rest for the pie.

To make the pie: Place the bones from the meat in a saucepan and cover with approximately 4 cups of the boiling liquor. Simmer for 2 hours, strain, and allow the liquid to cool. Remove all the fat from the jellied surface. Place the slices of hard-boiled egg in the bottom of a pie dish, and add alternately layers of calf's head meat and jellied stock, until the dish is full. On a floured board, roll out the pastry. Dampen the edges of the pie dish, and place a strip of pastry around the edge. Dampen the pastry, and cover the pie dish with the pastry. Press the edges together to seal. Make a hole in the centre. Bake at 220°C (425°F) for approximately 20 minutes, until the crust is browned. Remove from the oven, and allow to cool, and the jelly to set. To serve, turn the pie out, upside down on a plate.

DINING WITH MR SMALLWEED—STUFFED ROAST OF VEAL AND MARROW PUDDING

'Into the dining-house, unaffected by the seductive show in the window, of artificially whitened cauliflowers and poultry, verdant baskets of peas, coolly blooming cucumbers, and joints ready for the spit, Mr. Smallweed leads the way ... It is no use trying him with anything less than full-sized 'bread', or proposing to him any joint in cut, unless it is in the very best cut. In the matter of gravy he is adamant ... Chick, out of the profundity of his artfulness, preferring 'veal and ham and French beans—And don't you forget the stuffing, Polly' (with an unearthly cock of his venerable eye); Mr. Guppy and Mr. Jobling give the like order. Three pint pots of half-and-half are superadded. Then, amid a constant coming in, and going out, and running about, and a clatter of crockery, and a rumbling up and down of the machine which brings the nice cuts from the kitchen, and a shrill crying for more nice cuts down the speaking-pipe, and a shrill reckoning of the cost of nice cuts that have been disposed of, and a general flush and steam of hot joints, cut and uncut, and a considerable heated atmosphere in which the soiled knives and tablecloths seem to break out spontaneously into eruptions of grease and blotches of beer, the legal triumvirate appease their appetites ...

'Will you take any other vegetables? Grass? Peas? Summer cabbage?'

'Thank you, Guppy,' says Mr. Jobling. 'I really don't know but what I *will* take summer cabbage.'

Order given; with the sarcastic addition (from Mr. Smallweed) of 'Without slugs, Polly!' And cabbage produced ... Three marrow puddings being produced, Mr. Jobling adds, in a pleasant humour, that he is coming of age fast. To these succeed, by command of Mr. Smallweed, 'three Cheshires;' and to those, 'three small rums.' This apex of the entertainment happily reached, Mr. Jobling puts up his legs on the carpeted seat (having his own side of the box to himself), leans against the wall, and says, 'I am grown up now, Guppy. I have arrived at maturity.'

Bleak House Ch XX

STUFFED ROAST OF VEAL

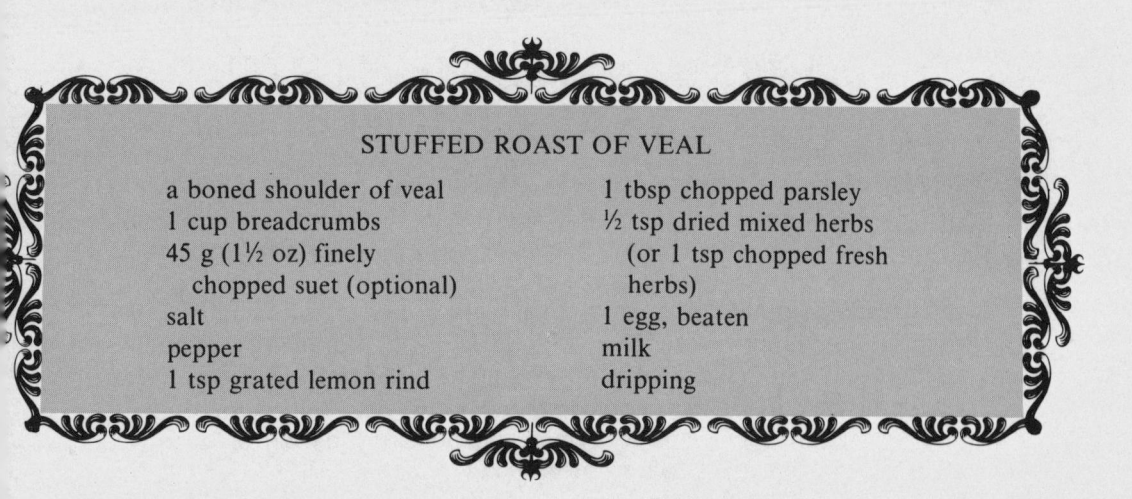

a boned shoulder of veal
1 cup breadcrumbs
45 g (1½ oz) finely
   chopped suet (optional)
salt
pepper
1 tsp grated lemon rind
1 tbsp chopped parsley
½ tsp dried mixed herbs
   (or 1 tsp chopped fresh
   herbs)
1 egg, beaten
milk
dripping

Make the stuffing by mixing together the breadcrumbs, suet (if used), salt, pepper, lemon rind, parsley, and mixed herbs, binding them together with the beaten egg. Add a little milk if the mixture needs more moisture. Stuff the meat with the mixture, then either sew up firmly or secure with skewers. Place the dripping in the roasting pan, and heat until smoking in an oven set at 230°C (450°F). Place the veal in the pan, baste with the dripping, and cook for 10 minutes; reduce the heat to 190°C (375°F) and continue to cook until the veal is done— 25 minutes for every half-kilo (or pound) and 25 minutes over. Veal should be well done, but moist. Baste well during cooking.

Note: As veal tends to dry out during cooking, a piece of pork skin can be tied around it until the last 30 minutes of cooking. Alternatively, the veal can be rubbed well with butter and wrapped in tin foil until the last 30 minutes of cooking. During the last stages, baste well to brown. Serve with gravy.

THE RELATIVE MERITS OF A VEAL CUTLET

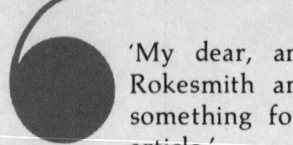

'My dear, and girls,' said the cherub-patriarch, 'between Mr. Rokesmith and me, there is a matter of eight sovereigns, and something for supper shall come of it, if you'll agree upon the article.'

This was a neat and happy turn to give the subject, treats being rare in the Wilfer household, where a monotonous appearance of a Dutch cheese at ten o'clock in the evening had been rather frequently commented on by the dimpled shoulders of Miss Bella. Indeed, the modest Dutchman himself seemed conscious of his want of variety, and generally came before the family in a state of apologetic perspiration. After some discussion on the subject of the relative merits of veal-cutlet, sweetbread, and lobster, a decision was pronounced in favour of veal-cutlet. Mrs. Wilfer then solemnly divested herself of her handkerchief and gloves, as a preliminary sacrifice to preparing the frying-pan, and R. W. himself went out to purchase the viand. He soon returned, bearing the same in a fresh cabbage-leaf, where it coyly embraced a rasher of ham. Melodious sounds were not long in rising from the frying-pan on the fire, or in seeming, as the firelight danced in the mellow halls of a couple of full bottles on the table, to play appropriate dance-music.

Our Mutual Friend Bk 1 Ch IV

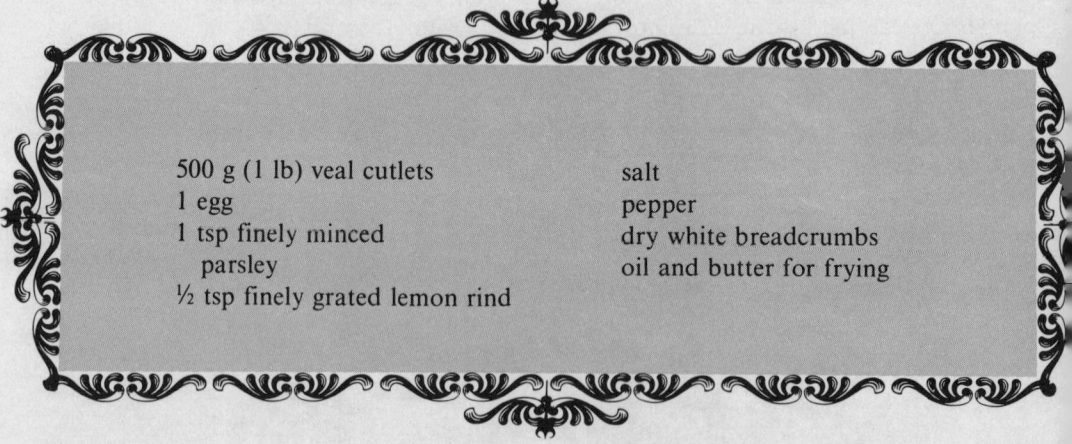

---

500 g (1 lb) veal cutlets
1 egg
1 tsp finely minced parsley
½ tsp finely grated lemon rind
salt
pepper
dry white breadcrumbs
oil and butter for frying

Beat each cutlet well, and trim the edges. Beat the egg, and mix in the parsley and lemon rind, seasoning with salt and pepper. Dip the cutlets in the mixture, then roll them in the breadcrumbs, pressing the crumbs on well. Heat a mixture of butter and oil in a frying pan, put in the cutlets, and fry them over a moderate to slow heat for 7-10 minutes, until golden, turning them once.

To make a quick gravy to serve with the cutlets: Pour off all but 1 tablespoon of the fat in the pan. Add 2-3 teaspoons of flour, brown it, and pour in half a cup of hot stock or water, stirring all the time. Season with salt and pepper, boil for 3 minutes, strain and serve. Alternatively, a piquant sauce or a tomato sauce was considered suitable to the meat.

Note: Mr Wilfer's rasher of ham was no chance purchase; it was taken as a natural accompaniment to veal, as were forcemeat balls (see Roast Chicken with Shrimp Stuffing and Forcemeat Balls).

VEAL IN SAVOURY JELLY

'Oh! but the master wins,' returned the jailer, with a passing look of no particular liking at the other man, 'and you lose. It's quite another thing. You get husky bread and sour drink by it; and he gets sausage of Lyons, veal in savoury jelly, white bread, strachino cheese, and good wine by it. Look at the birds, my pretty!'

Little Dorrit Ch I

500 g (1 lb) stewing veal
1 large onion
2 carrots
1 stalk celery
2 tsps chopped mustard pickle
2 tsps tomato sauce
2½ cups well-seasoned jelly stock (preferably made from veal bones)
60 g (2 oz) butter
parsley and lemon slices for garnish

Chop the meat into small pieces, and chop the vegetables. Melt the butter in a saucepan, add the vegetables, and saute for 5 minutes. Add the veal and the stock; bring to the boil. Simmer until the meat is tender, and test for seasoning. Strain the liquid into a basin, and leave it to cool. Mince together the veal, vegetables, pickles and sauce. Remove all traces of fat from the liquid, and add the liquid to the meat. Reheat the mixture, then pour it into a mould that has been rinsed in cold water. Leave in a cool place to set. To serve, turn it out on to a dish and garnish with parsley and lemon slices.

BEEFSTEAK PUDDING

'I don't know, Tom,' said his sister, blushing, 'I am not quite confident, but I think I could make a beef-steak pudding, if I tried, Tom.' ...
To see the butcher slap the steak, before he laid it on the block, and give his knife a sharpening, was to forget breakfast instantly. It was agreeable, too—it really was—to see him cut it off, so smooth and juicy. There was nothing savage in the act, although the knife was large and keen; it was a piece of art, high art; there was delicacy of touch, clearness of tone, skilful handling of the subject, fine shading. It was the triumph of mind over matter; quite. Perhaps the greenest cabbage-leaf ever grown in a garden was wrapped about this steak, before it was delivered over to Tom. But the butcher had a sentiment for his business, and knew how to refine upon it. When he saw Tom putting the cabbage-leaf into his pocket awkwardly, he begged to be allowed to do it for him; 'for meat,' he said with some emotion, 'must be humoured, not drove.' ...
Such a busy little woman she was! So full of self-importance, and trying so hard not to smile, or seem uncertain about anything! It was a perfect treat to Tom to see her with her brows knit, and her rosy lips pursed up, kneading away at the crust, rolling it out, cutting it up into strips, lining the basin with it, shaving it off fine round the rim, chopping up the steak into small pieces, raining down pepper and salt upon them, packing them into the basin, pouring in cold water for gravy, and never venturing to steal a look in his direction ... until, at last, the basin being quite full and only wanting the top crust, she clapped her hands all covered with paste and flour ...

Martin Chuzzlewit Ch XXXIX

Nicholas suggested cold meat, but there was no cold meat—poached eggs, but there were no eggs—mutton chops, but there wasn't a mutton chop within three miles, though there had been more last week than they knew what to do with, and would be an extraordinary supply the day after tomorrow. 'Then,' said Nicholas, 'I must leave it entirely to you, as I would have done at first, if you had allowed me.' 'Why, then I'll tell you what,' rejoined the landlord. 'There's a gentleman in the parlour that's ordered a hot beef-steak pudding and potatoes, at nine. There's more of it than he can manage, and I have very little doubt that if I ask leave, you can sup with him. I'll do that, in a minute.'

Nicholas Nickleby Ch XXII

First prepare the pastry. Sift the flour and salt into a bowl. Grate the suet finely, removing any pieces of membrane, and then dredge it with a little flour to prevent it sticking together. Stir the suet into the flour. Gradually add the cold water to make a dough. Knead. Place in a cool spot. Cut the steak into small pieces, trimming off any fat. Mix the flour with a little salt and pepper, and roll the meat in it. On a floured board,

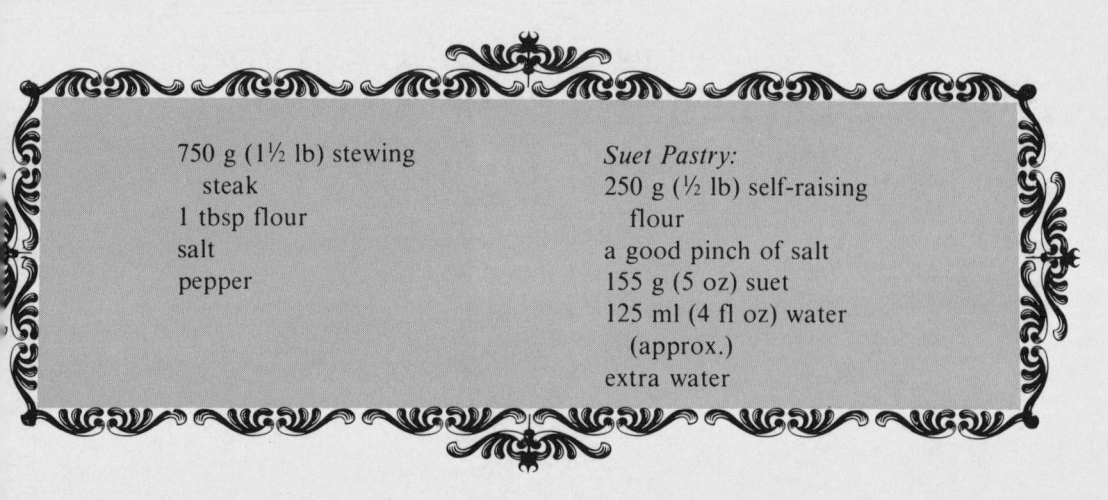

750 g (1½ lb) stewing steak 1 tbsp flour salt pepper	*Suet Pastry:* 250 g (½ lb) self-raising flour a good pinch of salt 155 g (5 oz) suet 125 ml (4 fl oz) water (approx.) extra water

roll out the pastry to line a pudding basin. Grease the basin with butter. Retaining enough pastry to make a lid for the pudding, gently lift the pastry with floured hands, and line the basin with it. Make sure that there are no breaks in the pastry. Leave a little of the pastry overlapping the edges. Place the floured meat in the lined basin, seasoning between layers. Three-quarters fill the bowl with cold water. Dampen the top rim of the pastry lining the bowl, and add the pastry lid, pressing well down around the edges so that there are no spaces to allow the gravy to escape. Trim. Take a large piece of greaseproof paper, put a large pleat in the centre, and tie it securely over the bowl. Take a large piece of linen cloth, scald it, wring it out, and flour well the underside. Wrap it completely around the bowl, and tie it very securely, making a loop with string or the top knots of the cloth to enable you to place it in the water and to remove it. Have ready a large pan of boiling water, submerge the pudding in it, and boil for 3½ hours. Serve from the basin.

Note: This can become a Beefsteak and Kidney Pudding by the addition of some chopped kidney; a little minced onion or some mushrooms can also be added.

THE GRATEFUL INFLUENCE OF COLD BOILED BEEF AND BEER, WITH SUET DUMPLINGS

'With which mournful review of their proceedings, Mr. Dennis sought consolation in cold boiled beef and beer; but without at all relaxing the grim and dissatisfied expression of his face, the gloom of which was rather deepened than dissipated by their grateful influence.

Barnaby Rudge Ch L

The supper was ready laid, the chairs were drawn round the table, bottles, jugs, and glasses were arranged upon the sideboard, and everything betokened the approach of the most convivial period in the whole four-and-twenty hours ... There was a gigantic round of cold beef upon the table, and Mr. Pickwick was supplied with a plentiful portion of it.

The Pickwick Papers Ch IX

'There were more dances, and there were forfeits, and more dances, and there was cake, and there was negus, and there was a great piece of Cold Roast, and there was a great piece of Cold Boiled, and there were mince-pies, and plenty of beer. But the great effect of the evening came after the Roast and Boiled, when the fiddler (an artful dog, mind! The sort of man who knew his business better than you or I could have told it him!) struck up 'Sir Roger de Coverley.'

A Christmas Carol Stave II

The following recipe is devised for initially eating a hot meal from the beef; if it is intended solely as a cold cut, let the meat stand overnight in the water in which it was cooked, to make it sweet and juicy. Either salted or unsalted meat can be used; if the latter, add salt to the cooking water. Again, if a cold meat only is intended, omit the cabbage, and use less of the other vegetables, as their function will be to add flavour, not substance. This dish was commonly served with suet dumplings, and a recipe for these is also given below.

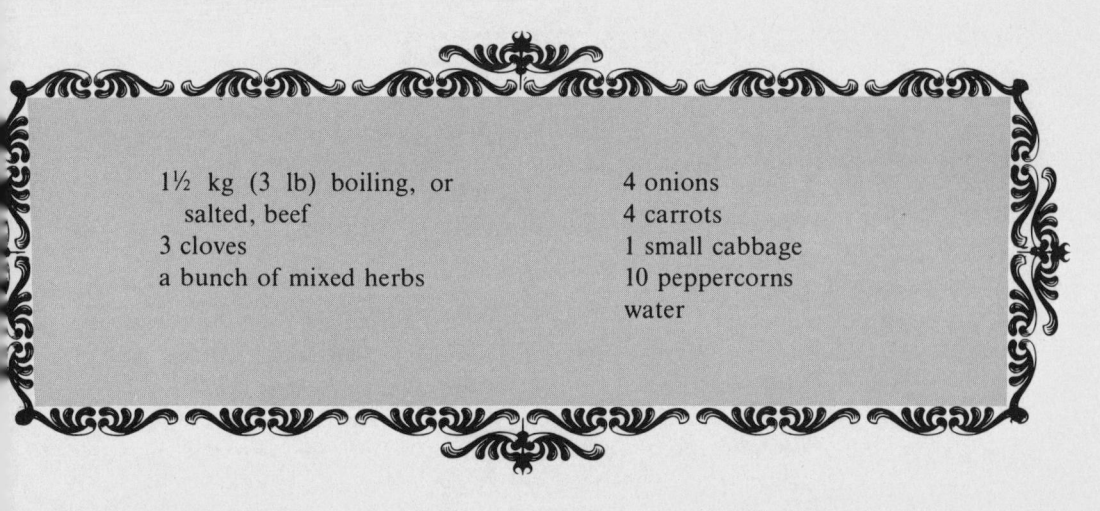

1½ kg (3 lb) boiling, or salted, beef	4 onions
3 cloves	4 carrots
a bunch of mixed herbs	1 small cabbage
	10 peppercorns
	water

If the meat is not already tied, tie it securely in a net shape with string. If using unsalted meat, put the meat into a saucepan, cover with boiling water, then boil for 5 minutes to seal the meat. Reduce to simmering point. If using salted meat, place it in lukewarm water, and gradually bring it to simmering point. Add the peppercorns, cloves, and herbs. Keep the liquid clear of fat and scum as it cooks. The slower the meat cooks the more tender it will be. Cook for approximately 30 minutes for each half-kilo (or pound). Peel the onions and leave them whole. Scrape the carrots, and cut them into halves or quarters; quarter the cabbage. Add the onions and carrots 50 minutes before the end of cooking time; add the cabbage 40 minutes before the end of cooking time. If using suet dumplings, add then 20-30 minutes before the end. To serve, place the dumplings around the outside of the serving dish, place the meat and a little of the liquor in the dish and surround it with the vegetables. Have a little of the liquor available separately for individual moistening of the meat.

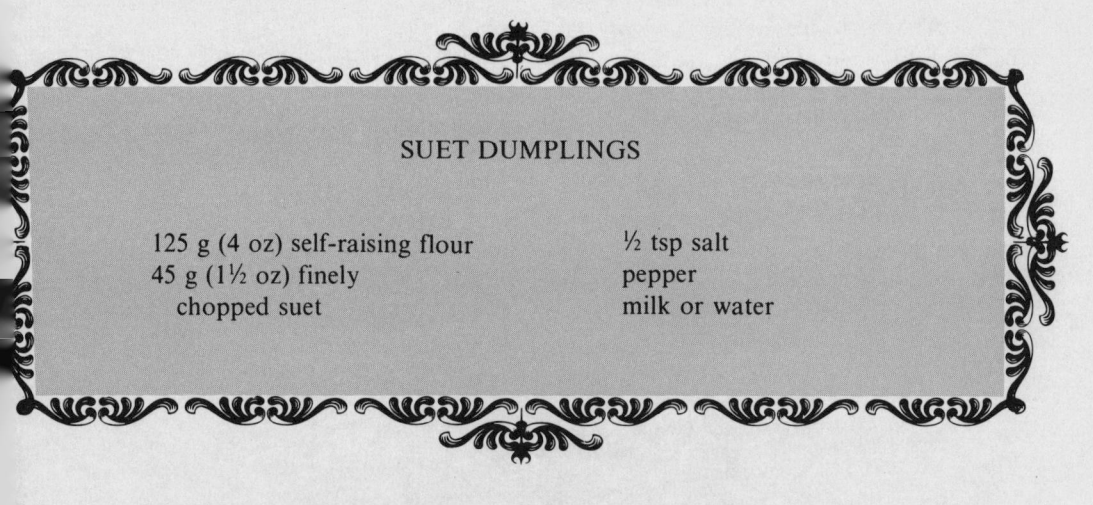

SUET DUMPLINGS

125 g (4 oz) self-raising flour	½ tsp salt
45 g (1½ oz) finely chopped suet	pepper
	milk or water

Sift the flour and the salt into a bowl, add the suet and pepper. Using either milk or water, slowly add sufficient to form a soft dough. Form into small balls with floured hands—making them approximately 4 cm (1½ in.) in diameter. Bring to the boil the liquid in which they are to cook, and drop in the dumplings 30 minutes before serving time. Cover the pan and keep the liquid on a steady simmer. Remove the lid only once during cooking time to turn the dumplings.

MR PINCH'S STEAK

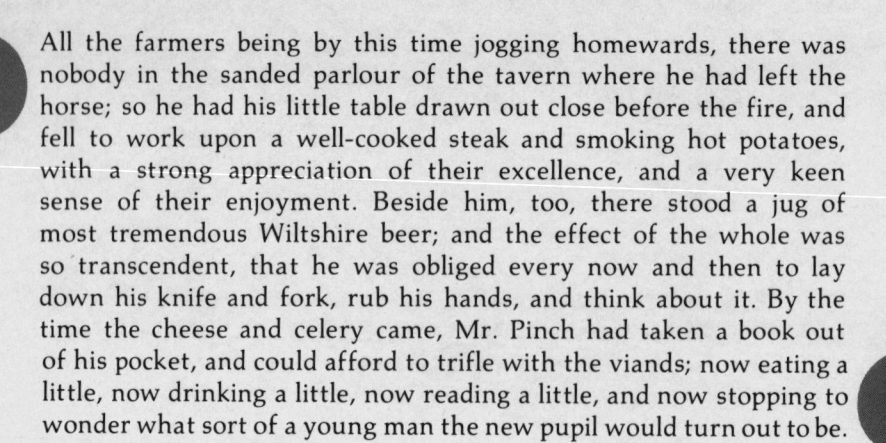

> All the farmers being by this time jogging homewards, there was nobody in the sanded parlour of the tavern where he had left the horse; so he had his little table drawn out close before the fire, and fell to work upon a well-cooked steak and smoking hot potatoes, with a strong appreciation of their excellence, and a very keen sense of their enjoyment. Beside him, too, there stood a jug of most tremendous Wiltshire beer; and the effect of the whole was so transcendent, that he was obliged every now and then to lay down his knife and fork, rub his hands, and think about it. By the time the cheese and celery came, Mr. Pinch had taken a book out of his pocket, and could afford to trifle with the viands; now eating a little, now drinking a little, now reading a little, and now stopping to wonder what sort of a young man the new pupil would turn out to be.

Martin Chuzzlewit Ch V

Being set ashore, with very little money in their pockets, and no definite plan of operations in their heads, they sought out a cheap tavern, where they regaled upon a smoking steak, and certain flowing mugs of beer, as only men just landed from the sea can revel in the generous dainties of the earth.

Martin Chuzzlewit Ch XXXV

If Mr Pinch had his steak grilled (or broiled, as it was then termed), and if it was as excellent as he found it, then it must have been nicely thick—about 20 mm ($^4/_5$ in.)—and cooked over a bright clear fire that was free from smoke. The gridiron would have been placed over a fire that had had a little salt sprinkled on it, and left until the iron was hot. Suet would have then been rubbed over the gridiron, and the steak added, to be cooked for 8-10 minutes, depending on taste, and being turned with steak-tongs, or, if those were unavailable, with a fork used in the edge of the fat, to make sure no juices escaped. Everything else would have been ready for serving while the steak was cooking, as it had to be sent to table very hot. The warmed plate might have had a little ketchup and minced shallot placed upon it, while the cooked steak would be finally rubbed with butter and seasoned with salt and pepper. 'Oyster, tomato, onion and many other sauces are frequent accompaniments to rump-steak, but true lovers of this English dish generally reject all additions but pepper and salt.'

WEMMICK'S STEWED STEAK

'Now, I'll tell you what I have got for supper, Mr. Pip. I have got a stewed steak—which is of home preparation—and a cold roast fowl—which is from the cook's shop. I think it's tender, because the master of the shop was a Juryman in some cases of ours the other day, and we let him down easy. I reminded him of it when I bought the fowl, and I said, "Pick us out a good one, old Briton, because if we had chosen to keep you in the box another day or two, we could easily have done it." He said to that, "Let me make you a present of the best fowl in the shop." I let him, of course. As far as it goes, it's property and portable ...'

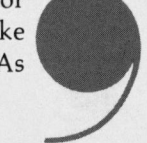

Great Expectations Ch XXV

'Take two pounds of steaks, and put them in a stewpan with just sufficient water to cover them, and let them simmer for half an hour; then add six large onions whole, with a little pepper and salt, a carrot cut up, and some thickening, consisting of two table-spoonfuls of flour and some ketchup, and a teaspoonful of mustard. Let it simmer for an hour longer, and the steaks will be done. They must be sufficiently cooked, and at the same time not "done to rags", or they are spoilt.'

Another simple and homely dish such as Wemmick might have served is:

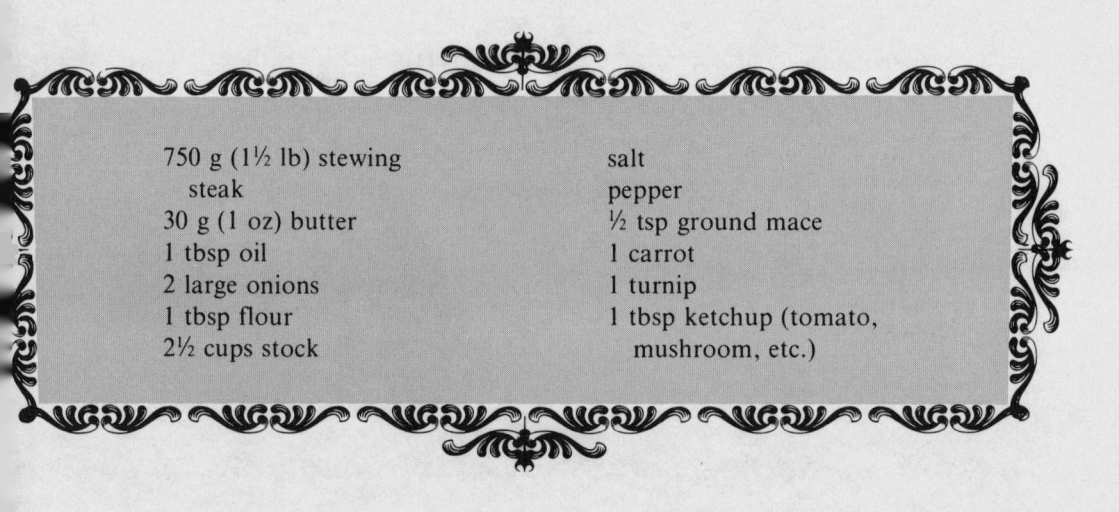

750 g (1½ lb) stewing steak
30 g (1 oz) butter
1 tbsp oil
2 large onions
1 tbsp flour
2½ cups stock
salt
pepper
½ tsp ground mace
1 carrot
1 turnip
1 tbsp ketchup (tomato, mushroom, etc.)

Cut the meat into small pieces, slice the onion, and cut the turnip and carrot into strips. Heat the butter and oil in a heavy saucepan, and in it brown the meat, adding it slowly, so that the temperature of the pan is not too quickly reduced. Drain the meat on to a plate. Lightly fry the onion rings in the remaining butter and oil in the saucepan; add the flour and stir it in, allowing it to brown a little. Very slowly add the stock, stirring all the time until it thickens and boils. Add the meat, carrot, turnip, salt and pepper, and mace. Simmer for 1-1½ hours, depending upon the quality of the meat. Remove the meat and vegetables to their serving dish, skim the liquid of any remaining fat, and reheat. Add some ketchup to taste, and pour the sauce over the meat. Serve with plain boiled vegetables.

A DISH OF STEWED BEEF

It was a remarkable instance of want of forethought on the part of the ironmonger who had made Mrs. Crupp's kitchen fireplace, that it was capable of cooking nothing but chops and mashed potatoes. As to a fish-kittle, Mrs. Crupp said, well! would I only come and look at the range? She couldn't say fairer than that. Would I come and look at it? As I should not have been much the wiser if I *had* looked at it, I declined, and said, 'Never mind the fish.' But Mrs. Crupp said, 'Don't say that; oysters was in, why not them?' So *that* was settled. Mrs. Crupp then said that what she would recommend would be this. A pair of hot roast fowls—from the pastry-cook's; a dish of stewed beef, with vegetables—from the pastry-cook's; two little corner things, as a raised pie and a dish of kidneys—from the pastry-cook's; a tart, and (if I liked) a shape of jelly—from the pastry-cook's. This, Mrs. Crupp said, would leave her at full liberty to concentrate her mind on the potatoes, and to serve up the cheese and celery as she could wish to see it done.

I acted on Mrs. Crupp's opinion, and gave the order at the pastry-cook's myself. Walking along the Strand, afterwards, and observing a hard, mottled substance in the window of a ham and beef shop, which resembled marble, but was labelled 'Mock Turtle', I went in and bought a slab of it, which I have since seen reason to believe would have sufficed for fifteen people. This preparation, Mrs. Crupp, after some difficulty, consented to warm up; and it shrunk so much in a liquid state, that we found it what Steerforth called 'a rather tight fit' for four.

David Copperfield Ch XXIV

A dish of stewed beef usually took the form of a pot roast; 'Mock Turtle' was customarily made from a calf's head:

1¼ kg (2½ lb) topside beef	salt
1 tbsp dripping	pepper
1 onion	3 slices bacon, trimmed
1 bunch mixed herbs	200 ml (7 fl oz) beef stock
1 carrot	2 tsps flour
	extra stock

Take a heavy-based pot, place the dripping in it, and heat until hot. Brown the meat in the dripping, then pour off all but 1 tablespoon of fat. Lay the bacon rashers over the meat. Slice the carrot and the onion, and add them to the pot, along with the herbs. Season with salt and pepper, and pour in the stock. Make sure that the lid is a tightly fitting one; if not, use some tin foil between the lid and the top of the pot. Cook over a very low heat on the top of the stove, or place in a slow oven at 150°-160°C (300°-325°F).

Cook for approximately 3 hours, or until the meat is very tender. Remove the herbs and discard the vegetables. Place the meat on a serving dish, and keep warm. Skim the fat from the liquid and reserve. Place the liquid in a bowl. Place 1 tablespoon of the fat back in the cooking pot, and stir in the flour over the heat. Add the liquid, stirring all the time, then add extra stock to make a gravy. Season to taste. Simmer for 5 minutes. Serve the gravy in a gravy boat, accompanying the meat.

THE PASSION FOR GRAVY

'Presiding over an establishment like this, makes sad havoc with the features, my dear Miss Pecksniffs,' said Mrs. Todgers. 'The gravy alone, is enough to add twenty years to one's age, I do assure you.'
'Lor!' cried the two Miss Pecksniffs.
'The anxiety of that one item, my dears,' said Mrs. Todgers, 'keeps the mind continually upon the stretch. There is no such passion in human nature, as the passion for gravy among commercial gentlemen. It's nothing to say a joint won't yield—a whole animal wouldn't yield—the amount of gravy they expect each day at dinner. And what I have undergone in consequence,' cried Mrs. Todgers, raising her eyes and shaking her head, 'no one would believe!'

Martin Chuzzlewit Ch IX

He resumed this occupation when he was replete with beef, had sucked up all the gravy in the baking-dish with the flat of his knife, and had drawn liberally on a barrel of small beer in the scullery.

Little Dorrit Ch V

Pure gravy consists of the juices from the roasted meat; made gravy is when these are increased by the addition of flour and water. Mrs Todgers possibly alleviated her cares by adding some good brown sauce to the juices. Alternatively, she might have undergone adding 1 tablespoon of flour to a little of the dripping left in the pan, scraping up the sediment well, and then stirring in over the heat about 1½ cups of good stock. This would have been simmered to reduce it slightly, being then seasoned with salt and pepper. Mrs Joe, in *Great Expectations*, must have inclined at times to make gravy. Joe, who 'always aided and comforted me when he could, in some way of his own, ... always did so at dinner-time by giving me gravy, if there were any. There being plenty of gravy to-day, Joe spooned into my plate, at this point, about half a pint.' (Ch IV)

Pork and its Sauces

ROAST SUCKING PIG

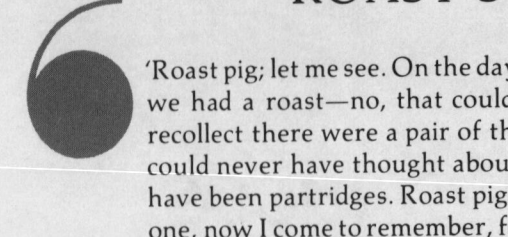

'Roast pig; let me see. On the day five weeks after you were christened, we had a roast—no, that couldn't have been a pig, either, because I recollect there were a pair of them to carve, and your poor papa and I could never have thought about sitting down to two pigs—they must have been partridges. Roast pig! I hardly think we ever could have had one, now I come to remember, for your papa could never bear the sight of them in the shops, and used to say that they always put him in mind of very little babies, only the pigs had much fairer complexions; and he had a horror of little babies, too, because he couldn't very well afford any increase to his family, and had a natural dislike to the subject...'

Nicholas Nickleby Ch XLI

By using the first of the following recipes, you will be able to cope successfully with a sucking pig; by following some of the instructions in the second, you will be able to understand the nineteenth-century treatment, when sucking pigs were a common dish, and add a few flourishes to what is today a rare and luxurious treat.

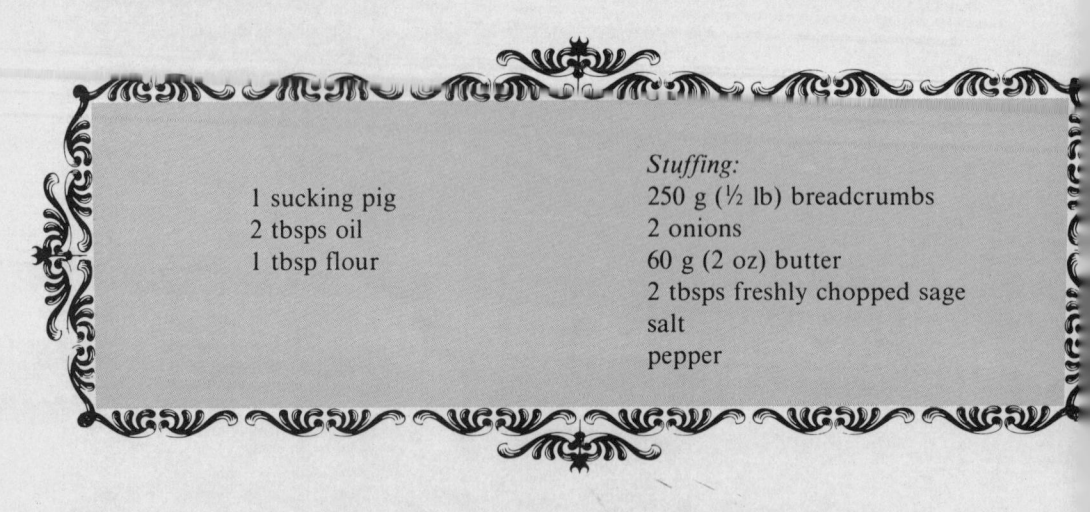

1 sucking pig
2 tbsps oil
1 tbsp flour

Stuffing:
250 g (½ lb) breadcrumbs
2 onions
60 g (2 oz) butter
2 tbsps freshly chopped sage
salt
pepper

Make sure the pig is well cleaned; wipe it over with a cloth. Make a stuffing by chopping the onions, and then sautéing them for 5 minutes in the butter in a saucepan. In a bowl, mix together the breadcrumbs, sage, salt, pepper, and the onion and butter. Stuff the pig with the mixture, and sew up. Brush oil over the pig, and place it in a roasting tin, with the legs tucked along the sides if there is not room to truss the legs back. Cook at 200°C (400°F) for approximately 2 hours, basting frequently throughout the cooking. Half-way through the cooking process, dredge the pig with flour. Send whole to the table.

'A sucking pig, to be eaten in perfection, should not be more than three weeks old, and should be dressed the same day that it is killed. After preparing the pig for cooking ... stuff it with finely grated breadcrumbs, minced sage, pepper, salt, and a piece of butter the size of an egg, all of which should be well mixed together, and put into the body of the pig. Sew up the slit neatly, and truss the legs back, to allow the inside to be roasted, and the underpart to be crisp. Put the pig down to a bright clear fire, not too near, and let it lay until thoroughly dry; then have ready some butter tied up in a piece of thin cloth, and rub the pig with this in every part. Keep it well rubbed with the butter the whole of the time it is roasting, and do not allow the crackling to become blistered or burnt. When half-done, hang a pig-iron before the middle part (if this is not obtainable, use a flat iron), to prevent its being scorched and dried up before the ends are done. Before it is taken from the fire, cut the head, and part that and the body down the middle. Chop the brains and mix them with the stuffing; add ½ pint of good gravy, a tablespoon of lemon-juice, and the gravy that flowed from the pig; put a little of this on the dish with the pig, and the remainder send to the table in a tureen. Place the pig back to back in the dish, with one half of the head on each side, and one of the ears at each end, and send it to table as hot as possible. Instead of butter, many cooks take salad oil for basting, which makes the crackling *crisp*; and as this is one of the principal things to be considered, perhaps it is desirable to use it; but be particular that it is very pure, or it will impart an unpleasant flavour to the meat. The brains and stuffing may be stirred into a tureen of melted butter instead of gravy, when the latter is not liked. Apple sauce and the old-fashioned currant sauce are not yet quite obsolete as an accompaniment to roast pig.'

MRS MICAWBER'S LOIN OF PORK AND APPLE SAUCE

> I passed my evenings with Mr. and Mrs. Micawber, during the remaining term of our residence under the same roof; and I think we became fonder of one another as the time went on. On the last Sunday they invited me to dinner; and we had a loin of pork and apple sauce, and a pudding. I had bought a spotted wooden horse over-night as a parting gift to little Wilkins Micawber—that was the boy—and a doll for little Emma. I had also bestowed a shilling on the Orfling, who was about to be disbanded.

David Copperfield Ch XII

> I soon fell asleep before Wemmick's fire, and the Aged and I enjoyed one another's society by falling asleep before it more or less all day. We had loin of pork for dinner, and greens grown on the estate, and I nodded at the Aged with a good intention whenever I failed to do it drowsily.

Great Expectations Ch XLV

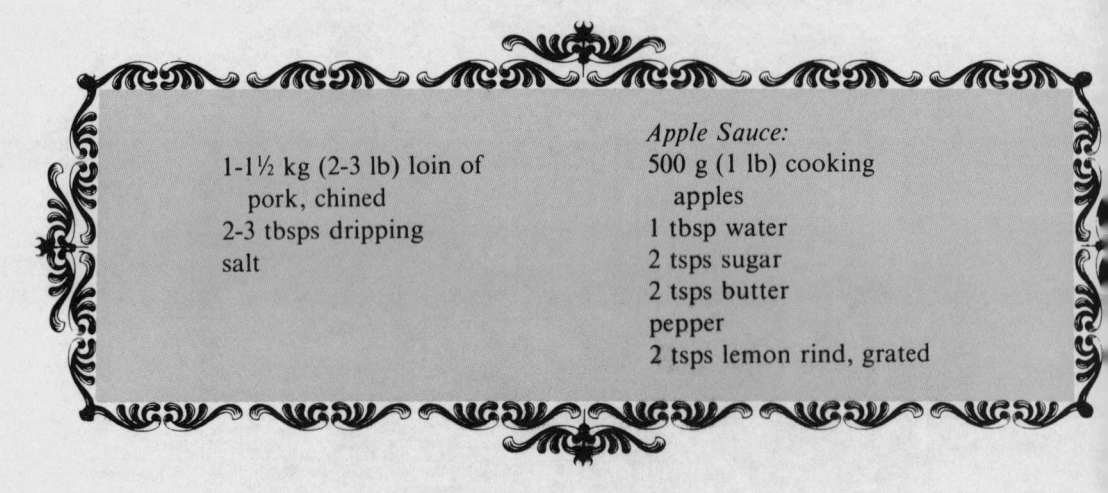

1-1½ kg (2-3 lb) loin of pork, chined
2-3 tbsps dripping
salt

Apple Sauce:
500 g (1 lb) cooking apples
1 tbsp water
2 tsps sugar
2 tsps butter
pepper
2 tsps lemon rind, grated

Score the rind of the pork well, and rub in plenty of salt. If you have sufficient time, leave the pork to stand for ¾ hour, then rub off the salt, which will have absorbed much of the moisture from the rind. Re-salt. Melt the dripping in a roasting tin, and place the pork in it. Cook in an oven set at 200°C (400°F) for 55-60 minutes a kilo (or 2 pounds), allowing an extra 25 minutes, basting frequently. Serve with gravy and apple sauce.

To make the sauce: Peel and core the apples, then quarter them, placing them in a bowl of cold water to retain their colour. Place the apples in a saucepan with the lemon rind and a good dash of pepper. Add 1 tablespoon of water to begin the cooking. Bring to the boil, cover, and cook gently until pulpy. Beat well, then stir in the sugar and the butter.

MRS BAGNET'S BOILED PORK

In the distribution of these comestibles, as in every other household duty, Mrs. Bagnet develops an exact system; sitting with every dish before her; allotting to every portion of pork its own portion of pot-liquor, greens, potatoes, and even mustard! and serving it out complete. Having likewise served out the beer from a can, and thus supplied the mess with all things necessary, Mrs. Bagnet proceeds to satisfy her own hunger, which is in a healthy state.

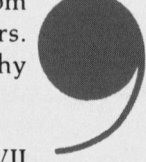

Bleak House Ch XXVII

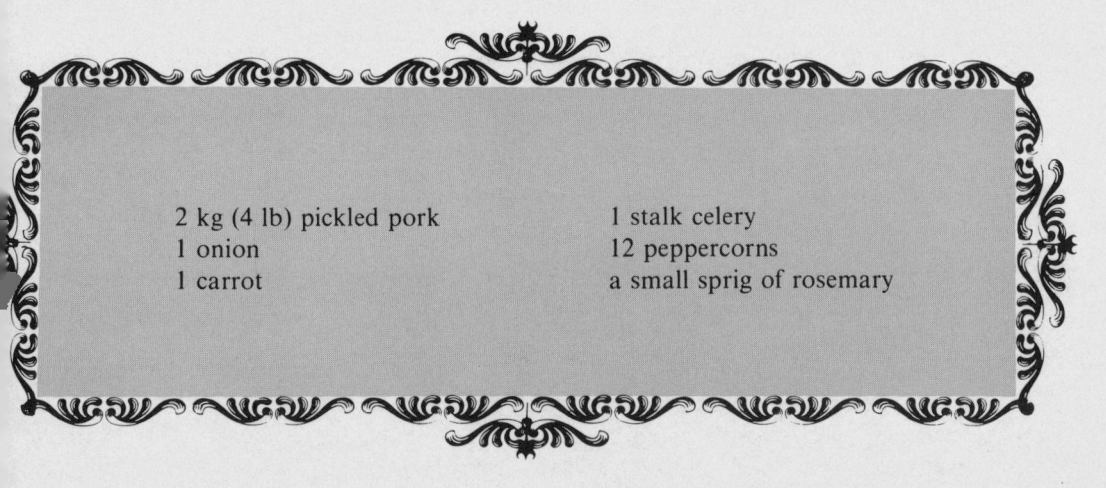

2 kg (4 lb) pickled pork
1 onion
1 carrot
1 stalk celery
12 peppercorns
a small sprig of rosemary

If the pork is very salty, first soak it for 2 hours in cold water. Drain. Place the pork in a saucepan, cover with cold water, and bring to the boil. Remove any scum. Add the onion, carrot, celery, peppercorns, and rosemary. Simmer gently until the meat is well done, allowing approximately 30 minutes to each half-kilo (or pound). Serve, Mrs Bagnet style, with boiled vegetables.

RASHERS OF BROILED HAM, DONE TO A TURN

'That done, they sat down to tea in the bar, where there was an uncommon display of buttered toast, and—in order that they might not grow faint for want of sustenance, and might have a decent halting-place or half-way house between dinner and supper—a few savoury trifles in the shape of great rashers of broiled ham, which being well-cured, done to a turn, and smoking hot, sent forth a tempting and delicious fragrance.

Barnaby Rudge Ch XXI

In the meantime the youngest Miss Pecksniff brought from the kitchen a smoking dish of ham and eggs, and, setting the same before her father, took up her station on a low stool at his feet: thereby bringing her eyes on a level with the teaboard.'

Martin Chuzzlewit Ch II

The home-curing of hams and bacon (the flitches) provided a ready source of smoked meat to serve the year round. After their month or so hanging above the wood fire, hams were often placed in stout paper sacks, or several wrappings of brown paper secured with twine, and then placed in flour sacks. This kept them free from attack by flies and other insects. One recipe which advised that it gave positive security against insect attack was:

'First fill a large kettle or boiler full of water and let it come to a boil, then dip your hams in and let them remain three minutes, then remove to a board or table and cover them with a thick paste made of flour, water and cayenne pepper. Have the paste red with pepper. Let them lay in the sun until dry. Then put in paper sacks and tie closely, and hang in a dark place. This will keep them nice the year round, if they are put up before fly time.' The writer promised 'a positiveness that no fly nor bug can pierce this peppery paste'.

To broil, or grill, ham:

'If the ham is very salty freshen it in a little hot water, as salt pork is freshened, except to remove from the stove as soon as it boils, and let it soak about 20 minutes. Drain nicely, and broil as beefsteak, which see. Turning 2 or 3 times; season with pepper and a little butter upon it. To be served at once, while hot.'

To 'broil as beefsteak', the following directions were given:

'Be sure that next you have, to broil the steak,
Good coal in plenty: nor a moment leave,
But turn it over this way, and then that;
The lean should be quite rare—not so the fat.
The platter now and then the juice receive,
Put on your butter, place it on your meat,
Salt, pepper, turn it over, serve, and eat.'

And if Mr Pecksniff's ham and eggs are to be enjoyed, the following recipe, sent to *Country Gentleman* by a cook might well serve:

'Cut the ham not quite ½ inch thick, boil in plenty of water until barely cooked through; put in a pan and brown the fat part slightly; remove from the fire, take out the meat and pour off the fat into a cup; wipe the pan until it shines like a mirror. Then put in a spoonful of the clear part of the fat, break in the eggs, and set the pan in a place scarcely hotter than boiling water, cover, and let the eggs cook slowly, for four or five minutes, taking them out as soon as they can be lifted. Place them around the dish of ham, but do not put the fat on the dish. Eat with mashed potatoes.'

Chicken and Goose and their Sauces

ROAST CHICKEN WITH SHRIMP STUFFING AND FORCEMEAT BALLS

❛'But my dear young friend,' said Mr. Pumblechook, 'you must be hungry, you must be exhausted. Be seated. Here is a chicken had round from the Boar, here is a tongue had round from the Boar, here's one or two little things had round from the Boar, that I hope you may not despise ...'
Mr. Pumblechook helped me to the liver wing, and to the best slice of tongue (none of those out-of-the-way No Thoroughfares of Pork now), and took, comparatively speaking, no care of himself at all. 'Ah! poultry, poultry! You little thought,' said Mr. Pumblechook, apostrophising the fowl in the dish, 'when you was a young fledgling, what was in store for you. You little thought you was to be refreshment beneath this humble roof ...'

Great Expectations Ch XIX

Further conversation is prevented, for the time, by the necessity under which Mr. Bagnet finds himself of directing the whole force of his mind to the dinner, which is a little endangered by the dry humour of the fowls in not yielding any gravy, and also by the made-gravy acquiring no flavour, and turning out of a flaxen complexion. With a similar perverseness the potatoes crumble off forks in the process of peeling, upheaving from their centres in every direction, as if they were subject to earthquakes. The legs of the fowls, too, are longer than could be desired, and extremely scaly ...
It is well for the old girl that she has but one birthday in a year, for two such indulgences in poultry might be injurious. Every kind of finer tendon and ligament that is in the nature of poultry to possess, is developed in these specimens in the singular form of guitar strings. Their limbs appear to have struck roots into their breasts and bodies, as aged trees strike roots into the earth. Their legs are so hard, as to encourage the idea that they must have devoted the greater part of their long and arduous lives to pedestrian exercises, and the walking of matches.❜

Bleak House Ch XLIX

The following recipe is more akin to the culinary intention of Mr Bagnet, rather than to his practice:

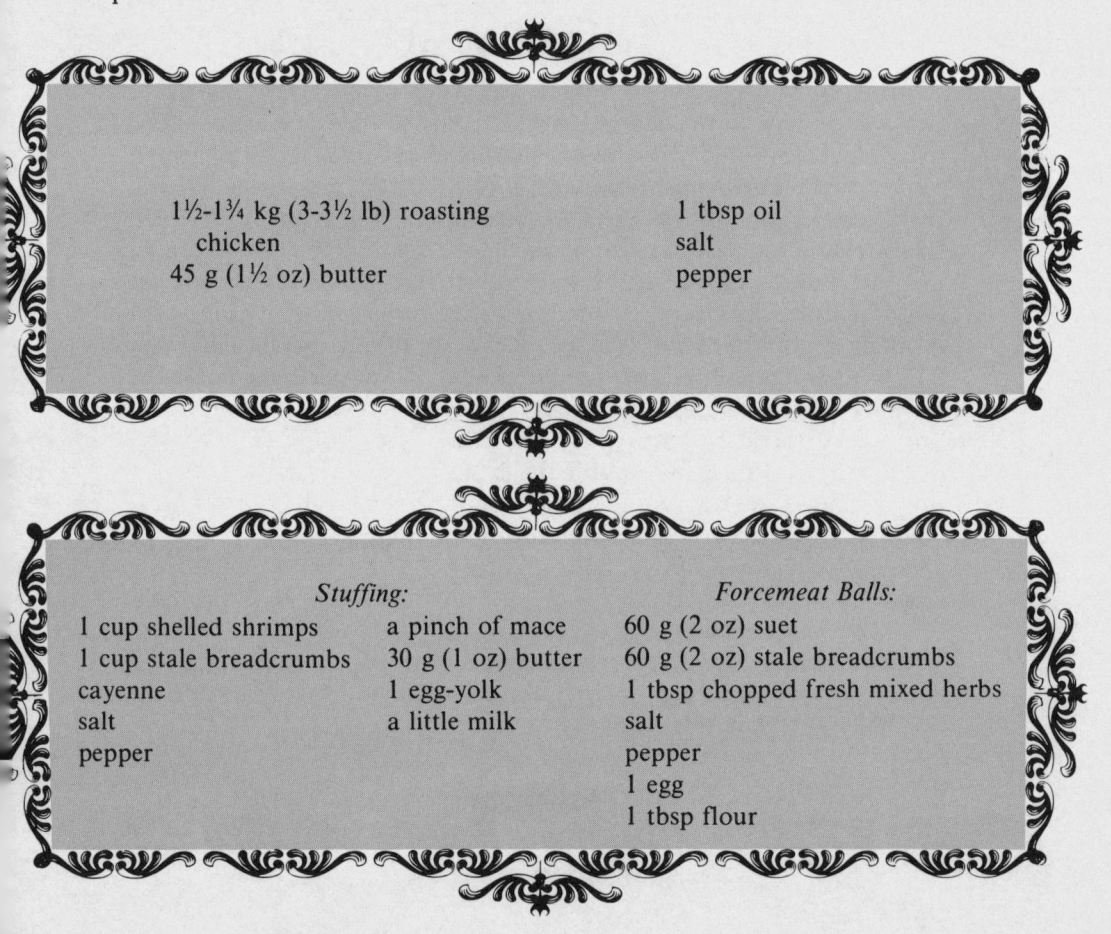

1½-1¾ kg (3-3½ lb) roasting chicken
45 g (1½ oz) butter
1 tbsp oil
salt
pepper

Stuffing:
1 cup shelled shrimps
1 cup stale breadcrumbs
cayenne
salt
pepper
a pinch of mace
30 g (1 oz) butter
1 egg-yolk
a little milk

Forcemeat Balls:
60 g (2 oz) suet
60 g (2 oz) stale breadcrumbs
1 tbsp chopped fresh mixed herbs
salt
pepper
1 egg
1 tbsp flour

Prepare the stuffing by placing the shrimps, breadcrumbs, cayenne, salt and pepper, and mace in a bowl. Cut the butter into shreds, add it to the other ingredients and mix well. Lightly beat the egg-yolk and use it to bind together the mixture. Add a little milk if the mixture is too dry.

Wipe the chicken inside and out with a damp cloth, and fill the cavity with the stuffing. Truss the bird, and rub the outside with butter, then season with salt and pepper. Heat the oil in a roasting pan, and place the bird in the pan breast-side up. Place it in an oven at 200°C (400°F) and cook for 1-1½ hours, depending upon the size and age of the bird. To test when it is done, place a skewer in the thigh meat—the juices that run out should be quite clear. The chicken should be well basted during cooking, being turned first on one side after 20 minutes, and then on the other 20 minutes later.

Towards the end of the chicken's cooking time, make the forcemeat balls. Chop the suet finely, then blend it with the breadcrumbs, herbs, and salt and pepper. Beat the egg and use it to bind together all the ingredients. Form into small balls and roll them in flour. Have ready a saucepan of boiling water. Gently add the forcemeat balls to the water and simmer for 10 minutes. Remove them with a slotted spoon, and serve them surrounding the roast chicken. Alternatively, the balls can be fried. Roll the balls in the flour, then in a beaten egg, then in breadcrumbs. Fry them over a moderate heat in oil until they are golden. Surround the chicken with forcemeat balls to serve.

A VERY LORD MAYOR'S FEAST OF BOILED CHICKEN AND PARSLEY BUTTER

It was a nice little dinner—seemed to me then, a very Lord Mayor's Feast—and it acquired additional relish from being eaten under those independent circumstances, with no old people by, and with London all around us. This again was heightened by a certain gipsy character that set the banquet off: for, while the table was, as Mr. Pumblechook might have said, the lap of luxury—being entirely furnished forth from the coffee-house—the circumjacent region of sitting-room was of a comparatively pastureless and shifty character: imposing on the waiter the wandering habits of putting the covers on the floor (where he fell over them), the melted butter in the arm-chair, the bread in the bookshelves, the cheese in the coal-scuttle, and the boiled fowl into my bed in the next room—where I found much of its parsley and butter in a state of congelation when I retired for the night.

Great Expectations Ch XXII

'Melted butter' often referred to Melted Butter Sauce (see recipe for Celery Sauce)—although melted butter, seasoned, was also a frequent accompaniment to plain meats.

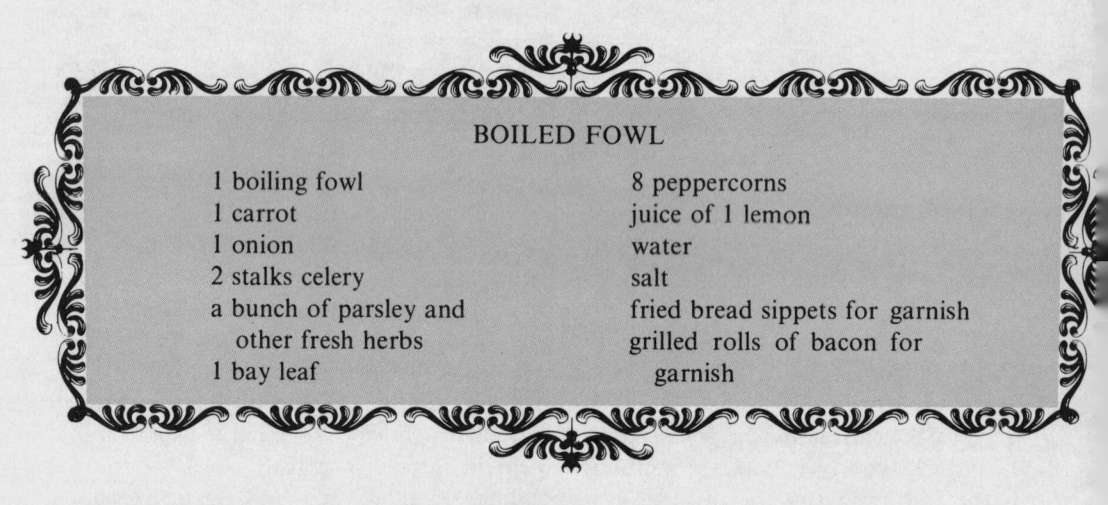

BOILED FOWL

1 boiling fowl
1 carrot
1 onion
2 stalks celery
a bunch of parsley and other fresh herbs
1 bay leaf
8 peppercorns
juice of 1 lemon
water
salt
fried bread sippets for garnish
grilled rolls of bacon for garnish

Place the fowl in a large saucepan, resting on its back. Quarter the vegetables and add them to the saucepan, along with the herbs, bay leaf, peppercorns, lemon juice and salt. Just cover the bird with water, and slowly bring to a simmer. (Remember the words of a nineteenth-century cookery book: 'Cooks should be made to comprehend the difference between a boiling simmer and a boiling gallop'.) Simmer the bird for 2-3 hours, depending upon its age and size. To serve, remove the skin from the fowl, carve, and pour over a little parsley butter. Serve the rest of the sauce on individual serves. Boiled rice, cooked in the stock from the bird, makes an excellent addition. Garnish the meat with fried bread sippets and rolls of grilled bacon.

PARSLEY BUTTER

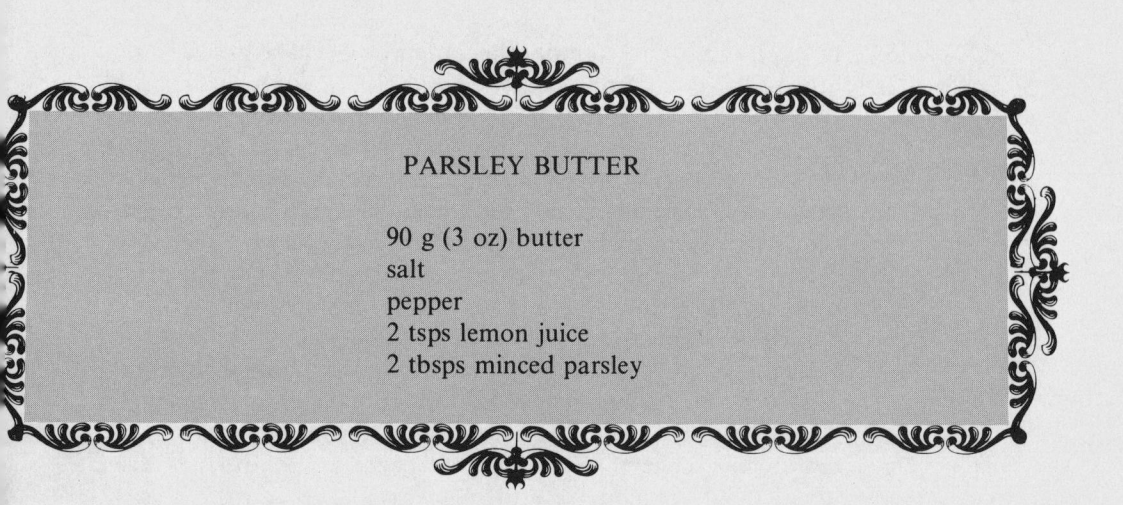

90 g (3 oz) butter
salt
pepper
2 tsps lemon juice
2 tbsps minced parsley

Melt the butter in a saucepan, season with salt and pepper, and add the lemon juice. Stir in the parsley, and allow to infuse for 2 minutes. Serve.

MRS CHIRRUP'S ROAST GOOSE

But if there be one branch of housekeeping in which she excels to an utterly unparalleled and unprecedented extent, it is in the important one of carving. A roast goose is universally allowed to be the great stumbling block in the way of young aspirants to perfection in this department of science; many promising carvers, beginning with legs of mutton, and preserving a good reputation through fillets of veal, sirloins of beef, quarters of lamb, fowls, and even ducks, have sunk before a roast goose, and lost caste and character for ever. To Mrs. Chirrup the resolving the goose into its smallest component parts is a pleasant pastime—a practical joke—a thing to be done in a minute or so, without the smallest interruption to the conversation of the time ... The legs of the bird slide gently down into a pool of gravy, the wings seem to melt from the body, the breast separates into a row of juicy slices, the smaller and more complicated parts of his anatomy are perfectly developed, a cavern of stuffing is revealed, and the goose is gone!

Sketches of Young Couples

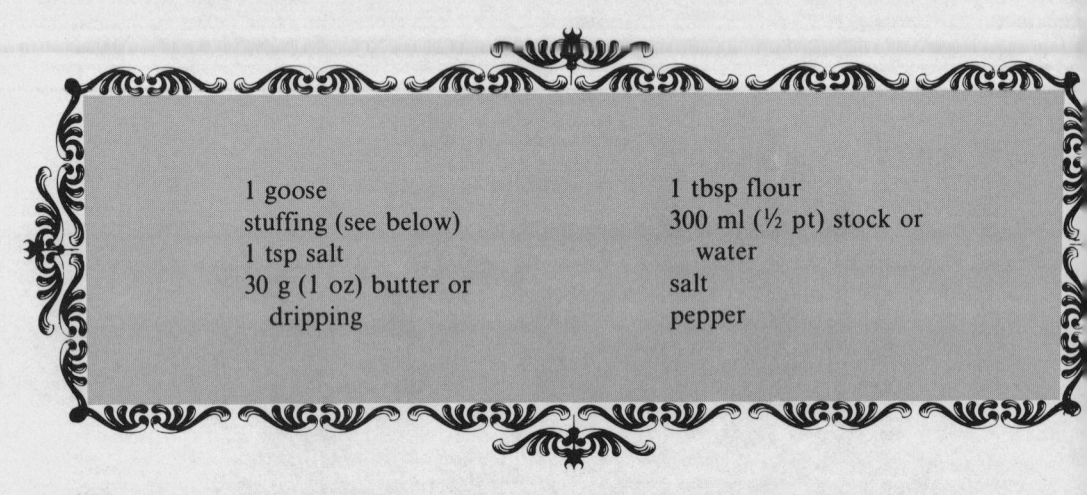

1 goose
stuffing (see below)
1 tsp salt
30 g (1 oz) butter or
    dripping

1 tbsp flour
300 ml (½ pt) stock or
    water
salt
pepper

Stuff the goose and truss it securely. Rub the salt over the skin. Place the goose breast-side up in a roasting pan, which has been greased on the bottom with the butter or dripping. As a goose is very fatty, no extra fat is required, and only a little basting is essential during cooking. There is no point in pricking the goose to release the extra fat, as the process makes little difference to the final result, and can release juices that should be retained under the skin. Pour off excess fat from time to time, keeping it for use in other cookery, as it is delicious and highly prized. Cook until tender, allowing 20 minutes a half-kilo (or pound) for a bird weighing 4-5 kilos (8-10 lb). Pour off all but 2 tablespoons of fat and juice, and stir the flour into what remains in the pan. Scrape well around the pan, then, over a moderate heat, pour in the stock or water to make the gravy. Stir until the gravy boils, then leave to simmer for a couple of minutes. Season to taste with salt and pepper. The tradition with poultry was to pour the gravy around the bird on the platter, but as goose is a difficult bird to carve, it was usually suggested that only a little gravy be used to moisten the dish, the rest being sent to the table separately.

Soyer's Goose Stuffing:

'Take 4 apples peeled and cored, 4 onions, 4 leaves of sage, and 4 leaves of lemon thyme not broken, and boil them in a stewpan with sufficient water to cover them; when done, pulp them through a sieve, removing the sage and thyme; then add sufficient pulp of mealy potatoes to cause it to be sufficiently dry without sticking to the hand; add pepper and salt, and stuff the bird.'

Goose Stuffing:

'Chop very fine about two ounces of onion, of *green* sage leaves about an ounce (both unboiled), four ounces of bread-crumbs, a bit of butter about as big as a walnut &c., the yolk and white of an egg, and a little pepper and salt; some add to this a minced apple.'

A particularly nice sauce to serve with goose is the following variant on bread sauce; it is also excellent with pork and all poultry:

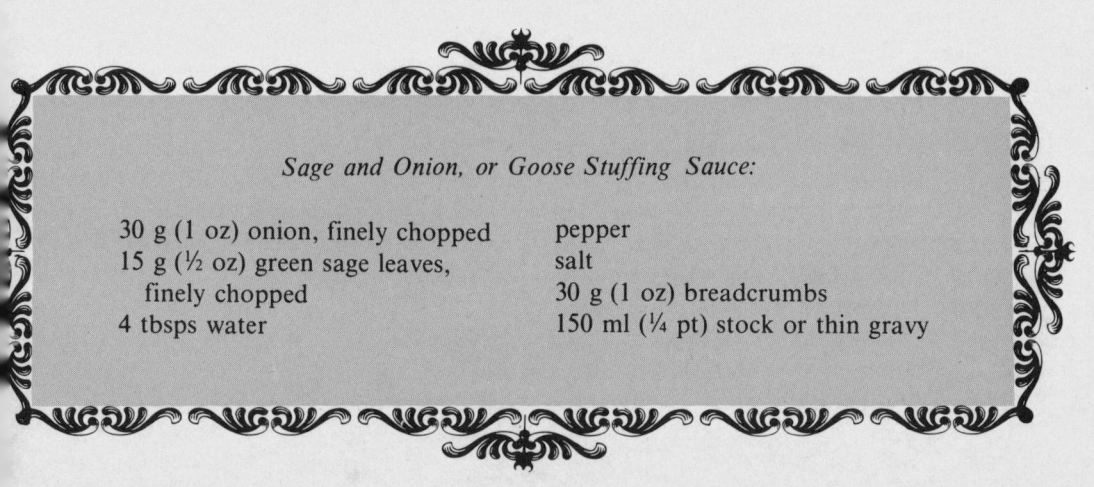

Sage and Onion, or Goose Stuffing Sauce:

30 g (1 oz) onion, finely chopped	pepper
15 g (½ oz) green sage leaves, finely chopped	salt
	30 g (1 oz) breadcrumbs
4 tbsps water	150 ml (¼ pt) stock or thin gravy

Place the onion, sage leaves, and water in a saucepan, and simmer them all together for 10 minutes. Add the breadcrumbs, stock or gravy, and seasonings. Stir well together, bring to the boil, and simmer for 5 minutes.

MELTED BUTTER CELERY SAUCE AT CHRISTMAS

'As a particularly Angular man, I do not fit smoothly into the social circle, and consequently I have no other engagement at Christmas time than to partake, on the twenty-fifth, of a boiled turkey and celery sauce with a—with a particularly Angular clerk I have the good fortune to possess, whose father, being a Norfolk farmer, sends him up (the turkey up), as a present to me, from the neighbourhood of Norwich ...'

The Mystery of Edwin Drood Ch IX

Melted Butter Sauce was the basic constituent of most English sauces, and, according to Tallyrand, it was the *only* one the English knew. A basic melted butter sauce was made thus: 'Cut about two ounces of butter into pieces, put it into a stewpan, with a dessert-spoonful of flour and two table-spoonfuls of milk; when well mixed add six table-spoonfuls more of water, hold it over the fire, and let it simmer till *thick*, turning it one way. No branch of cookery is so easily performed, yet how seldom do we have it well made—generally a watery fluid, from sheer neglect.'

Note: 'Turning it one way' refers to stirring; for use the sauce should be seasoned with salt and pepper.

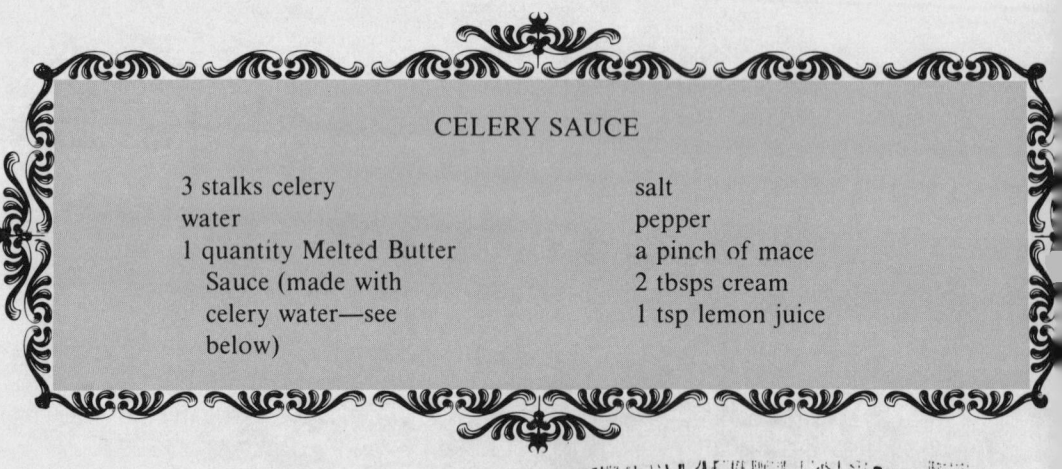

CELERY SAUCE

3 stalks celery	salt
water	pepper
1 quantity Melted Butter Sauce (made with celery water—see below)	a pinch of mace
	2 tbsps cream
	1 tsp lemon juice

Trim and remove fibres from the celery, then cut it into small dice. Place it in a saucepan and cover it with water; simmer until the celery is tender. Strain and reserve the liquid. Make a quantity of melted butter sauce, using liquid from the cooked celery rather than plain water. Add the celery to the sauce, season with salt and pepper, and a pinch of mace. Stir in the cream and the lemon juice, heat through, and serve.

Savoury Pies

Most of the following pies are made with a one-crust pastry, although usually they would have had a crust at the top and bottom. However, as we no longer need so much pastry shell either as a filler or as an aid to keeping the meat, it has been left out. The jellied stock used serves to hold the pie together if it is to be eaten cold. Simply increase the quantity of pastry if you prefer a two-crust pie.

BEEFSTEAK AND KIDNEY PIE

Flora accordingly led the way across the road to the pie-shop in question ... When the three 'kidney ones', which were to be a blind to the conversation, were set before them on three little tin platters, each kidney one ornamented with a hole at the top, into which the civil man poured hot gravy out of a spouted can as if he were feeding three lamps, Flora took out her pocket-handkerchief.

Little Dorrit Ch XXXIV

The formality of spreading a table-cloth, not being observed in Mr. Riderhood's establishment, the serving of the 'peck' was the affair of a moment; it merely consisted in the handing down of a capacious baking-dish with three-fourths of an immense meat-pie in it, and the production of two pocket-knives, an earthenware mug, and a large brown bottle of beer.
Both ate and drank, but Riderhood much the more abundantly. In lieu of plates, that honest man cut two triangular pieces from the thick crust of the pie, and laid them, inside uppermost, upon the table: the one before himself, and the other before his guest. Upon these platters he placed two goodly portions of the contents of the pie, thus imparting the unusual interest to the entertainment that each partaker scooped out the inside of his plate, and consumed it with his other fare, besides having the sport of pursuing the clots of congealed gravy over the plain of the table, and of successfully taking them into his mouth at last from the blade of his knife, in case of their not first sliding off it.

Our Mutual Friend Bk 4 Ch VII

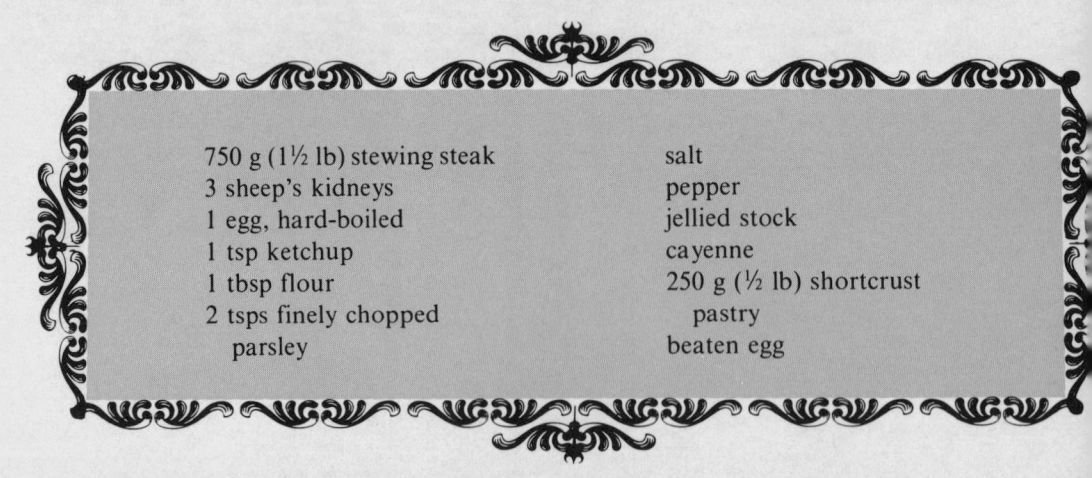

750 g (1½ lb) stewing steak
3 sheep's kidneys
1 egg, hard-boiled
1 tsp ketchup
1 tbsp flour
2 tsps finely chopped parsley
salt
pepper
jellied stock
cayenne
250 g (½ lb) shortcrust pastry
beaten egg

Trim the meat of fat and cut it into thin strips suitable for rolling up. Trim and core the kidneys, and cut them into small pieces. Blend together the flour, salt and pepper on a plate (this step should be omitted if the pie is only to be served cold; instead, season the meat well when it is placed in the pie dish). Coat the pieces of steak and kidney with the flour mixture. Roll up the pieces of meat, letting each roll contain a piece of kidney. Heap the rolls in a buttered pie dish, heaping them more in the middle to give support to the pastry. Sprinkle with some parsley and cayenne pepper, and season with salt and pepper. Chop the egg into about 8 pieces, and place these around the meat. Add the ketchup and sufficient stock to three-quarters fill the pie dish. Roll out the pastry on a floured board, and cut a strip to fit around the edge of the pie dish. Moisten the edge of the pie dish with water, place the strip of pastry on it, and moisten the top of the strip. Cover the pie dish with pastry, press to seal and trim the edges. Cut a hole in the centre. Glaze with beaten egg. Bake at 220°C (425°F) for 15 minutes, then reduce the heat to 180°C (350°F) and cook for a further 1½ hours approximately. The total cooking time will depend upon the quality of the meat. Test by running a skewer through the hole in the top. If the pastry shows signs of becoming overcooked, protect with layers of greaseproof paper. Remove from oven. Have ready some heated stock, and pour some of this into the pie by using a funnel placed in the hole in the centre. Serve hot or cold.

Note: As with all such pies, the top can be decorated with pastry roses or leaves. Again, instead of one large pie, individual pies can be made in the same manner.

BEEFSTEAK AND MUSHROOM PIE

I did not like to leave him [*Mr Peggotty*] under such circumstances, and we all three dined together off a beefsteak pie—which was one of the many good things for which Peggotty was famous—and which was curiously flavoured, on this occasion, I recollect well, by a miscellaneous taste of tea, coffee, butter, bacon, cheese, new loaves, firewood, candles, and walnut ketchup, continually ascending from the shop. After dinner we sat for an hour or so near the window, without talking much; and then Mr. Peggotty got up, and brought his oilskin bag and his stout stick, and laid them on the table.

David Copperfield Ch XXXII

'Chesney Wold, Thomas,' rejoins the housekeeper, with proud complacency, 'will set my Lady up! There is no finer air, and no healthier soil, in the world!'
Thomas may have his own personal opinions on this subject; probably hints them, in his manner of smoothing his sleek head from the nape of his neck to his temples; but he forbears to express them further, and retires to the servants' hall to regale on cold meat pie and ale.

Bleak House Ch XL

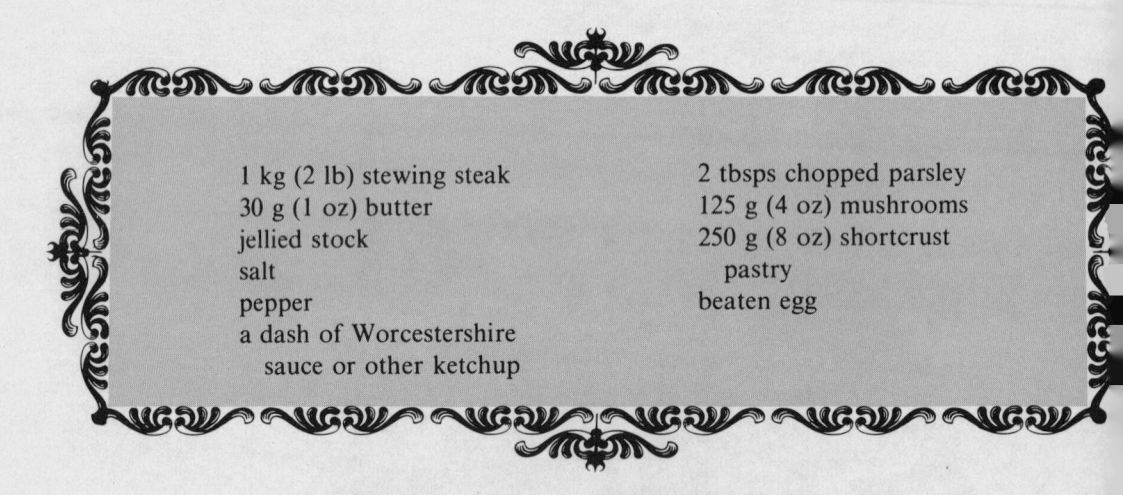

---

1 kg (2 lb) stewing steak
30 g (1 oz) butter
jellied stock
salt
pepper
a dash of Worcestershire sauce or other ketchup
2 tbsps chopped parsley
125 g (4 oz) mushrooms
250 g (8 oz) shortcrust pastry
beaten egg

Dice the stewing steak. Melt the butter in a saucepan, add the meat, and brown it over a moderate heat. Season with salt, pepper, and Worcestershire sauce or other ketchup. Add sufficient stock to cover, and simmer for 1½ hours or until the meat is tender. Trim and wipe the mushrooms. Layer the mushrooms, meat, and parsley in a pie dish, and pour in the cooking liquid. Add more stock if necessary to three-quarters fill the pie dish.

Roll out the pastry on a floured board, and cut a strip to fit around the edge of the pie dish. Moisten the edge of the pie dish with water, place the strip of pastry on it, and moisten the top of the strip. Cover the pie dish with pastry, pressing to seal, and trim the edges. Cut a hole in the centre. Glaze with beaten egg. Bake at 200°C (400°F) for 30 minutes, until the pastry is browned. Serve hot or cold.

'He has a proud stomach, this chap! He's too proud to eat it! Give him a meal of chaff!'

A VERY MELLERING VEAL AND HAM PIE

'*Have* I lost my smell for fruits, or is it a apple pie, sir?' asked Wegg.
'It's a veal and ham pie,' said Mr. Boffin.
'Is it, indeed, sir? And it would be hard, sir, to name the pie that is a better pie than a weal and hammer,' said Mr. Wegg, nodding his head emotionally.
'Have some, Wegg?'
'Thank you, Mr. Boffin, I think I will, at your invitation. I wouldn't at any other party's, at the present juncture; but at yours, sir!—And meaty jelly too, especially when a little salt, which is the case where there's ham, is mellering to the organ, is very mellering to the organ.'
Mr. Wegg did not say what organ, but spoke with a cheerful generality.

Our Mutual Friend Bk 1 Ch V

'Weal pie,' said Mr. Weller, soliloquising, as he arranged the eatables on the grass. 'Wery good thing is weal pie, when you know the lady as made it, and is quite sure it an't kittens; and arter all, though, where's the odds, when they're so like weal that the wery piemen themselves don't know the difference? ... Tongue; well, that's a wery good thing when it an't a woman's. Bread—knuckle o' ham, reg'lar picter—cold beef in slices, wery good. What's in them stone jars, young touch-and-go?'
'Beer in this one,' replied the boy, taking from his shoulder a couple of large stone bottles, fastened together by a leathern strap—'cold punch in t'other.'

Pickwick Papers Ch XIX

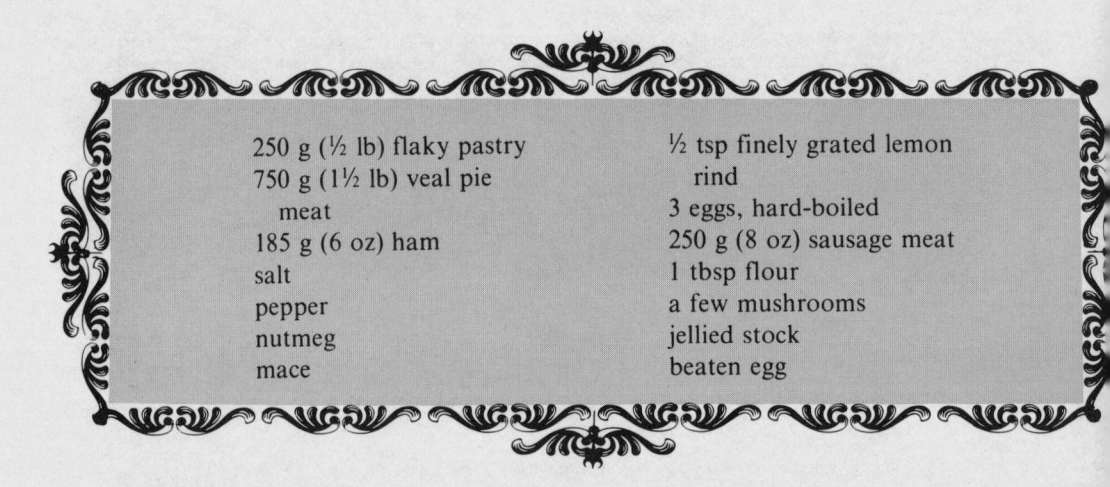

250 g (½ lb) flaky pastry
750 g (1½ lb) veal pie meat
185 g (6 oz) ham
salt
pepper
nutmeg
mace
½ tsp finely grated lemon rind
3 eggs, hard-boiled
250 g (8 oz) sausage meat
1 tbsp flour
a few mushrooms
jellied stock
beaten egg

Cut the veal and ham into pieces that are about 3 cm square, and season them with salt, pepper, nutmeg and mace. Quarter the eggs. Lightly season the sausage meat and roll it into small balls, then roll the balls in the flour. Place the veal, ham, eggs, meatballs and mushrooms in layers in a pie dish, and sprinkle with lemon rind. Add sufficient stock to three-quarters fill the pie dish. Roll out the pastry on a floured board, and cut a strip to fit around the edge of the pie dish. Moisten the edge of the pie dish with water, place the strip of pastry on it, and moisten the top of the strip. Cover the pie dish with pastry, and knock up the edges. Cut a hole in the centre. Glaze with beaten egg. Bake at 220°C (425°F) for 15 minutes, then reduce the heat to 180°C (350°F) and cook for a further 1-1¼ hours. If the pastry shows signs of becoming overcooked, protect it with layers of greaseproof paper. Remove from oven. Have ready some heated stock, and pour some of this into the heated pie by using a funnel placed in the hole in the centre. Serve hot or cold.

A ROUND COMPACT RAISED PORK PIE

I stole some bread, some rind of cheese, about half a jar of mincemeat (which I tied up in my pocket-handkerchief with my last night's slice), some brandy from a stone bottle (which I decanted into a glass bottle I had secretly used for making that intoxicating fluid, Spanish-liquorice-water, up in my room: diluting the stone bottle from a jug in the kitchen cupboard), a meat bone with very little on it, and a beautiful round compact pork pie. I was nearly going away without the pie, but I was tempted to mount upon a shelf, to look what it was that was put away so carefully in a covered earthenware dish in a corner, and I found it was the pie, and I took it, in the hope that it was not intended for early use, and would not be missed for some time.

Great Expectations Ch II

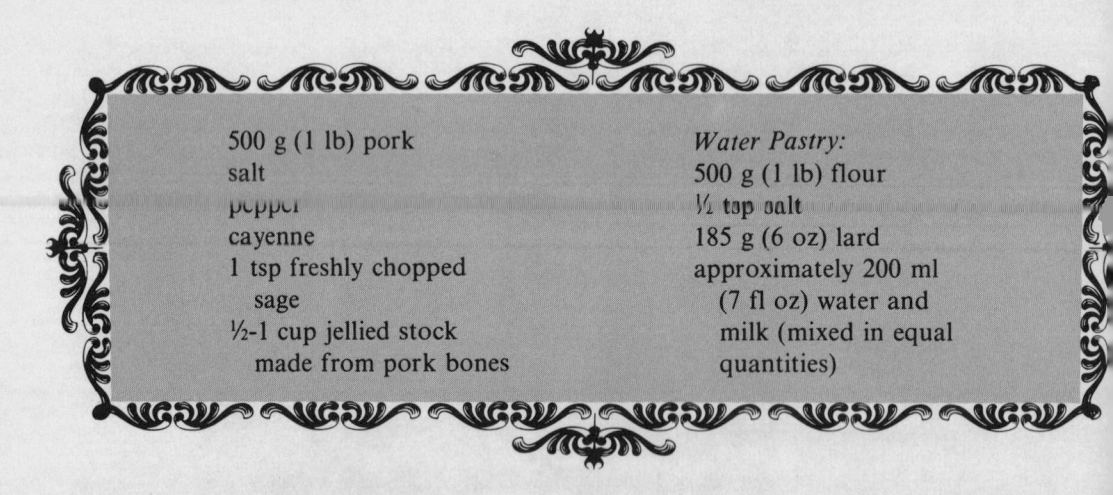

500 g (1 lb) pork
salt
pepper
cayenne
1 tsp freshly chopped sage
½-1 cup jellied stock made from pork bones

Water Pastry:
500 g (1 lb) flour
½ tsp salt
185 g (6 oz) lard
approximately 200 ml (7 fl oz) water and milk (mixed in equal quantities)

Dice both the lean and the fat of the pork; mix the meat with the salt, pepper, cayenne and sage. Sift the flour and the salt into a bowl. Heat together the lard, water and milk; stir until the fat has dissolved. While still boiling, pour the liquid into a well in the centre of the flour (do not at first use it all, as it may not be required). Knead the pastry well; it should form a stiff paste, but should be able to be moulded easily. Add a little more warm water and milk if needed. Rapid work is required, as the pastry must be used while it is still warm, otherwise the lard sets and the pastry cracks. The pie shell can be raised in three ways: a special mould can be used (these often have decorative patterns on them which imprint the pastry); the pastry can be shaped around the fist into a round or an oval (this is the simplest home method, but one reserved for the experienced maker of raised pies); or the pastry can be moulded around the outside of a large jar (this is simple; have the jar lightly floured for safe removal of the pastry). Turn the pastry out on to a lightly floured board, and knead with the hand (not a rolling pin) into a thick round, reserving some to make a lid. Place the reserved portion in a cloth in a warm place. Using the jar method, quickly mould the pastry round the base and up the sides of the jar, leaving no cracks or spaces; when the pastry cools sufficiently, lift out the jar. Pack the prepared meat closely into the pie shell; it must be quite full. Smoothly cut around the top edges of the pastry. Form a lid from the reserved pastry, and pinch it on to the shell, leaving no gaps. Make a hole in the top, and decorate if desired. Tie brown paper around the pie to help it keep its shape. Slide the pie on to a floured baking sheet and place it in an oven set at 180°C (350°F). If the meat is of good quality it should be cooked 1½-2 hours. Protect the top of the pie with paper if it browns too much. Remove the pie from the oven and allow to cool on the baking sheet. Remove the paper. Melt the jellied stock. Place a funnel in the hole in the top of the pie, and slowly pour in the stock. Leave to cool and set. Serve cold.

VENISON PIE

'Have you got anything to eat, any of you? I'm as ravenous as a hungry wolf. Which of you was in the larder—come?'

'I was, brother,' said Dennis, pulling off his hat, and fumbling in the crown. 'There's a matter of cold venison pasty somewhere or another here, if that'll do.'

... Mr. Dennis, having by this time succeeded in extricating from his hat a great mass of pastry, which had been wedged in so tightly that it was not easily got out, put it before him; and Hugh, having borrowed a notched and jagged knife from one of the company, fell to work upon it vigorously.

Barnaby Rudge Ch LIX

A venison pie should be made entirely of venison; the addition of other meats reduces it to being merely a game, or meat, pie. If a proper 'pasty' is required, line the pie dish with pastry, instead of placing a strip around the edge. In that case a greater quantity of pastry will be needed.

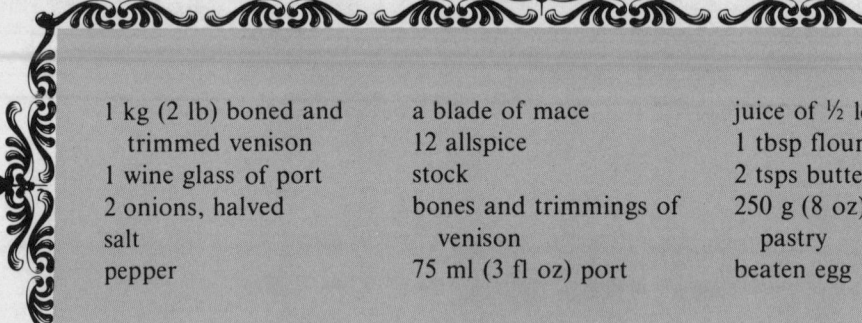

---

1 kg (2 lb) boned and trimmed venison
1 wine glass of port
2 onions, halved
salt
pepper
a blade of mace
12 allspice
stock
bones and trimmings of venison
75 ml (3 fl oz) port
juice of ½ lemon
1 tbsp flour
2 tsps butter
250 g (8 oz) shortcrust pastry
beaten egg

Cut the meat into pieces 5 cm (2 in.) square. Place the meat in a saucepan with the wine glass of port (more can be used, if liked; the original recipe called for 450 ml or ¾ pint), the onions, salt, pepper, mace, and allspice; cover with stock. Simmer until the meat is tender. Take out the meat and place it to cool in a dish along with about half a cup of the cooking liquor. Place the meat trimmings and bones in the saucepan with the remaining cooking liquor, and simmer for 1 hour. Strain, and reserve the liquid. Place the meat and its moistening liquid in a pie dish. Roll out the pastry on a floured board, and cut a strip to fit around the edge of the pie dish. Moisten the edge of the pie dish with water, place the strip of pastry on it, and moisten the top of the strip. Cover the pie dish with pastry, pressing to seal, and trim the edges. Cut a hole in the centre. Glaze with beaten egg. Bake at 230°C (450°F) for 10 minutes, reduce the heat to 180°C (350°F) and bake for a further 20-30 minutes, until the pie is golden brown. Meanwhile, place 300 ml (½ pint) of the strained stock in a saucepan. To it add the 75 ml (3 fl oz) of port and the lemon juice. Combine together the flour and the butter, and drop it in small pieces into the heated liquid, stirring all the time. Test for seasoning. Simmer for 3 minutes. When the pie is ready to serve, use a funnel through the hole in the centre of the pie to pour in the thickened gravy. Accompany with cranberry sauce.

SITCH A RABBIT PIE

'Sitch a rabbit-pie, Bill,' exclaimed that young gentleman, disclosing to view a huge pasty; 'sitch delicate creatures, with sitch tender limbs, Bill, that the wery bones melt in your mouth, and there's no occasion to pick 'em; half a pound of seven-and-sixpenny green, so precious strong that if you mix it with biling water, it'll go nigh to blow the lid of the tea-pot off; a pound and a half of moist sugar that the niggers didn't work at all at, before they got it up to sitch a pitch of goodness—oh, no! Two half-quartern brans; a pound of best fresh; piece of double Glo'ster; and, to wind up all, some of the richest sort you ever lushed!'

Oliver Twist Ch XXXIX

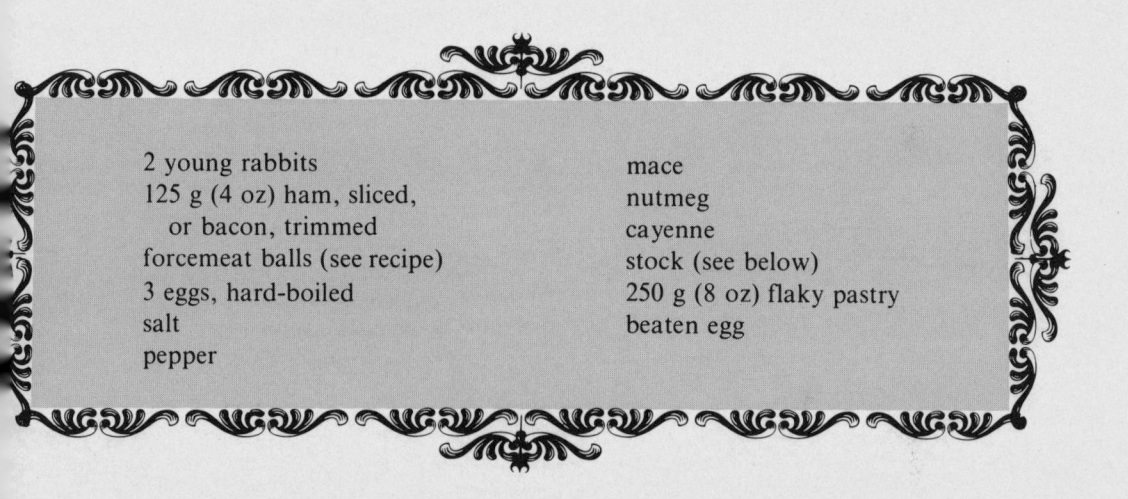

---

2 young rabbits
125 g (4 oz) ham, sliced, or bacon, trimmed
forcemeat balls (see recipe)
3 eggs, hard-boiled
salt
pepper
mace
nutmeg
cayenne
stock (see below)
250 g (8 oz) flaky pastry
beaten egg

Joint the rabbits, and soak them overnight in plenty of salted water. Drain. Use the bones from the wings and the rib-cage to make some stock by simmering them in water to cover with an onion, some fresh herbs, and a chopped carrot, for 2 hours. Strain and reserve the stock. Make the Forcemeat Balls (see recipe). If using bacon instead of ham, blanch it by simmering it in water for 2 minutes. Drain. Slice the eggs. Pack the rabbit pieces, forcemeat balls, eggs and ham or bacon, into a pie dish, seasoning well between each layer with salt, pepper, mace, nutmeg, and cayenne. Pour in sufficient stock to three-quarters fill the pie dish. Roll out the pastry on a floured board, and cut a strip to fit around the edge of the pie dish. Moisten the edge of the pie dish with water, place the strip of pastry on it, and moisten the top of the strip. Cover the pie dish with pastry, then trim and knock up the edges. Cut a hole in the centre. Glaze with beaten egg. Bake at 220°C (425°F) for 15 minutes, then reduce the heat to 180°C (350°F) and cook for a further hour. If the pastry shows signs of becoming overcooked, protect with layers of greaseproof paper. Remove from oven. Have ready some heated stock, and pour some of this into the pie by using a funnel placed in the hole in the centre.

PIGEON PIE

The fat boy jumped up: and the leaden eyes, which twinkled behind his mountainous cheeks, leered horribly upon the food as he unpacked it from the basket.

'Now, make haste,' said Mr. Wardle; for the fat boy was hanging fondly over a capon, which he seemed wholly unable to part with. The boy sighed deeply, and, bestowing an ardent gaze upon its plumpness, unwillingly consigned it to his master.

'That's right—look sharp. Now the tongue—now the pigeon-pie. Take care of that veal and ham—mind the lobsters—take the salad out of the cloth—give me the dressing.'

Pickwick Papers Ch IV

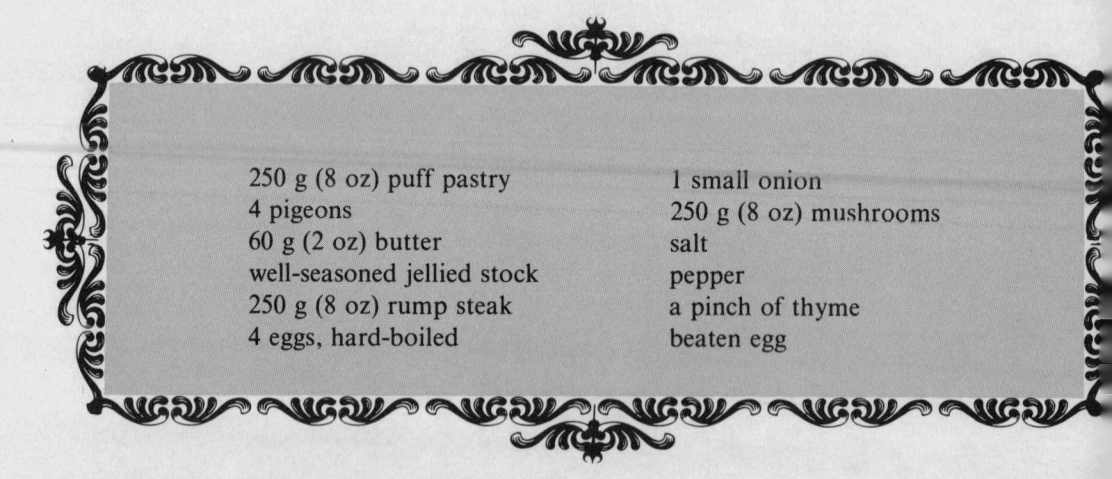

---

250 g (8 oz) puff pastry
4 pigeons
60 g (2 oz) butter
well-seasoned jellied stock
250 g (8 oz) rump steak
4 eggs, hard-boiled

1 small onion
250 g (8 oz) mushrooms
salt
pepper
a pinch of thyme
beaten egg

Heat the butter in a frying pan, and in it brown the prepared pigeons. Remove the pigeons to a saucepan, cover with stock, and simmer for 1½ hours. Cut the pigeons through the centre, remove the sharp breastbones and the meatless part of the legs. Retain the feet. Cut the steak into fairly thin pieces about 8 cm (3 in.) long, and place on the bottom of the pie dish. Season, and then lay the pigeon pieces over the top. Chop the eggs and the onion, and press these into the hollows between the birds. Add the trimmed and wiped mushrooms. Season with salt, pepper and thyme. Add sufficient stock to three-quarters fill the pie dish. Roll out the pastry on a floured board, and cut a strip to fit around the edge of the pie dish. Moisten the edge of the pie dish, place the strip of pastry on it, and moisten the top of the strip. Cover the pie dish with pastry, then trim and knock up the edges. Cut a hole in the centre. Glaze with beaten egg. Bake at 220°C (425°F) for 15 minutes; reduce the heat to 180°C (350°F) and cook for a further 1¼ hours. If the pastry shows signs of becoming overcooked, protect with layers of greaseproof paper. Remove from the oven. Have ready some heated stock, and pour some of this into the pie by using a funnel placed in the hole in the centre. Decorate the central hole with some of the reserved pigeon feet. Eat hot or cold.

Variety Meats and Sausages

TRIPE AND POTATO STEW

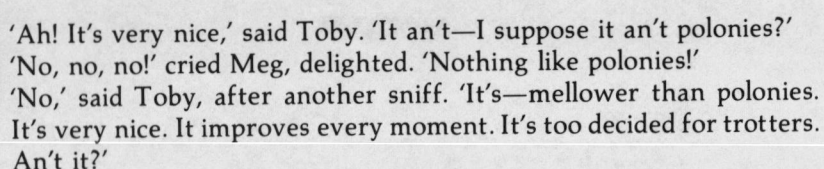

'Ah! It's very nice,' said Toby. 'It an't—I suppose it an't polonies?'
'No, no, no!' cried Meg, delighted. 'Nothing like polonies!'
'No,' said Toby, after another sniff. 'It's—mellower than polonies. It's very nice. It improves every moment. It's too decided for trotters. An't it?'
Meg was in an ecstasy. He could not have gone wider of the mark than trotters—except polonies.
'Liver?' said Toby, communing with himself. 'No. There's a mildness about it that don't answer to liver. Pettitoes? No. It an't faint enough for pettitoes. It wants the stringiness of cocks' heads. And I know it an't sausages. I'll tell you what it is. It's chitterlings!'
'No, it an't!' cried Meg in a burst of delight. 'No, it an't!'
'Why, what am I a-thinking of!' said Toby, suddenly recovering a position as near as the perpendicular as it was possible for him to assume. 'I shall forget my own name next. It's tripe!'
Tripe it was; and Meg, in high joy, protested he should say, in half a minute more, it was the best tripe ever stewed.

The Chimes First Quarter

'But who eats tripe?' said Mr. Filer, looking round. 'Tripe is without an exception the least economical, and the most wasteful article of consumption that the markets of this country can by possibility produce. The loss upon a pound of tripe has been found to be, in the boiling, seven-eighths of a fifth more than the loss upon a pound of any other animal substance whatever. Tripe is more expensive, properly understood, than the hot-house pineapple. Taking into account the number of animals slaughtered yearly within the bills of mortality alone; and forming a low estimate of the quantity of tripe which the carcasses of those animals, reasonably well butchered, would yield; I find that the waste on that amount of tripe, if boiled, would victual a garrison of five hundred men for five months of thirty-one days each and a February over. The Waste, the Waste!'

The Chimes First Quarter

Toby's potato came hot and separate, along with half a pint of fresh-drawn beer; he might well have readily appreciated this dish where the tripe and potato are cooked together:

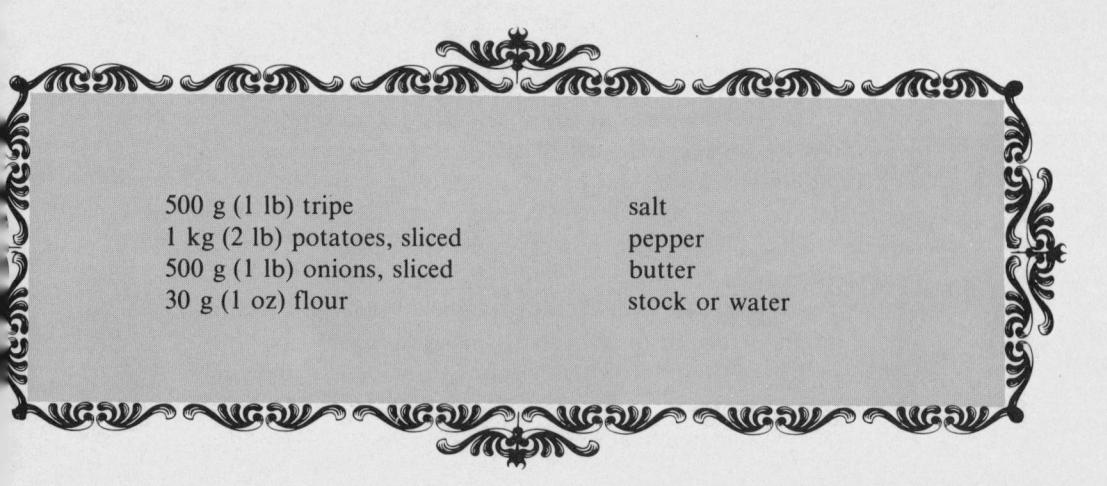

500 g (1 lb) tripe
1 kg (2 lb) potatoes, sliced
500 g (1 lb) onions, sliced
30 g (1 oz) flour
salt
pepper
butter
stock or water

Wash the tripe well, dry it, and cut it into cubes. Season the flour with salt and pepper, and roll the cubes of tripe in the flour. Shake to remove excess flour. Well grease a cassserole dish with butter, and fill it with alternating layers of tripe, potatoes and onions, finishing with a layer of potatoes, and seasoning well between layers. Add sufficient stock or water to three-quarters fill the dish. Dot with butter and cover tightly. Cook for 2 hours or more at 190°C (or 375°F) until the tripe is tender, checking occasionally to make sure that the liquid has not evaporated too much, adding more if necessary. Remove the the lid 10 minutes before the end of cooking time.

A SAVOURY STEW OF TRIPE

A mighty fire was blazing on the hearth and roaring up the wide chimney with a cheerful sound, which a large iron cauldron, bubbling and simmering in the heat, lent its pleasant aid to swell. There was a deep, red, ruddy blush upon the room; and when the landlord stirred the fire, sending the flames skipping and leaping up—when he took off the lid of the iron pot and there rushed out a savoury smell, while the bubbling sound grew deeper and more rich, and an unctuous steam came floating out, hanging in a delicious mist above their heads—when he did this, Mr. Codlin's heart was touched ...
'It's a stew of tripe,' said the landlord, smacking his lips, 'and cow-heel,' smacking them again, 'and bacon,' smacking them once more, 'and steak,' smacking them for the fourth time, 'and peas, cauliflowers, new potatoes, and sparrow-grass, all working up together in one delicious gravy.'

The Old Curiosity Shop Ch XVIII

In the course of five minutes after his arrival at that house of entertainment, he was enrolled among the gallant defenders of his native land; and within half an hour, was regaled with a steaming supper of boiled tripe and onions, prepared, as his friend assured him more than once, at the express command of his most Sacred Majesty the King.

Barnaby Rudge Ch XXXI

A stew of tripe such as the landlord's can quite easily be devised along the lines of putting in a casserole dish tripe and whatever vegetables appeal that are available. Celery, cauliflower sprigs, peas, potatoes (either new or quartered), tomatoes, and of course sliced onions, are all possibilities. If a little stewing steak is added it should be chopped, as should the tripe; some rinded bacon can also be used. If a cow-heel is to be added, it should be cleaned and split into four pieces. The whole should be well seasoned and then covered with stock or water. Cover the casserole tightly, and bake at 160°C (325°F) for 3-4 hours, or until tender.

TRIPE AND ONIONS

500-750 g (1-1½ lb)
   prepared tripe
4 onions, sliced
2½ cups water
salt
pepper

¾ cup milk, or milk and
   cream
2 tbsps finely chopped
   parsley
a pinch of nutmeg
2 tsps flour
2 tsps butter

Cut the tripe into squares, place it in a saucepan and cover with cold water. Bring to the boil, drain, and discard the water. Add the 2½ cups of water to the tripe, the sliced onions, and salt and pepper. Simmer for 1½-2 hours, until the tripe is tender. Strain off the tripe and onions, and return the liquid to the heat. Simmer until reduced by half. To the reduced liquid add the milk or milk and cream, nutmeg, and the parsley. Bring to the boil. Blend together the butter and flour, and add it in small pieces to the liquid, stirring all the time. Add the tripe and onions, test for seasoning, and re-heat. Serve in bowls.

Note: More milk or cream can be added, or alternatively the quantity of thickening can be increased, depending upon the texture required.

A SUPPER OF STEWED KIDNEYS

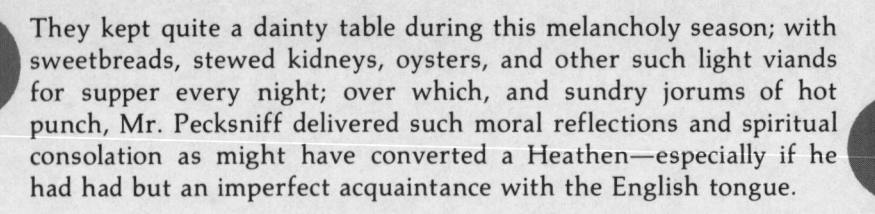

They kept quite a dainty table during this melancholy season; with sweetbreads, stewed kidneys, oysters, and other such light viands for supper every night; over which, and sundry jorums of hot punch, Mr. Pecksniff delivered such moral reflections and spiritual consolation as might have converted a Heathen—especially if he had had but an imperfect acquaintance with the English tongue.

Martin Chuzzlewit Ch XIX

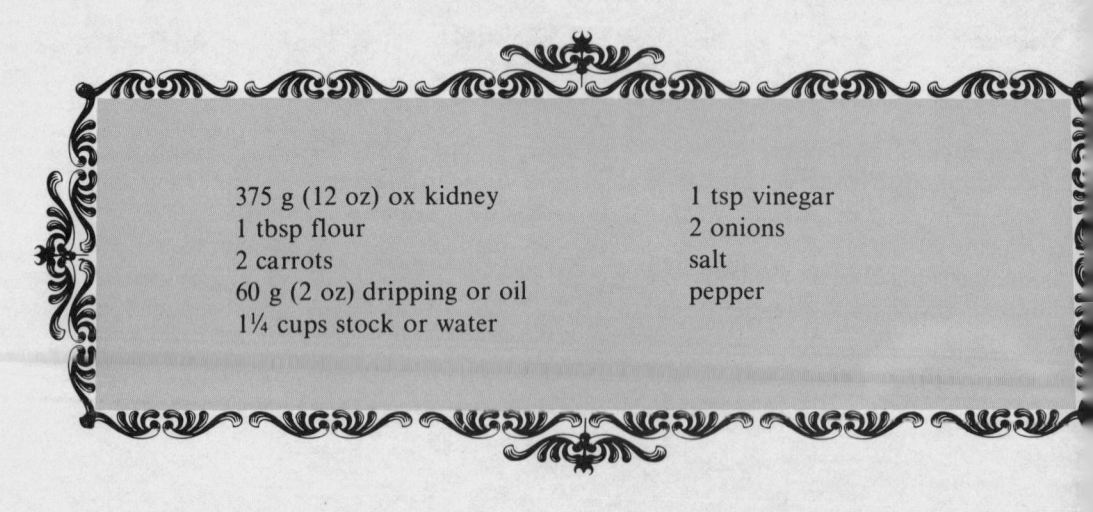

375 g (12 oz) ox kidney
1 tbsp flour
2 carrots
60 g (2 oz) dripping or oil
1¼ cups stock or water
1 tsp vinegar
2 onions
salt
pepper

Core and trim the kidney, and cut it into thin slices. Mix salt and pepper with half the flour and dredge the kidney in it. Heat the dripping or oil in a saucepan, and add the kidney. Sauté for 3 minutes until browned. Chop the carrots, slice the onions, and add them to the saucepan. Sauté for a further 3 minutes, then pour in the stock or water and vinegar. Bring to the boil, season, and simmer until the meat is tender—approximately 30-45 minutes. Mix the remaining flour with a little water, and add it to the saucepan, stirring while doing so. Cook for a further 5 minutes. Serve hot with mashed potatoes.

Note: This dish can be made even more substantial by the addition of turnips, quartered potatoes, or swedes. Add when the stock first boils, then more liquid and thickening if necessary.

A DEVILLED GRILL AND KIDNEYS

'Dombey,' said the Major, glancing at the Native as he arranged the table, and encouraging him with an awful shake of his fist when he upset a spoon, 'here is a devilled grill, a savoury pie, a dish of kidneys and so forth. Pray sit down, Old Joe can give you nothing but camp fare, you see.'

Dombey and Son Ch XX

The Major accompanied this with such a look, and, between eating, drinking, hot tea, devilled grill, muffins and meaning, was altogether so swollen and inflamed about the head, that even Mr. Dombey showed some anxiety for him.

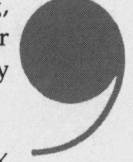

Dombey and Son Ch XX

A devil: 'a favourite dish with the epicure after he has sacrificed sufficiently to the jolly god, and requires a little stimulant: or it may be partaken of with great *gusto* at a hunting breakfast'. The Major had apparently reached a stage of requiring perpetual stimulation; he 'daily scorched himself' on private zests and flavours kept on a side table, mixing up the contents of every sauce and cruet on his plate. A devil was simply a pepper-hot dish; it was a very satisfactory way of dealing with the gizzard, rump or legs of a goose or fowl, as well as kidney; grilled with much pepper and covered with relish, the dish added to both the breakfast and the dinner table. An 'unexceptional devil' was made by warming in oil and butter the cold meat of turkey, fowl or duck, adding to the pan 'mushroom ketchup, Harvey or Worcester, superlative and Chilli vinegar, along with mustard, pepper, salt, and chutney, a moderate amount of cayenne, a few pickles cut in small pieces'.

A savoury combination of whatever spices and relishes you wish to lay your hand to seems to be in order; however, as some have taken the trouble to record their preferred quantities, here are two devilled sauces for pouring over grilled meat:

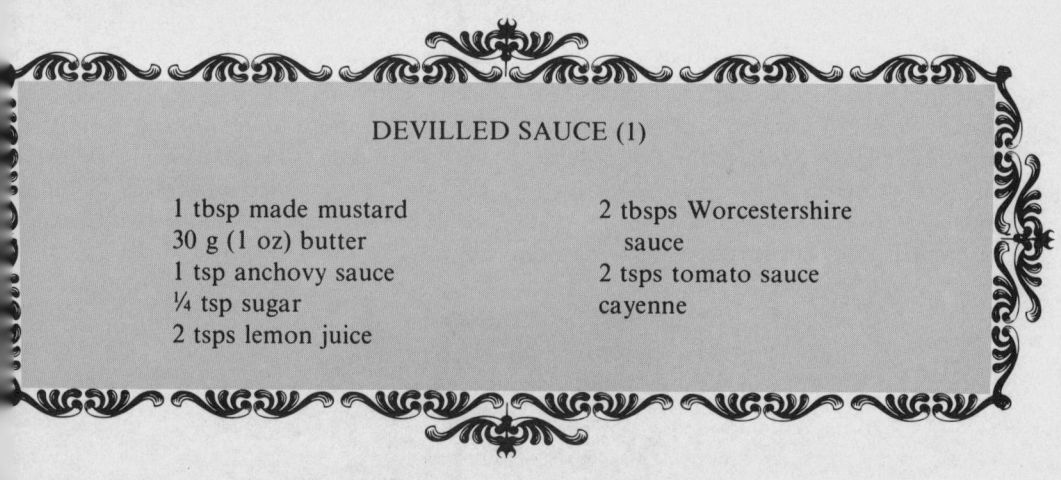

DEVILLED SAUCE (1)

1 tbsp made mustard
30 g (1 oz) butter
1 tsp anchovy sauce
¼ tsp sugar
2 tsps lemon juice
2 tbsps Worcestershire sauce
2 tsps tomato sauce
cayenne

Heat all ingredients together in a saucepan. Transfer to a gravy boat, and serve with grilled meat.

Continued overpage

DEVILLED SAUCE (2)

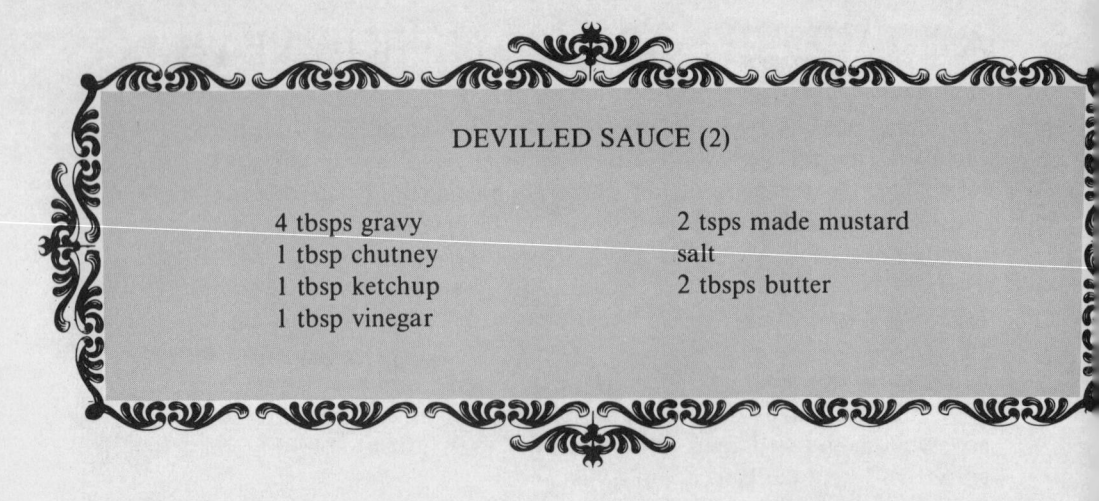

4 tbsps gravy	2 tsps made mustard
1 tbsp chutney	salt
1 tbsp ketchup	2 tbsps butter
1 tbsp vinegar	

Heat all ingredients except the gravy together in a saucepan. Three minutes before the meat has finished grilling, spread some of the mixture over it. Complete the grilling of the meat. Add the gravy to what remains of the mixture in the saucepan, heat through, and spoon it over the grilled meat to serve.

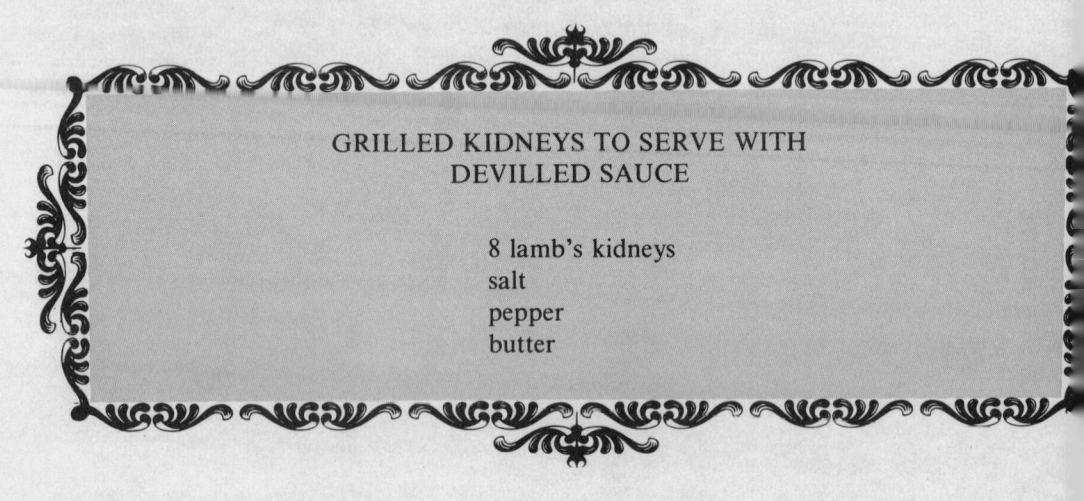

GRILLED KIDNEYS TO SERVE WITH DEVILLED SAUCE

8 lamb's kidneys
salt
pepper
butter

Skin and core the kidneys; cut them evenly, down to the root, but do not entirely separate them. Spread the kidneys on skewers, keeping them flat. Brush with melted butter. Grill under a good heat, beginning with the cut side, then turning them. They should be ready in 6-8 minutes. Brush with more butter during cooking to keep them moist. To serve, season well with salt and pepper, placing a piece of butter inside each kidney. Accompany with devilled sauce.

PETTITOES AND TOASTED CHEESE

> The two caps, reflected on the window-blind, were the respective head-dresses of a couple of Mrs. Bardell's most particular acquaintance, who had just stepped in, to have a quiet cup of tea, and a little warm supper of a couple of sets of pettitoes and some toasted cheese. The cheese was simmering and browning away, most delightfully, in a little Dutch oven before the fire; the pettitoes were getting on deliciously in a little tin saucepan on the hob; and Mrs. Bardell and her two friends were getting on very well, also ...
>
> *The Pickwick Papers* Ch XXVI

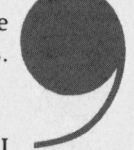

Pettitoes, or pig's feet, make a meal which today few of us would actually find ourselves indulging in, but it is one which nevertheless has a delightful aroma of nostalgia around it—it wafts comfort and well-being, luxury from cheap cuts. The cleaned and halved pig's feet were simmered in a good gravy seasoned with a sliced onion, a blade of mace, some sprigs of thyme, peppercorns, and salt, along with a slice of bacon; finally this was thickened with some knobs of butter blended with flour. A more substantial dish used to include the heart and liver of the pig, these being cooked for the first 15 minutes with the pig's feet, then removed, minced, and added again 10 minutes before the dish was served. At the end of cooking, when the feet had split, a little cream was added.

The cheese was simplicity itself, but again a gustatory pleasure. Mrs Bardell, possibly bereft of the silver individual dishes which her betters placed in a cheese toasting dish, nevertheless knew how to adapt. A little butter in the bottom of the Dutch oven, a little ale, thin slices of cheese; then: 'it is then exposed to the fire until done. This dish must not be attempted unless it can be served hot; and on such an occasion, if perfection is aimed at, ceremony must be disregarded. Even to wait for pepper, salt and mustard is time that cannot be spared by the real *gourmet* on this *plât*.'

A LITTLE FRY FOR SUPPER

Cook's state of mind is similar. She promises a little fry for supper, and struggles about equally against her feelings and the onions.

Dombey and Son Ch XVIII

A fry used to consist of the liver, heart and lungs, the heart and lungs being chopped finely and fried for 10 minutes before the addition of the sliced liver. In the nineteenth century the term was altering, coming to mean, as we take it today, the liver only. Again, our treatment of such a traditional dish has simplified; usually a coating of seasoned flour is considered sufficient for tastiness, but it used to be more common to dip the slices of liver in egg and then coat them with breadcrumbs, before frying, or alternatively the slices were coated with a batter and then shallow-fried. The dish was garnished with parsley and had the juice of a lemon squeezed over it before sending it to the table, or else a melted butter sauce accompanied it.

---

500 g (1 lb) lamb's liver
seasoned flour
a pinch of mixed herbs
2 onions, sliced or chopped
45 g (1½ oz) butter
3 tsps flour
approx. 300 ml (½ pt) stock or water
salt
pepper
lemon wedges

Cut the liver into slices 7-12 mm (¼-½ in.) thick, trimming away any tubes or blood vessels. Place the butter in a frying pan, and in it fry the onions until they are brown. Dip each liver slice in seasoned flour. Add the liver slices to the pan, and a little extra butter if required. Sprinkle with mixed herbs. Fry the slices fairly quickly, allowing about 3 minutes for each side. The slices should be pink in the middle, not grey. Remove the liver and onions to a hot plate. Pour off all but about 3 teaspoons of butter from the frying pan, and stir the flour into the pan juices. Cook until browned. Gradually add the stock, stirring all the time. Bring to the boil, cook for 3 minutes, and season to taste. Serve the liver and onion with the gravy poured around the dish. Accompany with lemon wedges.

The kettle sings a fireside song of comfort

THE SOPORIFIC AGENCY OF SWEETBREADS

"Mrs. Pipchin's constitution was made of such hard metal, in spite of its liability to the fleshly weakness of standing in need of repose after chops, and of requiring to be coaxed to sleep by the soporific agency of sweet-breads, that it utterly set at nought the predictions of Mrs. Wickam, and showed no symptoms of decline ...

Dombey and Son Ch IX

'Perhaps, my love, you will consult with the person of the house, whether she can procure us a lamb's fry: or, failing that, a roast fowl.'
On which the Billickin would retort (Rosa not having spoken a word), 'If you was better accustomed to butcher's meat, Miss, you would not entertain the idea of a lamb's fry. Firstly, because the lambs has long been sheep, and secondly, because there is such things as killing-days and there is not. As to roast fowls, Miss, why you must be quite surfeited with roast fowls, letting alone your buying, when you market for yourself, the agedest of poultry with the scaliest of legs, quite as if you was accustomed to picking 'em out for cheapness. Try a little inwention, Miss. Use yourself to 'ousekeeping a bit. Come now, think of somethink else.'

To this encouragement, offered with the indulgent toleration of a wise and liberal expert, Miss Twinkleton would rejoin, reddening:
'Or, my dear, you might propose to the person of the house, a duck.'
'Well, Miss!' the Billickin would exclaim (still no word being spoken by Rosa), 'you do surprise me when you speak of ducks! Not to mention that they're getting out of season and very dear, it really strikes to my heart to see you have a duck: for the breast, which is the only delicate cuts in a duck, always goes in a direction which I cannot imagine where, and your own plate comes down so miserably skin-and-bony! Try again, Miss. Think more of yourself, and less of others. A dish of sweetbreads, now, or a bit of mutton. Something at which you can get your equal chance.'

The Mystery of Edwin Drood Ch XXII

Misfortune in the family without feasting, in these lower regions, couldn't be. Therefore Cook tosses up a hot dish or two for supper, and Mr. Towlinson composes a lobster salad to be devoted to the same hospitable purpose. Even Mrs. Pipchin, agitated by the occasion, rings her bell and sends down word that she requests to have that little bit of sweet-bread that was left, warmed up for her supper, and sent to her on a tray with about a quarter of a tumbler-full of mulled sherry; for she feels poorly.

Dombey and Son Ch LIX

Either calves' sweetbreads or lambs' can be used; whatever the type, always pre-prepare them in the same way: Soak the sweetbreads for at least an hour in cold water with 1 tablespoon of salt. Drain. Place them in a saucepan, cover with water or stock and the juice of half a lemon. Simmer calves' sweetbreads for 10 minutes, lambs' sweetbreads for 2 minutes. Strain. Remove tubes, hard pieces, and some of the membrane (some membrane is useful for holding the pieces together, but too much causes them to be hard and to curl). Put them on a plate, place another plate on top, and add a weight. Leave to press for at least 2 hours before proceeding with the actual dish.

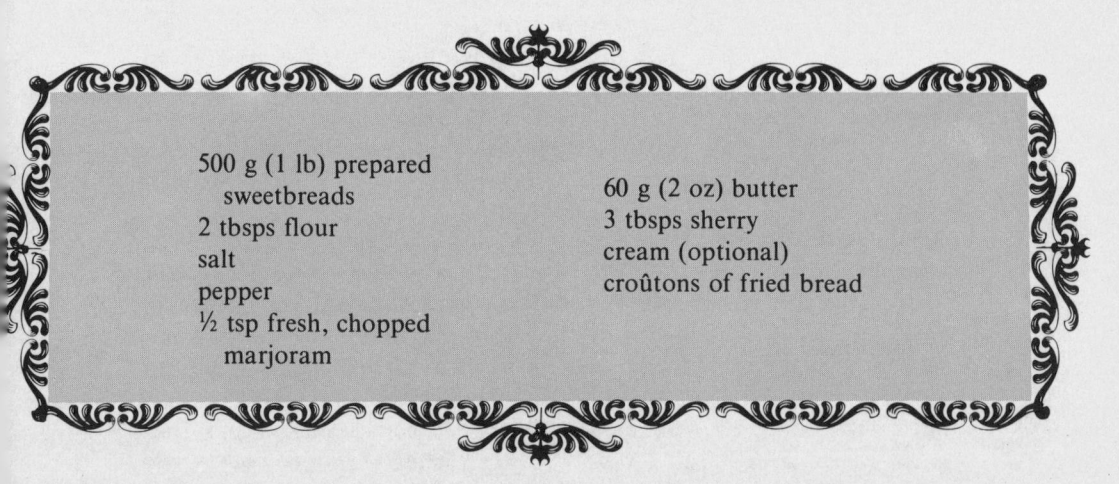

500 g (1 lb) prepared sweetbreads
2 tbsps flour
salt
pepper
½ tsp fresh, chopped marjoram
60 g (2 oz) butter
3 tbsps sherry
cream (optional)
croûtons of fried bread

Slice the sweetbreads if they are large. Mix together the flour, salt, pepper, and marjoram, and roll the sweetbreads in the mixture. Melt the butter in a frying pan and add the sweetbreads. Fry quickly until they are browned on one side; turn. Add some of the sherry and simmer to reduce, continuing to turn the sweetbreads. Add the rest of the sherry and reduce it a little. Just before serving, add a little cream (optional) to the contents of the pan. Serve the sweetbreads with croutons of fried bread, with a little of the pan juices poured over them.

For a plain dish, simply fry floured sweetbreads in butter. One nineteenth century recipe book suggests for the sauce: 'fried breadcrumbs, melted butter, with a little mushroom ketchup, and lemon juice, or served on buttered toast, garnished with egg sauce, or with gravy.'

DRESSED TONGUE CARVED WITH A PAIR OF SCISSORS

A noticeable relaxation of discipline had for some few days pervaded the Nuns House. Club suppers had occurred in the bedrooms, and a dressed tongue had been carved with a pair of scissors, and handed round with the curling tongs. Portions of marmalade had likewise been distributed on a service of plates constructed of curl paper; and cowslip wine had been quaffed from a small squat measuring glass in which Little Ricketts (a junior of weakly constitution) took her steel drops daily.

The Mystery of Edwin Drood Ch XIII

All the furniture is shaken and dusted, the portraits of Mr. and Mrs. Snagsby are touched up with a wet cloth, the best tea-service is set forth, and there is excellent provision made of dainty new bread, crusty twists, cool fresh butter, thin slices of ham, tongue and German sausage, and delicate little rows of anchovies nestling in parsley; not to mention new-laid eggs, to be brought up warm in a napkin, and hot buttered toast. For Chadband is rather a consuming vessel—the persecutors say a gorging vessel; and can wield such weapons of the flesh as a knife and fork, remarkably well.

Bleak House Ch XIX

... in one of the inn's smallest sitting-rooms, through whose open window there rose, in palpable steam, wholesome exhalations from reeking coach-horses, the usual furniture of a tea-table was displayed in neat and inviting order, flanked by large joints of roast and boiled, a tongue, a pigeon-pie, a cold fowl, a tankard of ale, and other little matters of the like kind, which, in degenerate towns and cities, are generally understood to belong more particularly to solid lunches, stage-coach dinners, or unusually substantial breakfasts.

Nicholas Nickleby Ch XLII

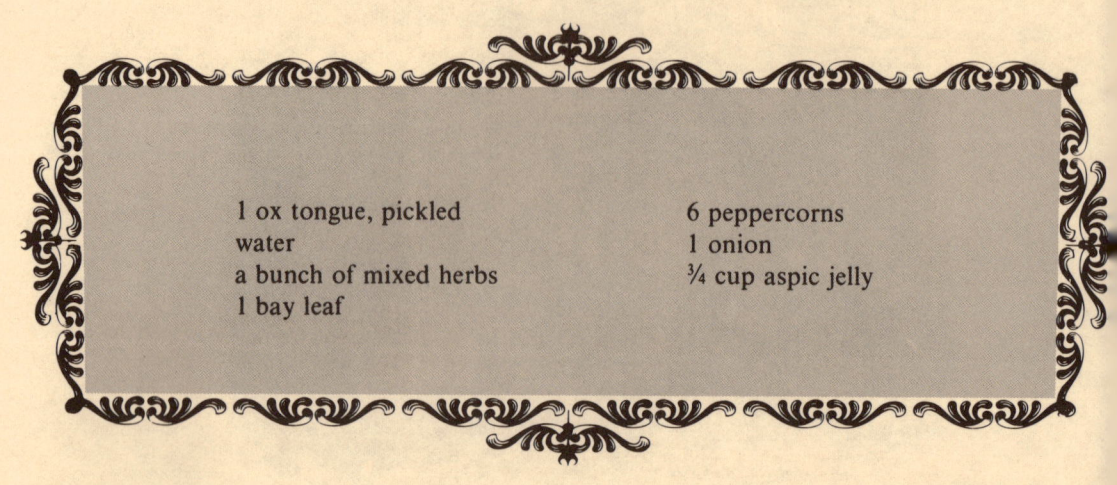

1 ox tongue, pickled
water
a bunch of mixed herbs
1 bay leaf

6 peppercorns
1 onion
¾ cup aspic jelly

Soak the tongue in cold water for at least 2 hours. Place the tongue in a saucepan, cover with cold water, and add the mixed herbs, bay leaf, peppercorns and onion. Bring to simmering point, and simmer gently for 4-5 hours, or until the meat is tender. Remove the scum as it rises during cooking. Remove the tongue from the saucepan, and place it in a dish of cold water to make it easier to remove the skin. Remove the skin, trim the roots, and remove any bones. If you do not have a tongue press (a container which has an inserted lid which can be screwed down tightly over the meat inside) then place the tongue in a cake tin which is just large enough to hold it. Place a dish or a circle of wood on the top, and upon that place a firm weight. Leave overnight. Next day, pour over the tongue the melted aspic jelly, and leave to set. To serve, turn out of container, and cut in thin slices.

PRESSED TONGUES OF SHEEP IN CURL-PAPER

It then begins to be Miss Tox's occupation to prepare little dainties—or what are such to her—to be carried into these rooms next morning. She derives so much satisfaction from the pursuit, that she enters on it regularly from that time; and brings daily in her little basket, various choice condiments selected from the scanty stores of the deceased owner of the powdered head and pigtail. She brings, in sheets of curl-paper, morsels of cold meats, tongues of sheep, halves of fowls, for her own dinner; and sharing these collations with Polly, passes the greater part of her time in the ruined house that the rats have fled from ...

Dombey and Son Ch LIX

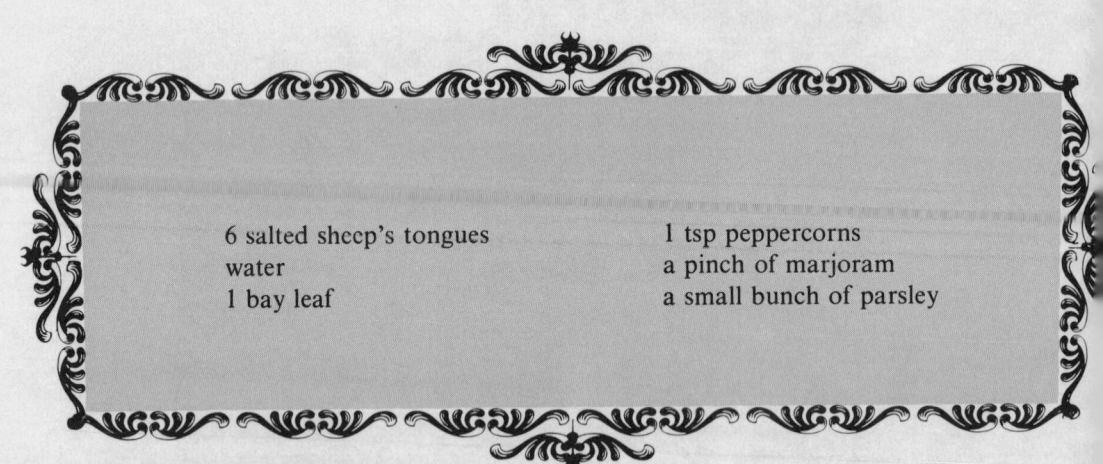

---

6 salted sheep's tongues
water
1 bay leaf

1 tsp peppercorns
a pinch of marjoram
a small bunch of parsley

Soak the tongues in cold water for 2 hours. Drain. Place the tongues in a saucepan and cover with cold water. Add the bay leaf, peppercorns, marjoram and parsley. Slowly bring to the boil, and simmer gently for approximately 1-1½ hours, until the tongues are tender. Remove any scum as it rises during cooking. Remove the tongues from the water, skin them, and remove any gristle or bone. Press the tongues into a bowl or dish just large enough to hold them. Place a piece of board on the top of them, if you do not have a meat-press, and place a weight on top. Leave overnight. To serve, turn out of the dish, and glaze if desired.

BRAWN

Heaped upon the floor, to form a kind of throne, were turkeys, geese, game, poultry, brawn, great joints of meat, sucking-pigs, long wreaths of sausages, mince-pies, plum-puddings, barrels of oysters, red-hot chestnuts, cherry-cheeked apples, juicy oranges, luscious pears, immense twelfth-cakes, and seething bowls of punch, that made the chamber dim with their delicious steam. In easy state upon this couch, there sat a jolly Giant, glorious to see; who bore a glowing torch, in shape not unlike Plenty's horn, and held it up, high up, to shed its light on Scrooge, as he came peeping round the door.

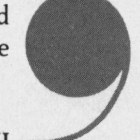

A Christmas Carol Stave III

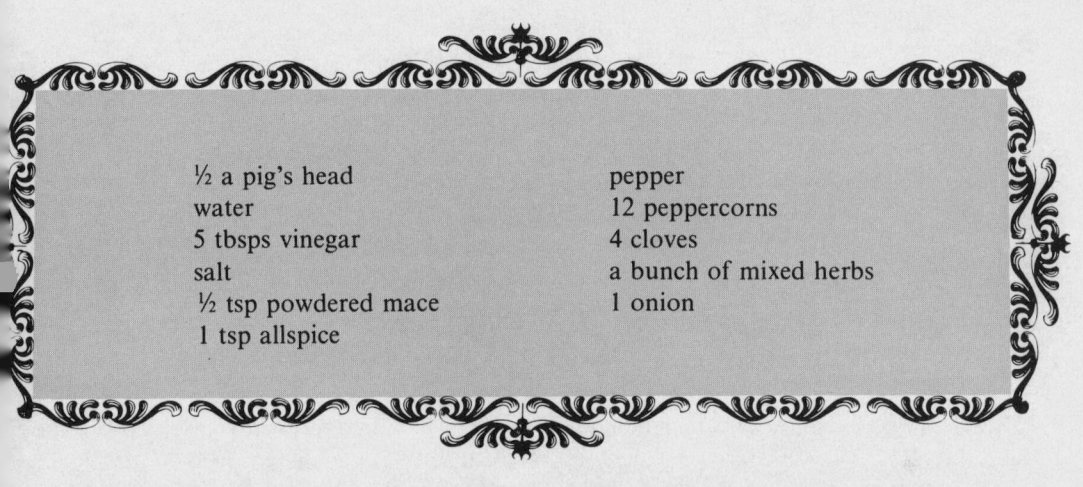

½ a pig's head
water
5 tbsps vinegar
salt
½ tsp powdered mace
1 tsp allspice
pepper
12 peppercorns
4 cloves
a bunch of mixed herbs
1 onion

Remove the brain from the head, and reserve for other cookery. Place the head in a bowl, cover with cold water, add the vinegar, and leave to soak for 1 hour. Drain, add lukewarm water to cover and 3 tablespoons of salt, and leave for another hour. Drain. Wipe the head clean, place it in a saucepan, cover with cold water, and slowly bring to the boil. Pour off the water and wipe the head free of any remaining scum. Re-cover with cold water, season with mace, allspice, salt, pepper, peppercorns, cloves, and the bunch of mixed herbs, and add the onion. Slowly bring to the boil, then simmer gently for approximately 3 hours, or until the meat is tender. Remove the meat from the pan and strain the cooking liquid, removing the fat also. Return the cooking liquid to the saucepan, and boil, uncovered, until it is reduced by half. Strain through a fine sieve. While the liquid is reducing, cut the meat from the head into small dice. Place the meat in small basins or moulds, and pour over some of the cooking liquid. Leave to cool and to form a jelly. Unmould to serve.

SOME POTTED MEATS

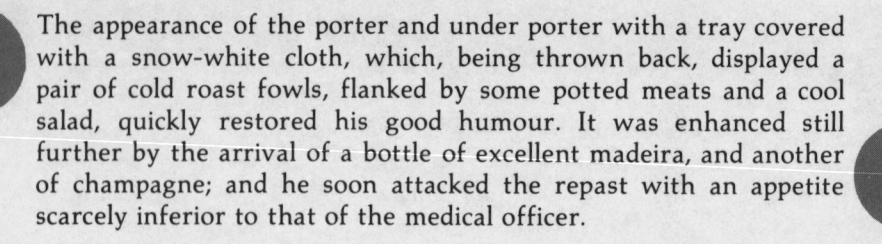

The appearance of the porter and under porter with a tray covered with a snow-white cloth, which, being thrown back, displayed a pair of cold roast fowls, flanked by some potted meats and a cool salad, quickly restored his good humour. It was enhanced still further by the arrival of a bottle of excellent madeira, and another of champagne; and he soon attacked the repast with an appetite scarcely inferior to that of the medical officer.

Martin Chuzzlewit Ch XXVII

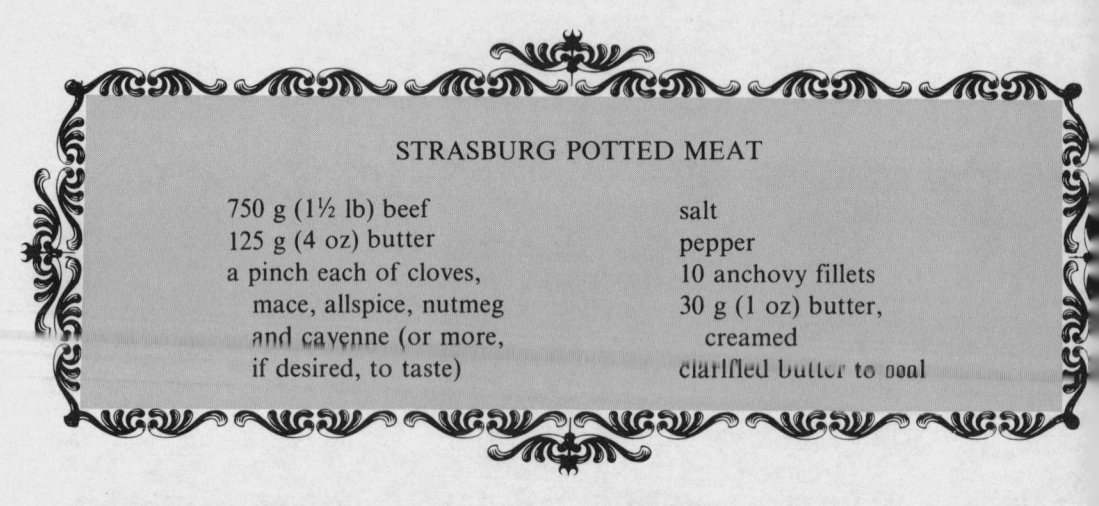

STRASBURG POTTED MEAT

750 g (1½ lb) beef
125 g (4 oz) butter
a pinch each of cloves, mace, allspice, nutmeg and cayenne (or more, if desired, to taste)
salt
pepper
10 anchovy fillets
30 g (1 oz) butter, creamed
clarified butter to seal

Dice the beef, and place it in an earthenware, or other heat-resistant, jar, with the 125 g (4 oz) of butter at the bottom. Seal well with a lid, and tie over it some strong paper or tin foil. Place in a saucepan of water, so that the water comes up the side of the jar, but has no chance to enter the top. Bring to the boil, and boil for 1½ hours, adding more boiling water if there is a loss from evaporation. Add the seasonings, re-cover, and cook in the same manner until done, which will be approximately half an hour. Allow to cool. Place the meat mixture in a container suitable for pounding. Add the anchovies and the creamed butter, and pound all together. Press into small pots and seal with clarified butter.

Note: Originally, this recipe required a few drops of cochineal to be added when pounding, to improve the colour. As well, melted mutton fat was used for sealing, instead of clarified butter.

PORK CHEESE

500 g (1 lb) cold roast pork
2 tsps finely chopped parsley
½ tsp chopped fresh sage
½ tsp chopped fresh thyme
½ tsp grated lemon rind
a pinch of grated nutmeg
salt
pepper
300 ml (½ pt) jellied stock

Cut the meat neatly into dice. Add the parsley, sage, thyme, lemon rind, nutmeg, salt and pepper, and blend all well together. Place the meat in a mould or earthenware container, and pour over the stock. Cover well with a tightly fitting lid, and bake at 180°C (350°F) for 1½ hours. Allow to cool. Unmould to serve.

A DELICATE RESTORATIVE— CALF'S-FOOT JELLY

... Mr. Abel started up, and hobbled to the door, and opened it; and behold! there stood a strong man, with a mighty hamper, which, being hauled into the room, and presently unpacked, disgorged such treasures of tea, and coffee, and wine, and rusks, and oranges, and grapes, and fowls ready trussed for boiling, and calf's-foot jelly, and arrowroot, and sago, and other delicate restoratives, that the small servant, who never thought it possible that such things could be, except in shops, stood rooted to the spot in her one shoe, with her mouth and eyes watering in unison, and her power of speech quite gone.

The Old Curiosity Shop Ch LXVI

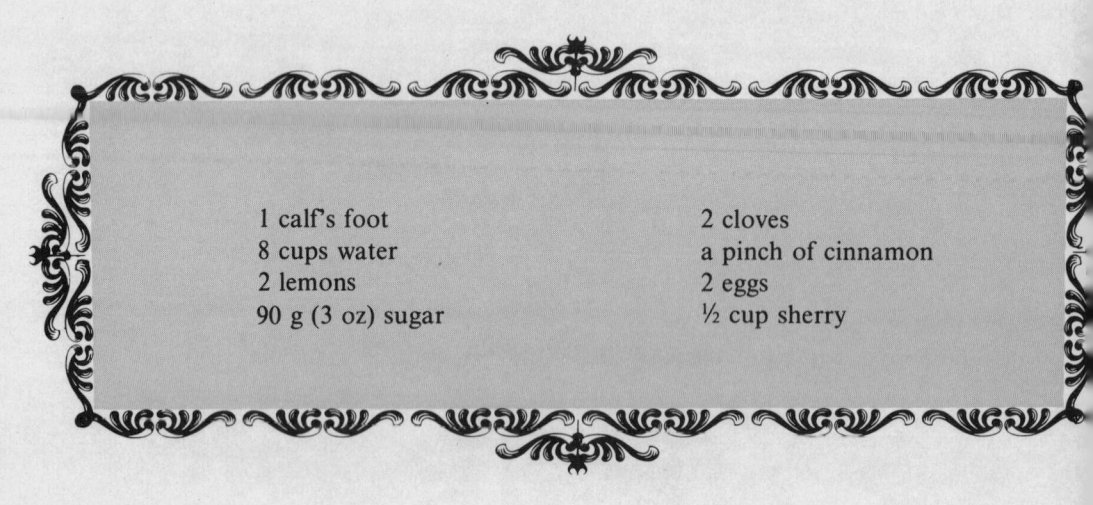

1 calf's foot
8 cups water
2 lemons
90 g (3 oz) sugar

2 cloves
a pinch of cinnamon
2 eggs
½ cup sherry

Chop the cleaned calf's foot into four pieces, place it in a saucepan, and cover it with water. Bring to the boil and strain off the water. Return the calf's foot to the saucepan, and pour in the 8 cups of water. Bring to a simmering point, and simmer for 7 hours, with the lid at a slant, skimming several times throughout the cooking. Remove the pieces of calf's foot, and strain the liquid through a fine sieve. Allow to cool. Remove all fat from the surface. Place the jelly in a clean saucepan, taking care not to include the sediment. Add the thinly pared rind of the lemons and their juice, along with the sugar, cloves, and cinnamon. Whip the egg-whites and crush the shells, then add the whites and shells to the liquid. Place the saucepan on the stove, and whisk until the liquid boils. After 5 minutes, add the sherry, and bring to the boil again. Strain the liquid through a very fine sieve. Re-strain if the liquid is not completely clear. Rinse a jelly mould in cold water, pour in the liquid and stand in a cool place until set. To serve, unmould on to a dish. Alternatively, the jelly can be cut into squares and served in tall glasses.

A LAMB'S HEAD AND A HAGGIS

'It was a glorious supper. There were kippered salmon, and Finnan haddocks, and a lamb's head, and a haggis—a celebrated Scotch dish, gentlemen, which my uncle always used to say looked to him, when it came to the table, very much like a cupid's stomach—and a great many other things besides, that I forget the names of, but very good things notwithstanding.'

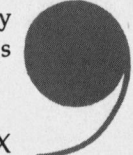

The Pickwick Papers Ch XLIX

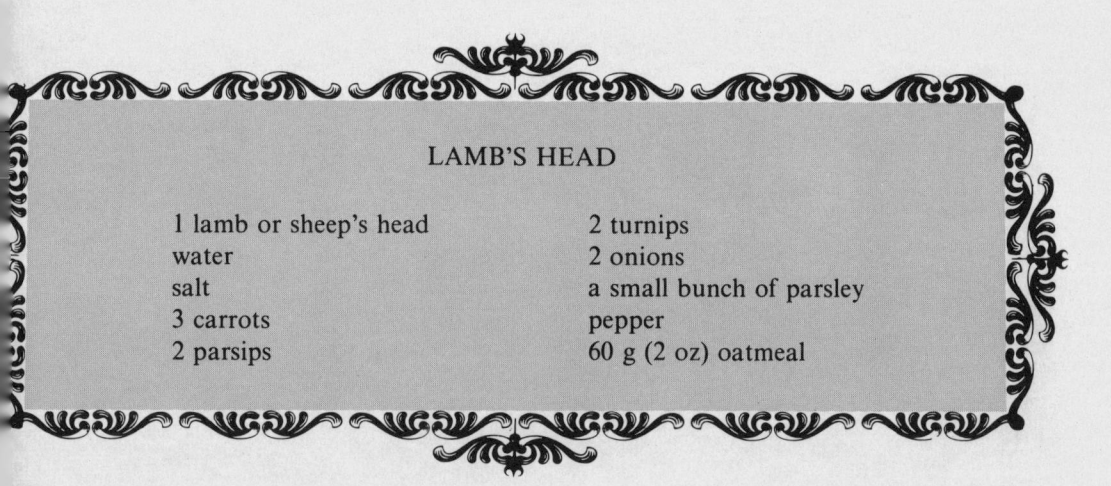

LAMB'S HEAD

1 lamb or sheep's head
water
salt
3 carrots
2 parsips

2 turnips
2 onions
a small bunch of parsley
pepper
60 g (2 oz) oatmeal

Clean the head and split it, if this makes it easier to accommodate in a saucepan. Soak the head for 2 hours in cold salted water to remove the blood. Drain. Place the head in a saucepan and cover with cold water. Bring to the boil and skim the surface well. Add the carrots, parsnips, turnips, onions (the vegetables should be left in large pieces except for the onions, which should be sliced) and the bunch of parsley. Moisten the oatmeal with a little of the liquid, and add to the saucepan. Season with salt and pepper. Stir until the liquid again comes to the boil, cover, and simmer for 2 to 3 hours, or until the meat is tender. The oatmeal serves to thicken the liquid; if a thicker juice is required, add more oatmeal in the last hour of cooking. Remove the head from the saucepan, and take the meat off it. Chop the brains; skin and slice the tongue. Keep hot. Serve the meat surrounded by the vegetables and some of the thickened liquid.

HAGGIS

'Take the stomach of a sheep. The washing and the cleaning is of more consequence than all, as it will be of a bad colour and a bad taste if not well cleansed: when clean, turn it inside out, then let it lie for a day or two in salt and water. Blanch the liver, lights and heart of the sheep, lay them in cold water, chop all very fine: the liver you had better grate, chop a pound of the suet very fine, dry in the oven a pound of oatmeal; mix all this well together; season with pepper and salt, a little chopped parsley and a little chopped onion; then sew up in the bag [the stomach]; before you finish sewing it add a few spoonfuls of a good white stock; put it in a stewpan with a drainer; boil it in water, keeping it well covered all the time, prick it all over with a small larding pin to keep it from bursting; it will take several hours to boil; be careful taking it up, and let your dish be large enough.'

A BEAUTIFUL LITTLE DINNER WITH FRIED SAUSAGE MEAT

But I was still more surprised, when I went to the little hotel next day, at the appointed dinner-hour, which was four o'clock, to find, from what Mr. Micawber said, that he had gone home with Uriah, and had drunk brandy-and-water at Mrs. Heep's ...
We had a beautiful little dinner. Quite an elegant dish of fish; the kidney-end of a loin of veal, roasted; fried sausage-meat; a partridge, and a pudding. There was wine, and there was strong ale; and after dinner Mrs. Micawber made us a bowl of hot punch with her own hands.

David Copperfield Ch XVII

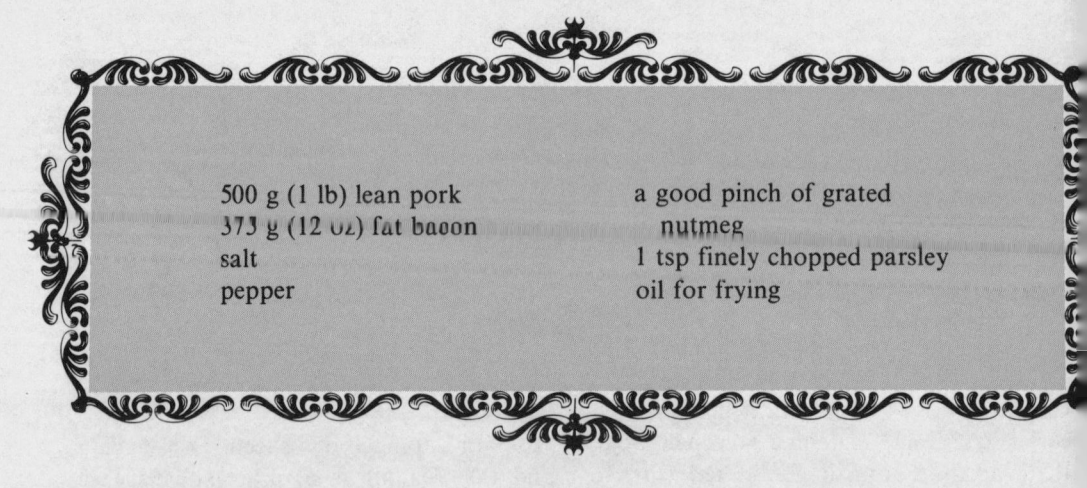

500 g (1 lb) lean pork
375 g (12 oz) fat bacon
salt
pepper
a good pinch of grated nutmeg
1 tsp finely chopped parsley
oil for frying

'Remove from the pork all skin, gristle, and bone, and chop it finely with the bacon; add the remaining ingredients, and carefully mix all together. Pound it well in a mortar, make it into convenient-sized cakes, flour these, and fry them a nice brown for about 10 minutes. This is a very simple method of making sausage-meat, and on trial will prove very good, its great recommendation being, that it is so easily made.'

MARROW BONES

'She's such a con-founded Idiot,' muttered Tackleton, 'that I was afraid she'd never comprehend me. Ah, Bertha! Married! Church, parson, clerk, beadle, glass-coach, bells, breakfast, bride-cake, favours, marrow-bones, cleavers, and all the rest of the tom-foolery. A wedding, you know; a wedding. Don't you know what a wedding is?'

The Cricket on the Hearth Chirp the Second

Those who count as a luxury the small piece of marrow that comes with chops should experiment with this old favourite; it has almost disappeared from the scene, although it is occasionally served with the traditional flourishes of white napkin and special long-handled spoon in some gentlemen's clubs: Have the marrow bones cut in half, and, if possible, have the uncut base trimmed so that the bone will stand upright in a saucepan. Clean the outside of the bones of any meat, finishing the process when they finally come from the pot. Make a paste of flour and water, and place it over the cut ends of the bones. To give extra security, tie a piece of tin foil around the cut ends. Tie the bones together, and place upright in a saucepan of water. Boil for 2 hours. Alternatively, after the paste has been placed on the ends of the bones, tie the bones in a scalded, floured pudding cloth, and boil for two hours. Serve in a white napkin, accompanied by thin toast.

Note: The marrow can be removed from the bones and spread on buttered toast. If it is not required immediately, sauté it in a little butter to heat it through before serving.

EGG SAUCE AND SAUSAGES

The Captain had spread the cloth with great care, and was making some egg-sauce in a little saucepan: basting the fowl from time to time during the process with a strong interest, as it turned and browned on a string before the fire ... The Captain pursued his cooking with extraordinary skill, making hot gravy in a second little saucepan, boiling a handful of potatoes in a third, never forgetting the egg-sauce in the first, and making an impartial round of basting and stirring with the most useful of spoons every minute. Besides these cares, the Captain had to keep his eye on a diminutive frying-pan, in which some sausages were hissing and bubbling in a most musical manner ...
'My lady lass,' said the Captain, 'cheer up and try to eat a deal. Stand by, my deary! Liver wing it is. Sarse it is. Sassage it is. And potato.' All which the Captain ranged symmetrically on a plate, and pouring hot gravy on the whole with the useful spoon, set before his cherished guest.

Dombey and Son Ch XLIX

EGG SAUCE

30 g (1 oz) butter	a pinch of mace
30 g (1 oz) flour	salt
1¼ cups milk	pepper
1 bay leaf	2 eggs, hard-boiled
2 cloves	15 g (½ oz) butter

Melt the butter in a saucepan, and stir in the flour. Heat over a low heat for 3 minutes, stirring all the time. Do not allow to brown. Slowly add the milk, stirring all the time until the sauce thickens and boils. Add the bay leaf, cloves, mace, salt and pepper. Simmer very gently for 10 minutes. Remove the bay leaf and cloves. Chop the eggs, and add them to the sauce. Allow the eggs to heat through. Stir in the 15 g (½ oz) butter and serve.

VARIOUS HOMEMADE SAUSAGES

It is no longer the custom to make one's own sausages: the butcher has the machinery, the recipe, the skins and the ingredients. And although, when one studies many of the last century's recipes, one is glad that there has been an improvement in the quality of meat available, such an affirmation of improved standards is tinged with regret. For sausages were (when prepared in the home, at least) of a succulent and tempting nature.

The intestines, for the skins, were first prepared by turning them inside out and stretching them on a stick; they were then washed and scraped in several waters. When they were thoroughly clean they were taken off the sticks, and soaked in salt water for 2-3 hours before being filled. *Oxford sausages* were made of half a kilo (1 lb) each of pork, veal, pork and veal fat, and breadcrumbs. These were minced and then mixed with thyme, parsley, sage leaves, garlic, salt and pepper. The white and the yolk of an egg were beaten separately, and used to bind the meat before it was filled into the skins. *Mutton sausages* consisted of half a kilo (1 lb) each of minced mutton and beef suet, finely chopped anchovies and seasoning to taste; *Worcester sausages* contained beef, suet, allspice, and herbs. Skins can, today, be obtained through a butcher, and from there on it is a matter of experimenting with different fillings.

David Copperfield makes himself known to his aunt

Potatoes and Yorkshire Pudding

THE CARBUNCULAR POTATO

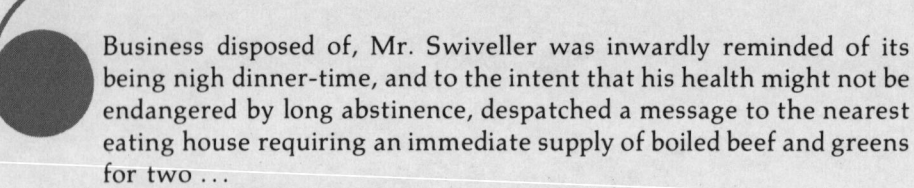

‘Business disposed of, Mr. Swiveller was inwardly reminded of its being nigh dinner-time, and to the intent that his health might not be endangered by long abstinence, despatched a message to the nearest eating house requiring an immediate supply of boiled beef and greens for two ...

'May the present moment,' said Dick, sticking his fork into a large carbuncular potato, 'be the worst of our lives! I like this plan of sending 'em with the peel on; there's a charm in drawing a potato from its native element (if I may so express it) to which the rich and powerful are strangers ...'

The Old Curiosity Shop Ch VIII

The Captain was dining (in his hat) off cold loin of mutton, porter, and some smoking hot potatoes, which he had cooked himself, and took out of a little saucepan before the fire as he wanted them. He unscrewed his hook at dinner-time, and screwed a knife into its wooden socket instead, with which he had already begun to peel one of these potatoes for Walter.

Dombey and Son Ch IX

'To obtain this wholesome and delicious vegetable cooked in perfection, it should be boiled and sent to table with the skin on. In Ireland, where, perhaps, the cooking of potatoes is better understood than any country, they are always served so. Wash the potatoes well, and if necessary, use a clean scrubbing-brush to remove the dirt from them; and, if possible, choose the potatoes so that they may all be as nearly the same size as possible. When thoroughly cleansed, fill the saucepan half full with them and just cover the potatoes with cold salted water: they are more quickly boiled with a small quantity of water, and, besides, are more savoury than when drowned in it. Bring them to boil, then draw the pan to the side of the fire, and let them simmer gently until tender. Ascertain when they are done by probing them with a fork: then pour off the water, uncover the saucepan, and let the potatoes dry by the side of the fire, taking care not to let them burn. Peel them quickly, put them in a very hot vegetable-dish, either with or without a napkin, and serve very quickly. After potatoes are cooked, they should never be entirely covered up, as the steam, instead of escaping, falls down on them, and makes them watery and insipid. In Ireland they are usually served up with the skins on, and a small plate is placed by the side of each guest.'

Note: Instead of letting the potatoes dry 'by the side of the fire', place the saucepan on an asbestos mat over a very low heat.

POTATOES IN A PUDDING DISH AND MASHED POTATOES

> 'Do you care for taters?' said the waiter, with an insinuating smile, and his head on one side. 'Young gentlemen generally has been overdosed with taters.'
> I commanded him, in my deepest voice, to order a veal cutlet and potatoes, and all things fitting; and to inquire at the bar if there were any letters for Trotwood Copperfield, Esquire—which I knew there were not, and couldn't be, but thought it manly to appear to expect. He soon came back to say that there were none (at which I was much surprised), and began to lay the cloth for my dinner in a box by the fire. While he was so engaged, he asked me what I would take with it; and on my replying 'Half a pint of sherry,' thought it a favourable opportunity, I am afraid, to extract that measure of wine from the stale leavings at the bottoms of several small decanters ... When the wine came, too, I thought it flat; and it certainly had more English crumbs in it, than were to be expected in a foreign wine in anything like a pure state; but I was bashful enough to drink it, and say nothing.
>
> *David Copperfield* Ch XIX

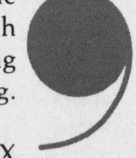

The 'oft abused potato' *can* be varied; these are two old-fashioned suggestions:

'The potatoes are sliced thin, as for frying, and allowed to remain in cold water for ½ hour. The slices are then put in a pudding dish, with salt, pepper and some milk—about ½ pint, to an ordinary pudding dish. They are then put into an oven (190°C or 375°F) and baked for an hour. When taken out, a lump of butter the size of a hen's egg is cut into small bits and scattered over the top. Those who have never eaten potatoes cooked thus, do not know all the capabilities of that esculent tuber. The slicing allows the interior of each potato to be examined, hence its value where potatoes are doubtful, though the poor ones are not of necessity required. The soaking in cold water hardens the slices, so that they will hold their shape. The milk serves to cook them through, and to make a nice brown on the top; the quantity can only be learned by experience; if just a little is left as a rich gravy, moistening all the slices, then it is right. In a year of small potatoes, this method of serving them will be very welcome to many a housekeeper.'

'Mashed potatoes; peel (thin), steam, place in a pan and mash, add milk, butter and salt, and then beat like cake batter, the longer the better, until they are nice and light. This steaming and beating will be found a great improvement.'

YORKSHIRE PUDDING AND ROAST POTATOES

> They walked on with him until they came to a dirty shop-window in a dirty street, which was made almost opaque by the steam of hot meats, vegetables, and puddings. But glimpses were to be caught of a roast leg of pork bursting into tears of sage and onion in a metal reservoir full of gravy, of an unctuous piece of roast beef and blisterous Yorkshire pudding, bubbling hot in a similar receptacle, of a stuffed fillet of veal in rapid cut, of a ham in a perspiration with the pace it was going at, of a shallow tank of baked potatoes glued together by their own richness, of a truss or two of boiled greens, and other substantial delicacies ... Fanny opened her reticule, as they surveyed these things, produced from that repository a shilling and handed it to Uncle. Uncle, after not looking at it a little while, divined its object, and muttering 'Dinner? Ha! Yes, yes, yes!' slowly vanished from them into the mist.
>
> *Little Dorrit* Ch XX

Yorkshire pudding, the traditional accompaniment to roast beef, was often served before the meat, in order to take some of the edge off the appetite, and to make the more expensive cut go further.

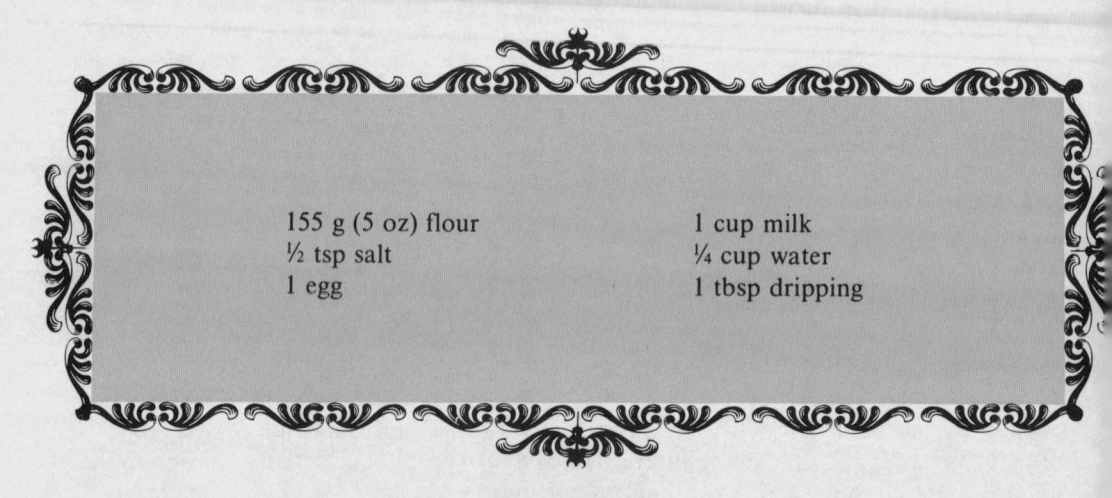

155 g (5 oz) flour
½ tsp salt
1 egg

1 cup milk
¼ cup water
1 tbsp dripping

Sift together the flour and salt into a bowl, and make a well in the centre. Place the egg in the centre of the flour, and work the flour in from the sides. Gradually add half the milk and water, continuing to beat to remove all lumps. Slowly add the rest of the flour and water, beating well. If possible, leave for 1 hour. There are several ways of proceeding from this point—the principal requirement with them all is that the dripping into which the batter is poured be smoking hot. One way is to melt the dripping in a tin dish until it is smoking hot, making sure that the sides of the dish are coated with fat. Beat the batter again, pour it into the tin, and bake at 200°-230°C (400°-450°F) on the top shelf of the oven for 30-40 minutes. The pudding should be crisp on the outside and light on the inside. The second way is to bake the pudding in the dripping in the tin the meat has been roasted in. Lift the meat on to a trivet, so that it rests above where the pudding is to cook. Have about 1 tablespoon of smoking hot dripping in the tin, and pour in the pudding. Cook in a hot oven for 30-40 minutes. Alternatively, the pudding can be cooked in its own tin, but 15 minutes before the end of cooking time it is placed below the meat to catch some of the juices that drip from the roast. Serve hot, cut into squares.

ROAST POTATOES

'Potatoes Roasted Under The Meat.—Half boil large potatoes; drain the water; put them into an earthen dish, or small tin pan, under meat roasting before the fire; baste them with the dripping. Turn them to brown on all sides; send up in a separate dish.'

The following directions are more explicit, and make an excellent roast potato:
Either choose small potatoes, or cut large ones into smaller pieces. Neaten the cut edges by paring around them with a knife. Scrape with a fork, place in cold water, bring to the boil, and boil for 3 minutes. Drain dry. Place the potatoes in the hot fat that surrounds the roast meat, and cook for 45-60 minutes, depending upon size. Baste and turn occasionally, sprinkling with salt during cooking. They should be brown and crisp on the outside. The par-boiling can be eliminated; if it is, place the potatoes in cold water and dry them before cooking.

Mrs Pipchin's present is a quencher to any number of candles

Pudding and Desserts

Only occasionally is Dickens explicit about the dishes served after the main course; 'a pudding', it seems, is of no great notice when one has already dined on roast beef and Yorkshire pie, or on boiled pork and partridge. So, while what in fact was served is unknown, some of the following recipes are attempts at possibilities ...

BAKED APPLE PUDDING

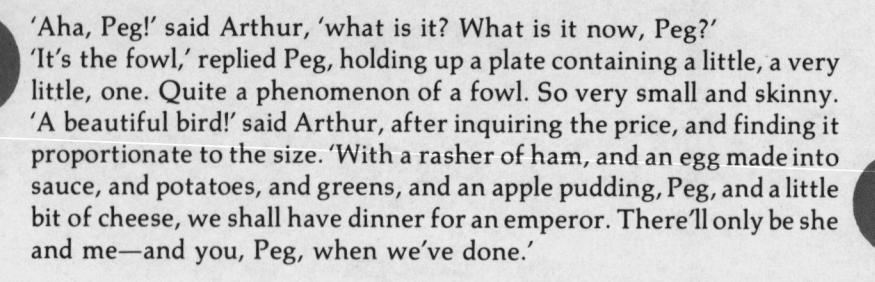

'Aha, Peg!' said Arthur, 'what is it? What is it now, Peg?'
'It's the fowl,' replied Peg, holding up a plate containing a little, a very little, one. Quite a phenomenon of a fowl. So very small and skinny.
'A beautiful bird!' said Arthur, after inquiring the price, and finding it proportionate to the size. 'With a rasher of ham, and an egg made into sauce, and potatoes, and greens, and an apple pudding, Peg, and a little bit of cheese, we shall have dinner for an emperor. There'll only be she and me—and you, Peg, when we've done.'

Nicholas Nickleby Ch LIII

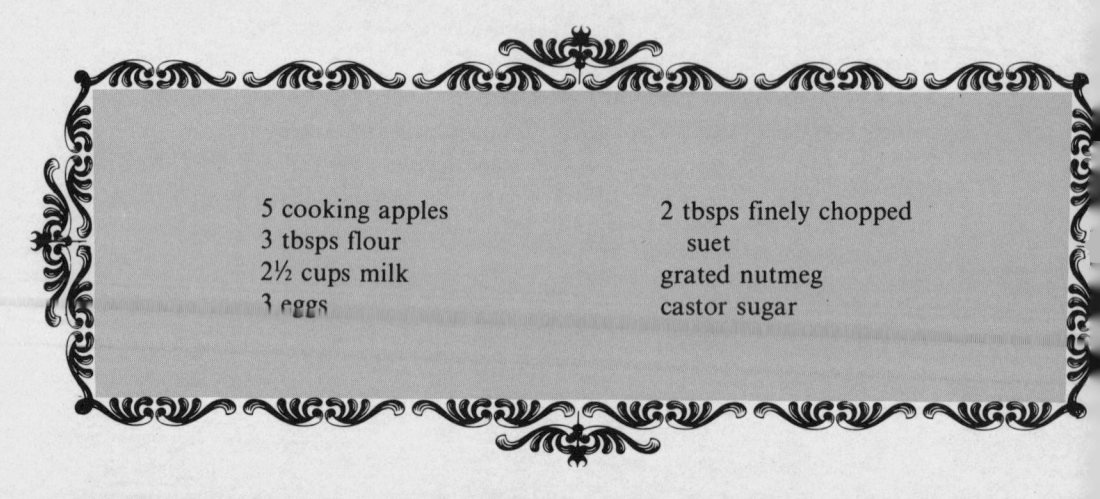

5 cooking apples
3 tbsps flour
2½ cups milk
3 eggs
2 tbsps finely chopped suet
grated nutmeg
castor sugar

Sift the flour into a bowl, make a well in the centre, and gradually beat in the milk. Beat the eggs, and then beat them into the flour and the milk. Have ready a buttered pie dish, and pour the batter into it. Wipe the apples, but do not peel them. Cut them in half and remove the cores. Place them in the batter with the skin turned upwards. Sprinkle the suet over the top and then sprinkle with nutmeg. Bake in a moderate oven for 1 hour. To serve, cover with castor sugar.

Note: Pared apples can be used instead of unpeeled ones. In that case, pare and then slice the apples before adding them to the batter.

THE WAITER'S FAVOURITE— A BATTER PUDDING

So he took a chop by the bone in one hand, and a potato in the other, and ate away with a very good appetite, to my extreme satisfaction. He afterwards took another chop, and another potato; and after that another chop, and another potato. When he had done, he brought me a pudding, and having set it before me, seemed to ruminate, and to become absent in his mind for some moments.
'How's the pie?' he said, rousing himself.
'It's a pudding,' I made answer.
'Pudding!' he exclaimed. 'Why, bless me, so it is! What!' looking at it nearer. 'You don't mean to say it's a batter-pudding?'
'Yes, it is indeed.'
'Why, a batter-pudding,' he said, taking up a table-spoon, 'is my favourite pudding! Ain't that lucky! Come on, little 'un, and let's see who'll get most.'

David Copperfield Ch V

Batter pudding, which belongs to the same family as Yorkshire pudding, was another of the great family fillers. Basically, it consists of a batter mixture to which is added anything that happens to be at hand—apples, currants, raisins, plums, gooseberries, prunes, or other dried fruit. The consistency of the batter varied from recipe to recipe—some cooks liked it quite thick in texture; others required it to be thin and creamy. Here are three recipes which provide for each alternative:

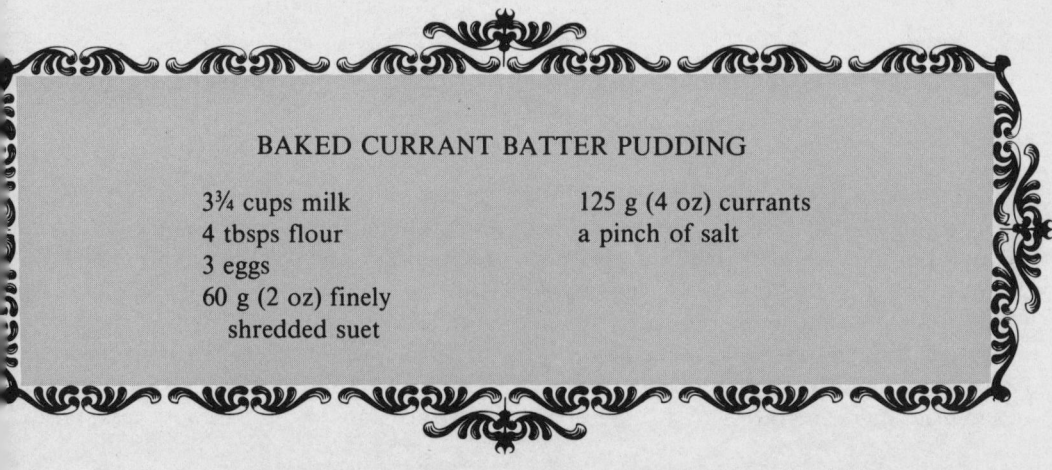

BAKED CURRANT BATTER PUDDING

3¾ cups milk
4 tbsps flour
3 eggs
60 g (2 oz) finely shredded suet
125 g (4 oz) currants
a pinch of salt

Sift the flour and salt into a bowl. Make a well in the centre and break in the eggs. Gradually work together the flour and the eggs and then slowly add the milk, beating all the time, to make a smooth batter. Stir in the suet and the currants. Have ready a buttered pie dish, and pour the mixture into it. Bake in a moderate oven for 1¼ hours.

Continued overpage

PLAIN BAKED BATTER PUDDING

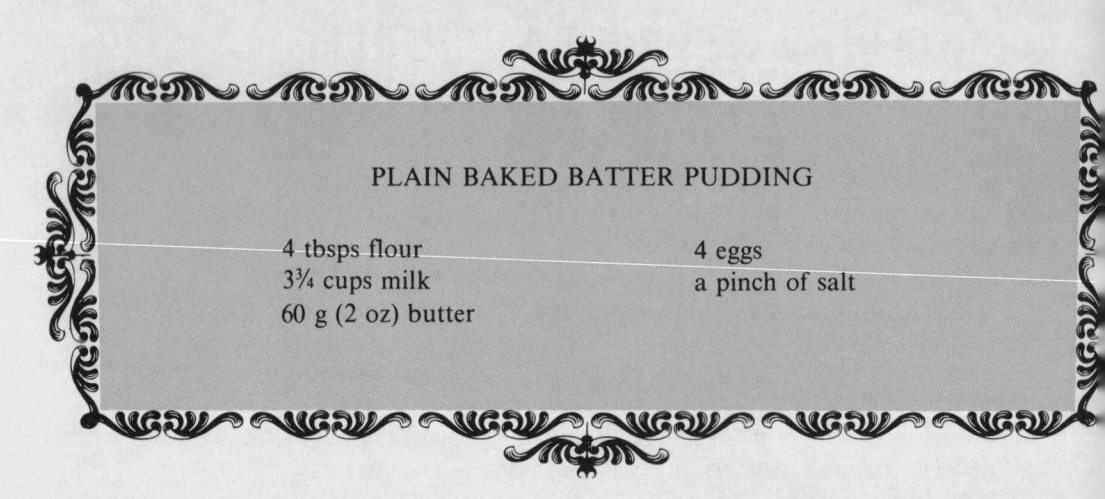

4 tbsps flour
3¾ cups milk
60 g (2 oz) butter

4 eggs
a pinch of salt

'Mix the flour with a small quantity of cold milk; make the remainder hot, and pour it on the flour, keeping the mixture well stirred; add the butter, eggs, and salt; beat the whole well, and put the pudding into a buttered pie-dish; bake for ¾ hour, and serve with a sweet sauce, wine sauce, or stewed fruit. Baked in small cups, very pretty little puddings may be made; they should be eaten with the same accompaniments as above.'

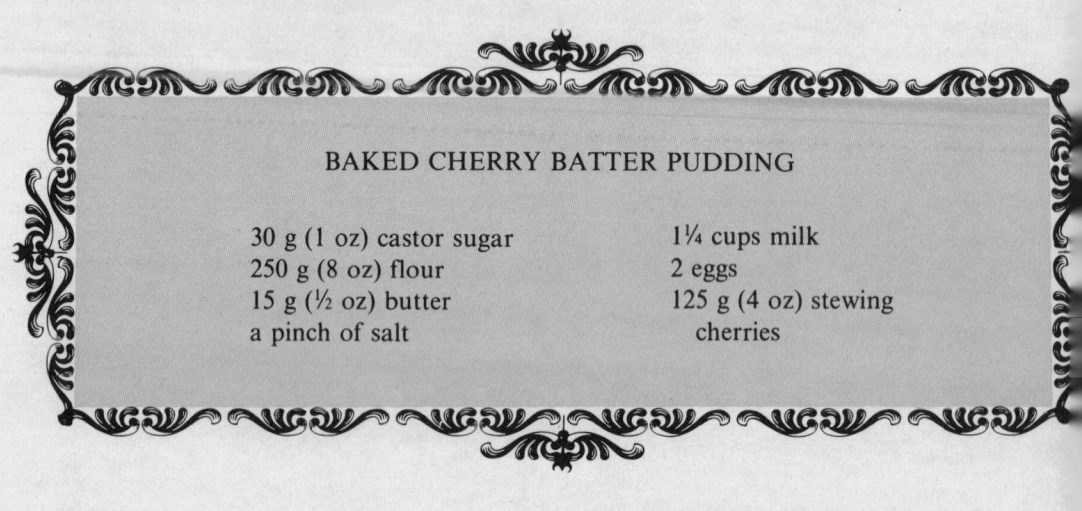

BAKED CHERRY BATTER PUDDING

30 g (1 oz) castor sugar
250 g (8 oz) flour
15 g (½ oz) butter
a pinch of salt

1¼ cups milk
2 eggs
125 g (4 oz) stewing cherries

Sift the flour and the salt into a bowl. Whisk the eggs and beat them into the flour. Melt the butter and add it to the flour mixture. Add the milk gradually (you may not need it all), beating all the time. The batter should be thick enough to drop from the spoon but not thick enough to pour. Stone the cherries, and place them and the sugar in a saucepan. Gently bring to simmering point, stirring to dissolve the sugar, and simmer until soft. Strain off and reserve the juice. Butter a pie-dish, add some batter to it, then add the cherries. Put in the remainder of the batter, and bake at 200°C (400°F) for approximately 30 minutes, until set and brown. Serve accompanied by the hot cherry syrup.

THE LITTLE APPARITION'S BAKED PUDDINGS

I was so young and childish, and so little qualified—how could I be otherwise?—to undertake the whole charge of my existence, that often, in going to Murdstone and Grinby's, of a morning, I could not resist the stale pastry put out for sale at half-price at the pastrycooks' doors, and spent in that, the money I should have kept for my dinner. Then, I went without my dinner, or bought a roll or a slice of pudding. I remember two pudding-shops, between which I was divided, according to my finances. One was in the court close to St. Martin's Church—at the back of the church,—which is now removed altogether. The pudding at the shop was made of currants, and was rather a special pudding, but was dear, twopennyworth not being larger than a pennyworth of more ordinary pudding. A good shop for the latter was in the Strand—somewhere in that part which has been rebuilt since. It was a stout pale pudding, heavy and flabby, and with great flat raisins in it, stuck in whole at wide distances apart. It came up hot at about my time every day, and many a day did I dine off it. When I dined regularly and handsomely, I had a saveloy and a penny loaf, or a fourpenny plate of red beef from a cook's shop: or a plate of bread and cheese and a glass of beer, from a miserable old public-house opposite our place of business, called the Lion, or the Lion and something else that I have forgotten. Once, I remember carrying my own bread (which I had brought from home that morning) under my arm, wrapped in a piece of paper, like a book, and going to a famous alamode beef-house near Drury Lane, and ordering a 'small plate' of that delicacy to eat with it. What the waiter thought of such a strange little apparition coming in all alone, I don't know; but I can see him now, staring at me as I ate my dinner, and bringing the other waiter to look. I gave him a halfpenny for himself, and I wish he hadn't taken it.

David Copperfield Ch XI

Continued overpage

The currants can be omitted, and the weight made up in raisins, or *vice versa*, in the following recipes:

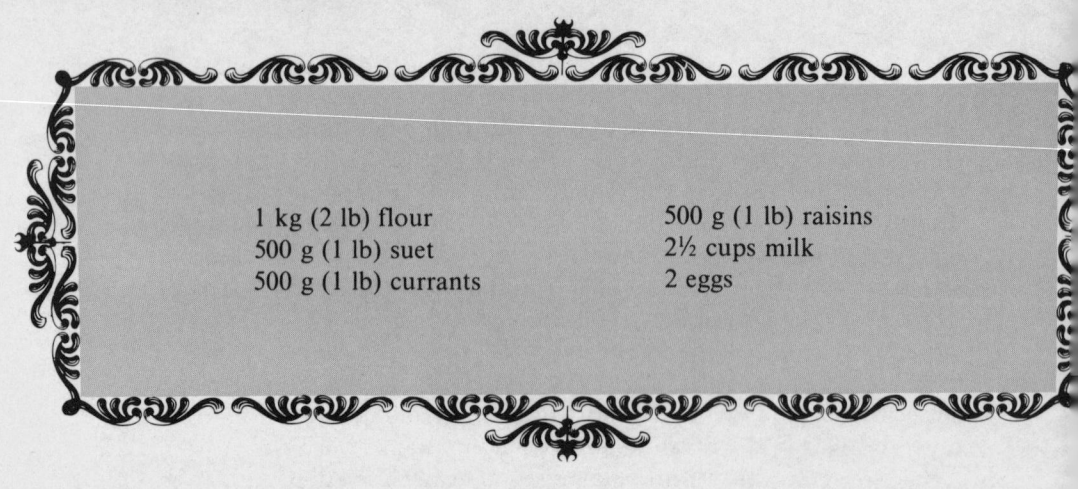

1 kg (2 lb) flour
500 g (1 lb) suet
500 g (1 lb) currants
500 g (1 lb) raisins
2½ cups milk
2 eggs

Finely shred the suet. Place the suet in a bowl, and sift in the flour. Add the raisins and currants. Beat the eggs well, then stir the milk into the eggs. Pour the egg mixture into the flour mixture, and blend, adding more milk if necessary, to make a stiff batter. Turn into a well buttered dish, and bake in a moderate oven for 2½-3 hours.

A less extravagant baked plum pudding:

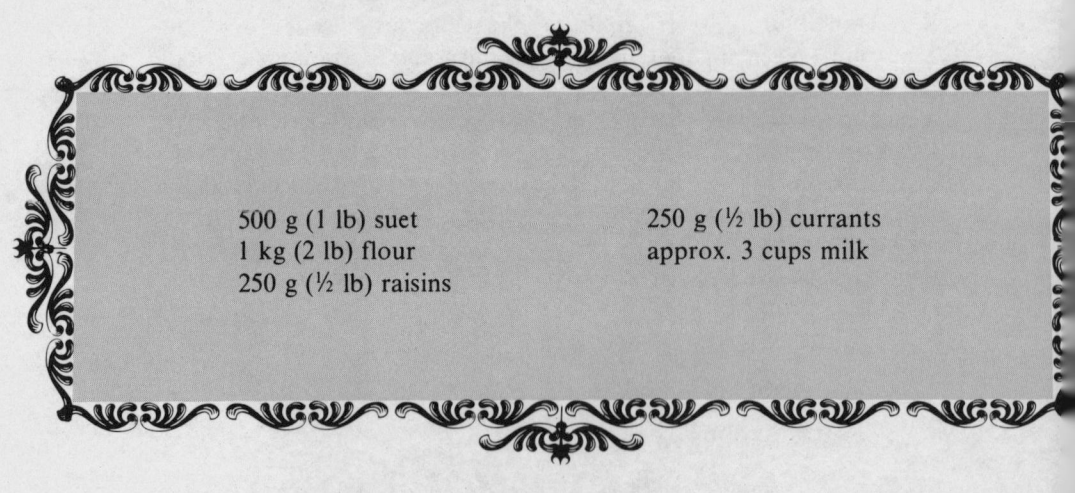

500 g (1 lb) suet
1 kg (2 lb) flour
250 g (½ lb) raisins
250 g (½ lb) currants
approx. 3 cups milk

Chop the suet finely. Place the suet in a bowl, and sift in the flour. Add the raisins and currants. Gradually stir in the milk, using sufficient to make a stiff batter. Turn into a well buttered dish, and bake in a moderate oven for 2-2½ hours.

TREACLE PUDDING

> We dined soon after I awoke, off a roast fowl and a pudding; I sitting at the table, not unlike a trussed bird myself, and moving my arms with considerable difficulty. But as my aunt had swathed me up, I made no complaint of being inconvenienced. All this time I was deeply anxious to know what she was going to do with me; but she took her dinner in profound silence, except when she occasionally fixed her eyes on me sitting opposite, and said, 'Mercy upon us!' which did not by any means relieve my anxiety.
> The cloth being drawn, and some sherry being put upon the table (of which I had a glass) my aunt sent up for Mr. Dick again ...
>
> *David Copperfield* Ch XIII

250 g (8 oz) breadcrumbs
125 g (4 oz) flour
1 tsp baking powder
125 g (4 oz) shredded suet
60 g (2 oz) dark brown sugar
1 lemon
2 eggs
15 g (½ oz) butter
2 tbsps golden syrup or treacle
150 ml (¼ pt) milk

Finely grate the lemon peel. In a bowl, mix together the breadcrumbs, flour, sugar, shredded suet and lemon rind. Add the juice of the lemon. Beat the eggs, add them to the mixture in the bowl, and blend well. Add the golden syrup or treacle, then the milk, and mix well. Sift in the baking powder, and evenly stir it into the mixture. Turn the mixture into a well buttered basin, and cover with a piece of well buttered greaseproof paper that has a large pleat in the middle. Tie on very securely. Steam for 2½ hours. Serve with extra golden syrup or treacle that has been heated with half its quantity of water.

MRS WALMERS'S BREAD-AND-BUTTER PUDDING

A biled fowl, and baked bread-and-butter pudding, brought Mrs. Walmers up a little; but Boots could have wished, he must privately own to me, to have seen her more sensible of the voice of love, and less abandoning of herself to currants.

The Holly-tree

Miss Rugg, perhaps making up some of her arrears, likewise took very kindly to the mutton, and it rapidly diminished to the bone. A bread-and-butter pudding entirely disappeared, and a considerable amount of cheese and radishes vanished by the same means. Then came the dessert.

Little Dorrit Ch XXV

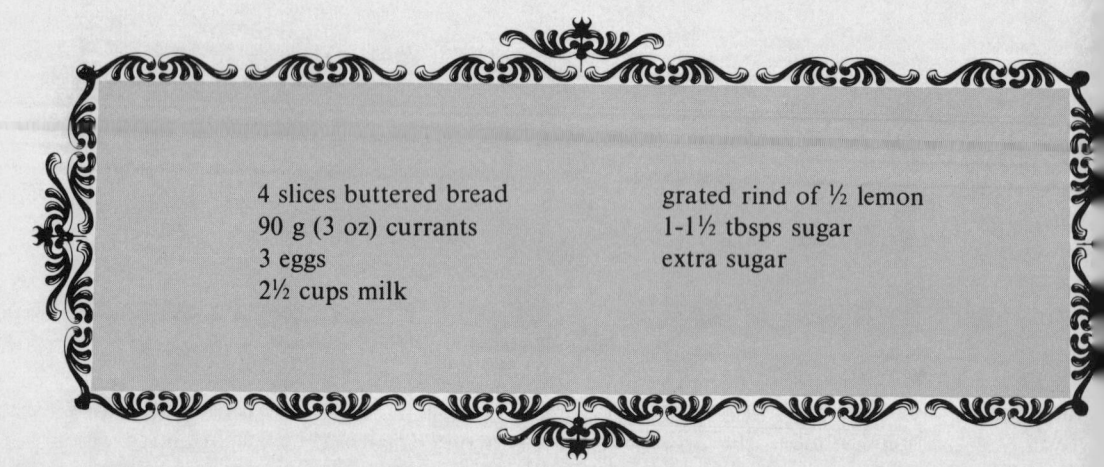

4 slices buttered bread
90 g (3 oz) currants
3 eggs
2½ cups milk
grated rind of ½ lemon
1-1½ tbsps sugar
extra sugar

The bread can be left in full slices, or, for a neater appearance, it can be cut into quarters. Place a layer of buttered bread in a greased pie dish and scatter on some currants. Continue to layer the bread and the currants, finishing with currants. Place the lemon rind and the milk in a saucepan, and bring to the boil. Stir in the sugar. Beat the eggs, and pour the milk over them, stirring well. Strain the mixture. Pour the egg and milk mixture on to the bread from the side of the dish, then sprinkle the top with a little extra sugar. Stand the dish in a *bain marie* and cook at 180°C (350°F) for 30-40 minutes, or until set and brown. Serve directly from the dish. 'This pudding may be very much enriched by adding cream, candied peel, or more eggs than stated above.'

FIG PUDDING

"Therefore a carriage was ordered, of capacity to take them all, and in the meantime Sloppy was regaled, feasting alone in the Secretary's room, with a complete realisation of that fairy vision—meat, beer, vegetables, and pudding. In consequence of which his buttons became more importunate of public notice than before, with the exception of two or three about the region of the waistband, which modestly withdrew into a creasy retirement."

Our Mutual Friend Bk 2 Ch IX

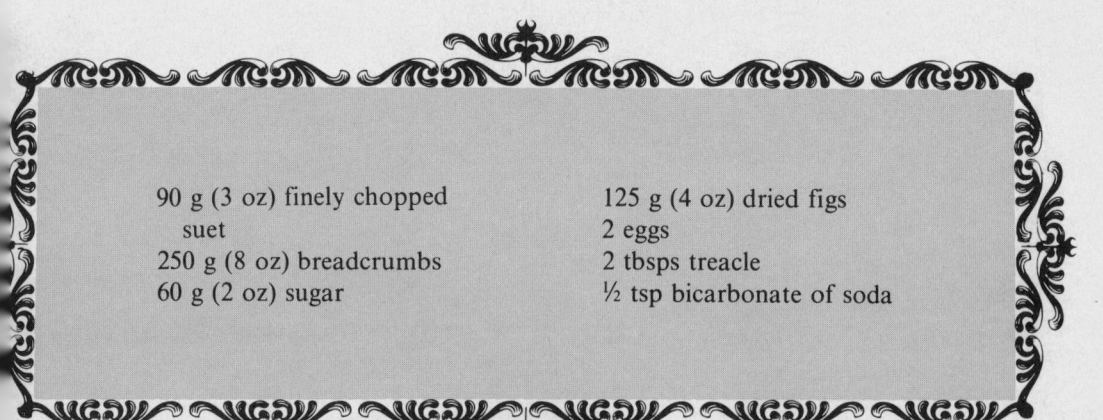

---

90 g (3 oz) finely chopped suet
250 g (8 oz) breadcrumbs
60 g (2 oz) sugar
125 g (4 oz) dried figs
2 eggs
2 tbsps treacle
½ tsp bicarbonate of soda

Mix together in a bowl the suet, breadcrumbs, and sugar. Chop the figs and add them to the bowl. Beat the eggs well, mix in the treacle, and stir in the bicarbonate of soda. Pour the liquid into the dry ingredients. Have ready a well greased pudding bowl. Pour the mixture into it. Prepare the pudding to boil it (see Damson Pudding). Immerse the pudding into a deep pan of boiling water, and boil for 3 hours. Keep the pudding covered with water, and do not allow it to go off the boil. Serve with a sweet sauce, warmed treacle, custard or cream.

JAM ROLY-POLY PUDDING

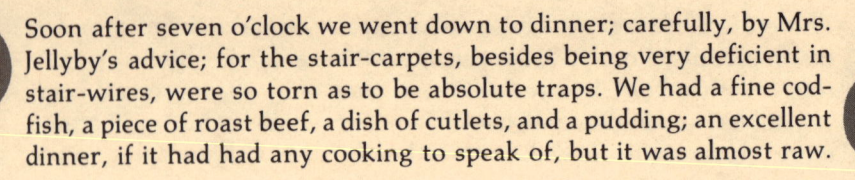

> Soon after seven o'clock we went down to dinner; carefully, by Mrs. Jellyby's advice; for the stair-carpets, besides being very deficient in stair-wires, were so torn as to be absolute traps. We had a fine cod-fish, a piece of roast beef, a dish of cutlets, and a pudding; an excellent dinner, if it had had any cooking to speak of, but it was almost raw.

Bleak House Ch IV

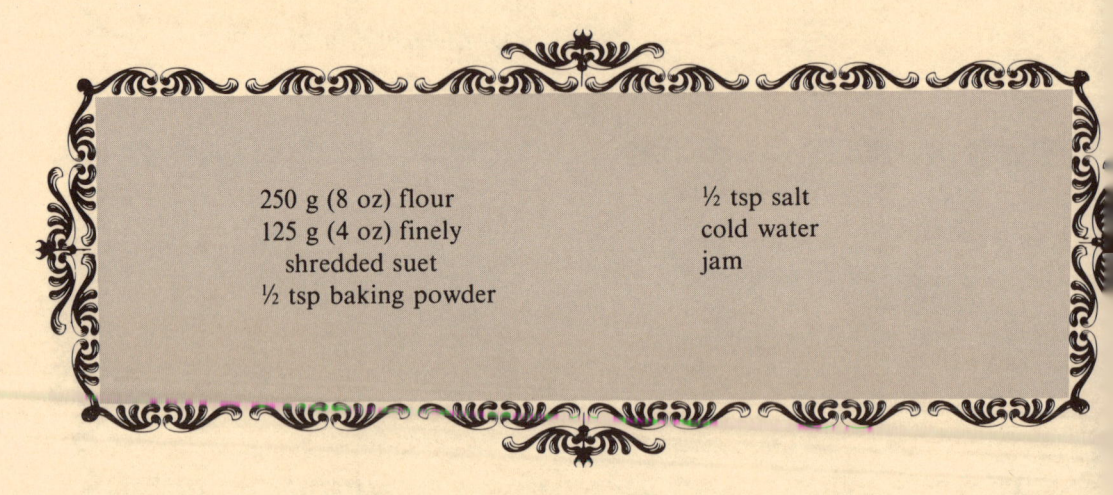

---

250 g (8 oz) flour
125 g (4 oz) finely shredded suet
½ tsp baking powder
½ tsp salt
cold water
jam

Sift the flour, baking powder, and salt into a bowl, and blend in the suet. Gradually add sufficient cold water to form a dough. Leave in a cool place for half an hour, if possible. On a floured board, roll out the dough in a strip that is approximately 7 mm (¼ in.) thick, and of an oblong shape. Fold in the edges of the larger two sides, and one of the shorter sides, to prevent the jam from oozing out. Spread inside this with jam. Moisten the folded edges with water. Roll up lightly and press the edges together to seal them. Have ready a scalded, floured pudding cloth. Place the pudding in the cloth, and tie the ends very securely with string. Boil or steam for 2 hours. Serve with a sweet white sauce or custard.

DAMSON PUDDING

Spoons are waved in the air, legs appear above the table-cloth in uncontrollable ecstasy, and eight short fingers dabble in damson syrup.
While the pudding is being disposed of, Mr. and Mrs. Whiffler look on with beaming countenances ...

Sketches of Young Couples

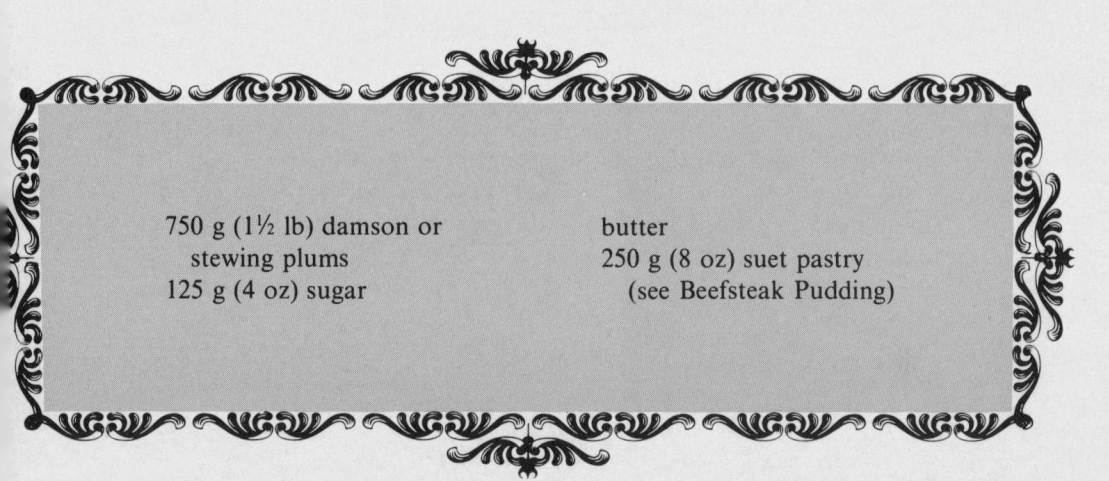

750 g (1½ lb) damson or stewing plums
125 g (4 oz) sugar
butter
250 g (8 oz) suet pastry (see Beefsteak Pudding)

Wash the plums, and remove any pieces of stem. Grease with butter a pudding basin. On a floured board, roll out the pastry (retaining some for the lid), making sure that there are no breaks in it. Lift the pastry gently with floured hands, and line the pudding basin with it, leaving some to overlap the top of the bowl. Fill the basin with plums (they should reach to the top of the bowl), sprinkling sugar between the layers. Fold in the trimmed but overlapping pieces of pastry. Roll out the remaining pastry to make a lid for the pudding. Dampen the top rim of the bottom layer of pastry, and add the lid, pressing well around the edges so that there are no spaces for the juice to escape. Trim. Take a large piece of greaseproof paper, put a large pleat in the centre, and tie it securely over the bowl. Take a large piece of linen cloth, scald it, wring it out, and flour well the underside. Wrap it completely around the bowl, and tie it very securely, making a loop with string or the top knots of the cloth to enable you to place it in the water and also to remove it. Have ready a large pan of boiling water, submerge the pudding in it, and boil for 2½-3 hours. The water should not go off the boil, and extra boiling water should be added to compensate for evaporation. Serve from the bowl.

A SPECKLED CANNON-BALL OF A CHRISTMAS PLUM PUDDING

Hallo! A great deal of steam! The pudding was out of the copper. A smell like a washing-day! That was the cloth. A smell like an eating house and a pastrycook's next door to each other, with a laundress's next door to that! That was the pudding! In half a minute Mrs. Cratchit entered—flushed, but smiling proudly—with the pudding, like a speckled cannon-ball, so hard and firm, blazing in half of half-a-quartern of ignited brandy, and bedight with Christmas holly stuck into the top.

Oh, a wonderful pudding! Bob Cratchit said, and calmly too, that he regarded it as the greatest success achieved by Mrs. Cratchit since their marriage. Mrs. Cratchit said that now the weight was off her mind, she would confess she had had her doubts about the quantity of flour. Everybody had something to say about it, but nobody said or thought it was at all a small pudding for a large family. It would have been flat heresy to do so. Any Cratchit would have blushed to hint at such a thing.

A Christmas Carol Stave III

We had previously left in the corner of the inn-yard a wall-eyed young man connected with the fly department, and well accustomed to the sound of a railway whistle which Ben always carries in his pocket, whose instructions were, so soon as he should hear the whistle blown, to dash into the kitchen, seize the hot plum-pudding and mince-pies, and speed with them to Watt's Charity, where they would be received (he was further instructed) by the sauce-female, who would be provided with brandy in a blue state of combustion.

The Seven Poor Travellers

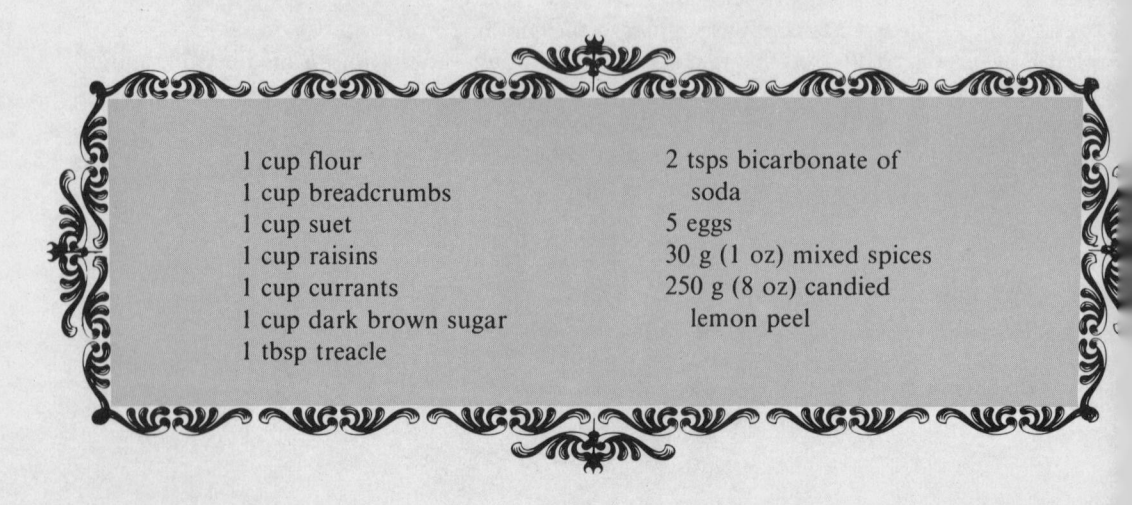

- 1 cup flour
- 1 cup breadcrumbs
- 1 cup suet
- 1 cup raisins
- 1 cup currants
- 1 cup dark brown sugar
- 1 tbsp treacle
- 2 tsps bicarbonate of soda
- 5 eggs
- 30 g (1 oz) mixed spices
- 250 g (8 oz) candied lemon peel

Chop the raisins, and sift together the flour, bicarbonate of soda, and the spice. Mix together in a bowl all the dry ingredients. Beat the eggs and warm the treacle, then add them to the dry ingredients. If using a pudding basin, grease it well, and grease a double thickness of greaseproof paper to go over the top of the pudding, allowing room for a large pleat. Either a pudding cloth or aluminium foil can go over the top. If a cloth is used, it should be prepared in the same way as a complete pudding cloth. If a pudding cloth instead of a basin is being used, scald the cloth just before using, wring it out, and flour it well. Place the pudding mixture in the basin or cloth. If a cloth is used, tie it very securely with string. If using a bowl, first top with greaseproof paper, which has been pleated to allow for swelling, then securely tie a cloth over and around the bowl. A clothed pudding must be immersed in steadily boiling water, having it resting on a plate or rack in the bottom of the saucepan to prevent it burning. If a basin is used, the water should come halfway up the sides of the bowl. Do not allow the water to go off the boil, and when adding extra water to replace that which has evaporated, always use boiling water. Boil for 8 hours. Allow to cool and dry completely, then hang a clothed pudding in a cool place, or store both types in a refrigerator. Boil for a further 2 hours before serving.

MRS JOE'S CHRISTMAS MINCE PIE

We were to have a superb dinner, consisting of a leg of pickled pork and greens, and a pair of roast stuffed fowls. A handsome mince-pie had been made yesterday morning (which accounted for the mincemeat not being missed), and the pudding was already on the boil. These extensive arrangements occasioned us to be cut off unceremoniously in respect of breakfast; 'for I an't,' said Mrs. Joe, 'I an't a-going to have no formal cramming and bursting and washing up now, with what I've got before me, I promise you!' ... We dined on these occasions in the kitchen, and adjourned, for the nuts and oranges and apples, to the parlour; which was a change very like Joe's change from his working clothes to his Sunday dress.

Great Expectations Ch IV

In Dickens's day the ingredients for mincemeat varied as much in their quantity and type as they do today, although the flavour of the finished preparation was succulently similar to that to which we are accustomed. Frequently (along with three pounds of beef suet and a 'pottle of apples'), minced lean beef was added, although the practice was gradually fading, leaving only the sweet dessert ingredients.

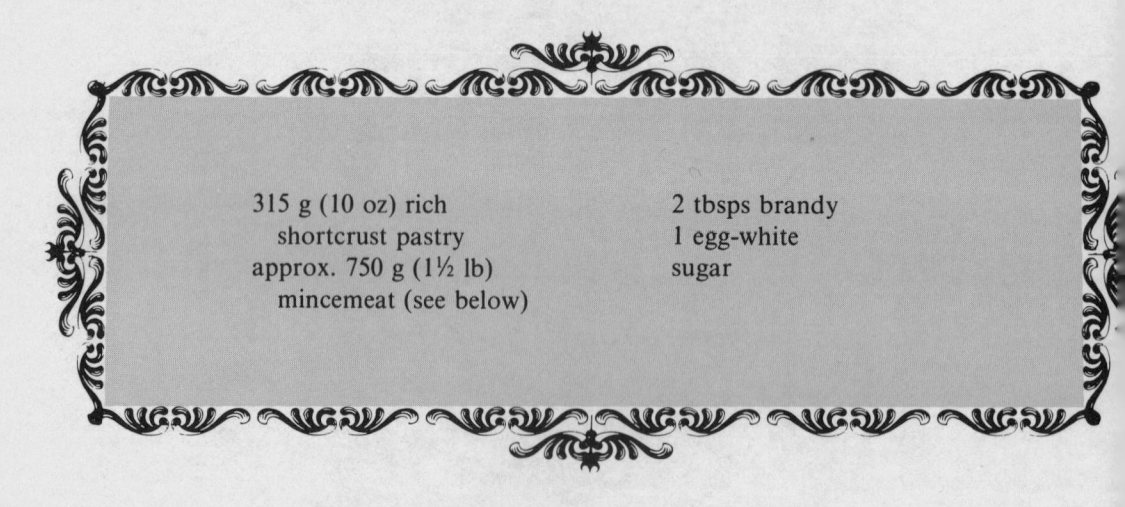

---

315 g (10 oz) rich shortcrust pastry
approx. 750 g (1½ lb) mincemeat (see below)

2 tbsps brandy
1 egg-white
sugar

Make the pastry and chill it for 1 hour. On a floured board, roll out half the pastry, and with it line a tart dish. Fill the centre with the mincemeat mixture which has been blended with the brandy. Roll out the rest of the pastry. Moisten with water the edges of the bottom layer of pastry, and cover the tart with the remaining pastry. Trim the edges, and press together to seal. Make a hole in the centre. Cook at 200°C (400°F) for approximately 35 minutes. Remove from the oven and brush the top with beaten egg-white. Sprinkle with sugar. Return to the oven for a couple of minutes to dry the egg-white. Serve hot or cold.

Note: Individual mince pies can also be made in a similar fashion, but will require a shorter cooking time.

Mincemeat for Preserving

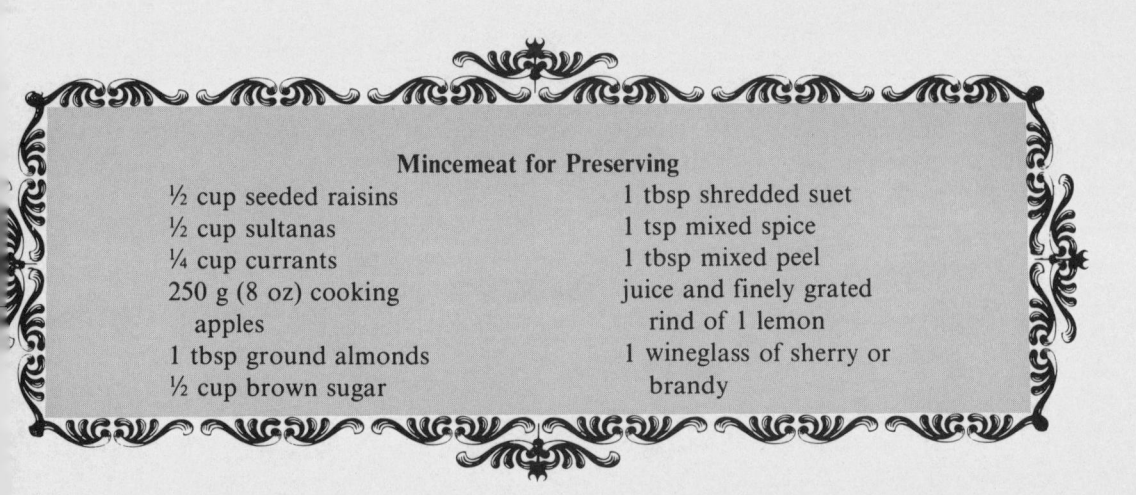

½ cup seeded raisins
½ cup sultanas
¼ cup currants
250 g (8 oz) cooking apples
1 tbsp ground almonds
½ cup brown sugar
1 tbsp shredded suet
1 tsp mixed spice
1 tbsp mixed peel
juice and finely grated rind of 1 lemon
1 wineglass of sherry or brandy

Wash and dry the dried fruit. Peel, core, and roughly chop the apples. Mince the dried fruit with the apples. Add the almonds, sugar, suet, mixed spice, mixed peel, and the lemon juice and rind. Blend in the sherry or the brandy. Pack the mixture tightly into jars and seal. Keep in a cool place for at least 1 month before using.

TREACLE TART

Salmon, lamb, peas, innocent young potatoes, a cool salad, sliced cucumber, a tender duckling, and a tart—all there.

Martin Chuzzlewit Ch XLV

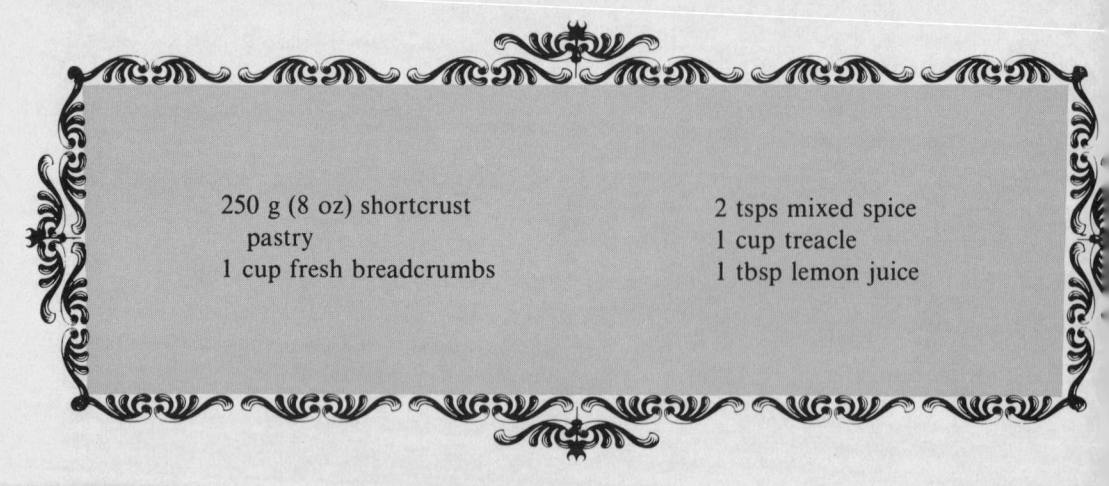

250 g (8 oz) shortcrust pastry
1 cup fresh breadcrumbs
2 tsps mixed spice
1 cup treacle
1 tbsp lemon juice

On a floured board, roll out the pastry to line a tart plate; trim and flute the edges of the tart. Mix the breadcrumbs with the spice, and sprinkle the mixture over the pastry case. Heat together the treacle and the lemon juice; pour it over the crumbs. Bake in a hot oven at 230°C (450°F) for 10 minutes, then reduce the heat to 180°C (350°F) and cook for 10 minutes longer.

THE PRECIOUS RASPBERRY JAM TART

A famous Inn! the hall a very grove of dead game, and dangling joints of mutton; and in one corner an illustrious larder, with glass doors, developing cold fowls and noble joints, and tarts wherein the raspberry jam coyly withdrew itself, as such a precious creature should, behind a lattice work of pastry.

Martin Chuzzlewit Ch XII

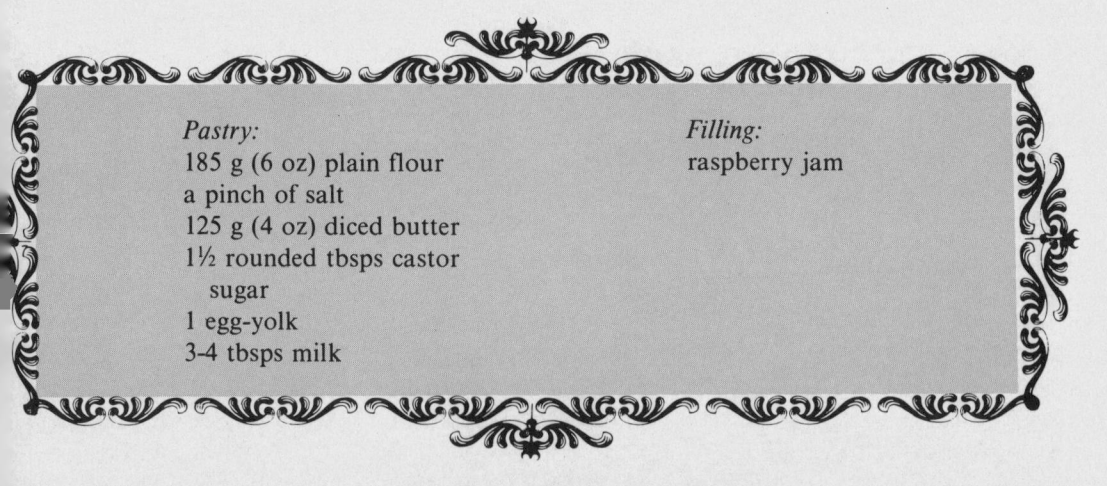

Pastry:
185 g (6 oz) plain flour
a pinch of salt
125 g (4 oz) diced butter
1½ rounded tbsps castor sugar
1 egg-yolk
3-4 tbsps milk

Filling:
raspberry jam

Sift the flour and salt into a mixing bowl. Lightly rub in the butter. Stir in the sugar. Beat the egg-yolk with the milk and mix it into the flour to make a dough. Chill for 30 minutes. Roll the pastry out on a floured board. Line a tart dish with the pastry, leaving enough trimmings to make a lattice top. Fill the centre with raspberry jam. Roll out the trimmings and cut into strips to make a lattice-work top across the tart. The strips can be glazed with milk or egg if preferred. Bake at 230°C (450°F) for 15 to 20 minutes. Serve hot or cold.

BAKEWELL TART

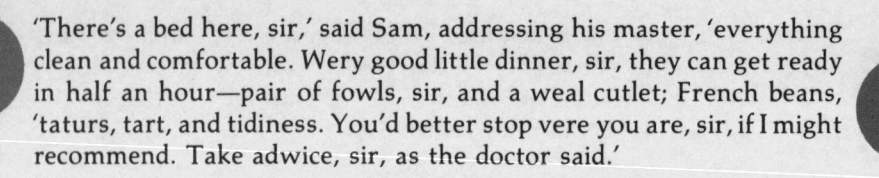

'There's a bed here, sir,' said Sam, addressing his master, 'everything clean and comfortable. Wery good little dinner, sir, they can get ready in half an hour—pair of fowls, sir, and a weal cutlet; French beans, 'taturs, tart, and tidiness. You'd better stop vere you are, sir, if I might recommend. Take adwice, sir, as the doctor said.'

The Pickwick Papers Ch LI

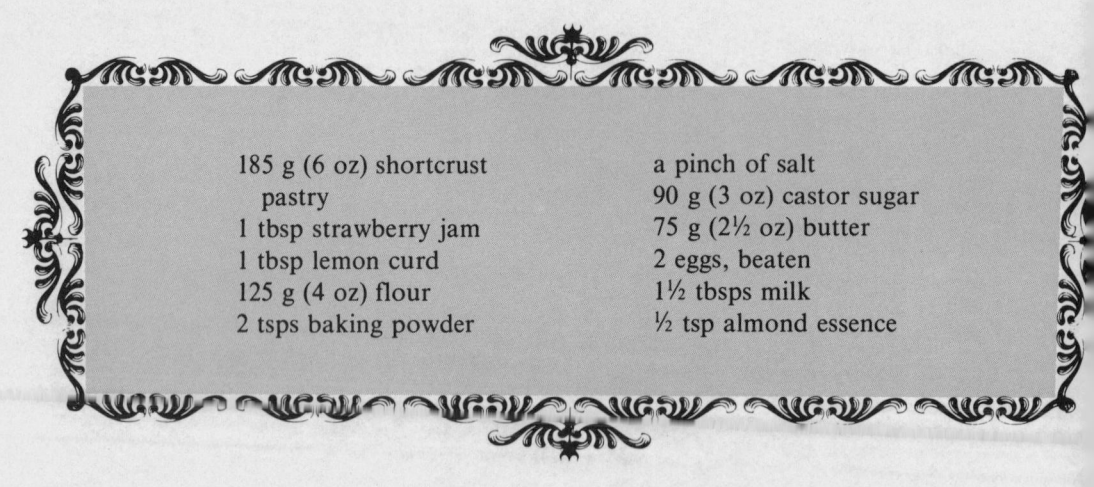

185 g (6 oz) shortcrust pastry	a pinch of salt
1 tbsp strawberry jam	90 g (3 oz) castor sugar
1 tbsp lemon curd	75 g (2½ oz) butter
125 g (4 oz) flour	2 eggs, beaten
2 tsps baking powder	1½ tbsps milk
	½ tsp almond essence

Chill the pastry, then roll it out to line an 18-cm (7-in.) sandwich tin. Spread the pastry first with the jam and then with the lemon curd. Sift the flour, baking powder, salt, and castor sugar into a mixing bowl and then rub in the butter. Stir in the eggs, milk, and almond essence, mixing until smooth. Pour into the pastry case. Bake for 30-35 minutes at 190°C (375°F).

APPLE PARSTIES

'So she makes,' said Mr. Barkis, after a long interval of reflection, 'all the apple parsties, and does all the cooking, do she?'
I replied that such was the fact.
'Well. I'll tell you what,' said Mr. Barkis. 'P'raps you might be writin' to her?'
'I shall certainly write to her,' I rejoined.
'Ah!' he said, slowly turning his eyes towards me. 'Well! If you was writin' to her, p'raps you'd recollect to say that Barkis was willin', would you?'

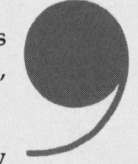

David Copperfield Ch V

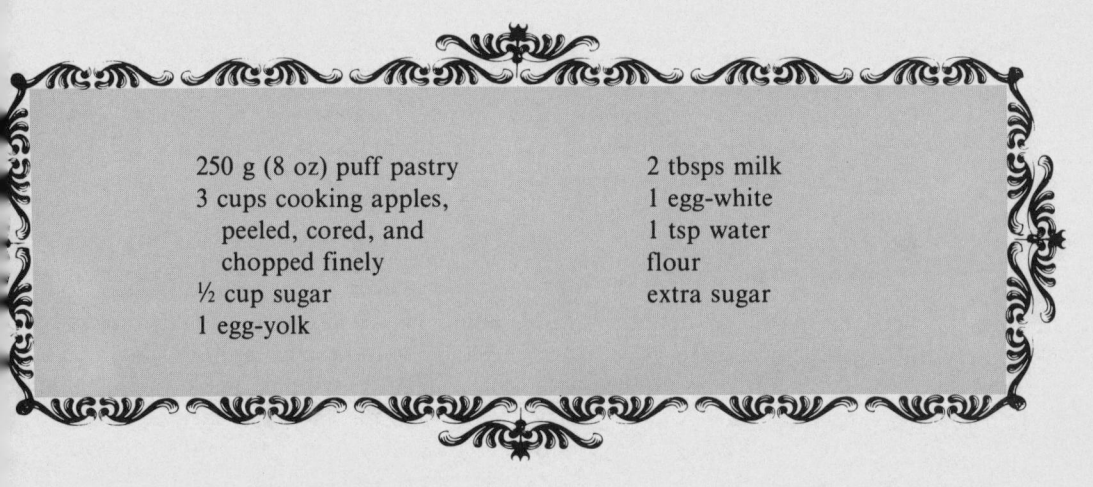

250 g (8 oz) puff pastry
3 cups cooking apples, peeled, cored, and chopped finely
½ cup sugar
1 egg-yolk
2 tbsps milk
1 egg-white
1 tsp water
flour
extra sugar

Working with a quarter of the pastry at a time, roll it out to a thickness of 7 mm (¼ in.), then cut it into 8-cm (3-in.) rounds with a sharp cutter. Leave the pastry to rest for 10 minutes. Mix the sugar and the apples. More sugar may be required if the apples are very tart. In a bowl, beat the egg-yolk, and stir in the milk to make an egg-glaze for the pastry. In another bowl, blend lightly together the egg-white and the water to make an egg-white glaze for the pastry. Roll out each pastry circle from the centre to make an oval approximately 23 cm (9 in.) long. Place heaps of the apple mixture on one half of each of the pastry ovals. Mix a little flour with some water to make a light paste, and very lightly brush it on the inside edges of each round. This will help to seal the pastry to prevent the juices from escaping. Fold each oval over and press together well around the edges. Using the yolk glaze only, brush the tops of each pastry, and place them on a baking sheet that has been dampened. Cover with a lightly dampened cloth, and leave to stand for half an hour. Bake at 230°C (450°F) for 20 minutes, then quickly remove the pasties from the oven, brush with the egg-white glaze, and sprinkle each with a little extra sugar. Return to the oven and bake for a further 5 minutes, until golden, making sure that you do not let them burn. Serve hot or cold.

ORANGES STEEPED IN WINE, AND 'A PRETTY DISH OF ORANGES'

> I was made very uneasy in my mind by Mrs. Pocket's falling into a discussion with Drummle respecting two baronetcies, while she ate a sliced orange steeped in sugar and wine, and forgetting all about the baby on her lap: who did most appalling things with the nut-crackers.
>
> *Great Expectations* Ch XXIII
>
> A quantity of oranges and halfpence thrust indiscriminately on each young Toodle, checked the first violence of their regret, and the family were speedily transported to their own home, by means of the hackney-coach kept in waiting for that purpose. The children, under the guardianship of Jemima, blocked up the window, and dropped out oranges and halfpence all the way along. Mr. Toodle himself preferred to ride behind among the spikes, being the mode of conveyance to which he was best accustomed.
>
> *Dombey and Son* Ch II

Mrs Pocket's dish was no doubt created simply and expeditely: an orange was peeled and sliced, placed in a bowl, sprinkled with pounded sugar, and white wine or sherry poured over the top—all of which was left to stand in a cool place until the sugar had dissolved and the orange had absorbed the flavour of the wine. A simple and refreshing similar dish is the following:

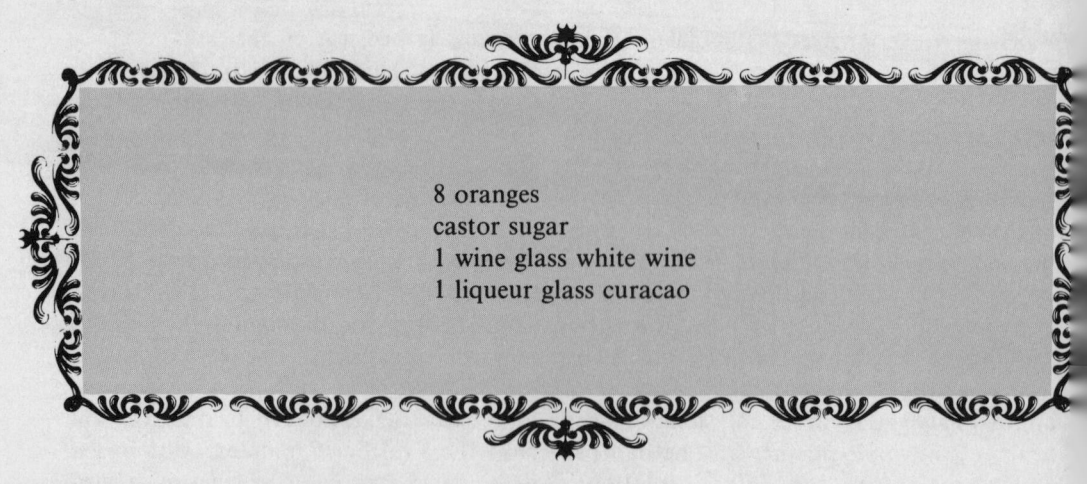

---

8 oranges
castor sugar
1 wine glass white wine
1 liqueur glass curacao

Peel the oranges, making sure that you peel through to the flesh, removing all the pith. (Treat the oranges over a bowl, so that all the juice will be collected.) Holding an orange in the hand, with a sharp knife cut through the inside edges of each segment, cutting towards the centre, so that the skin of each segment is removed, leaving pure flesh. Place the cut orange segments in a glass bowl, sprinkling each layer with castor sugar. Pour over the white wine and the curacao. Leave to stand in a cool place for two hours, then taste for sweetness. Sprinkle on more sugar if necessary. Chill until required. More wine can be used, of course, or a little of the caught orange juice can be strained over the dish.

Note: This is also excellent when made of equal parts of orange and grapefruit segments.

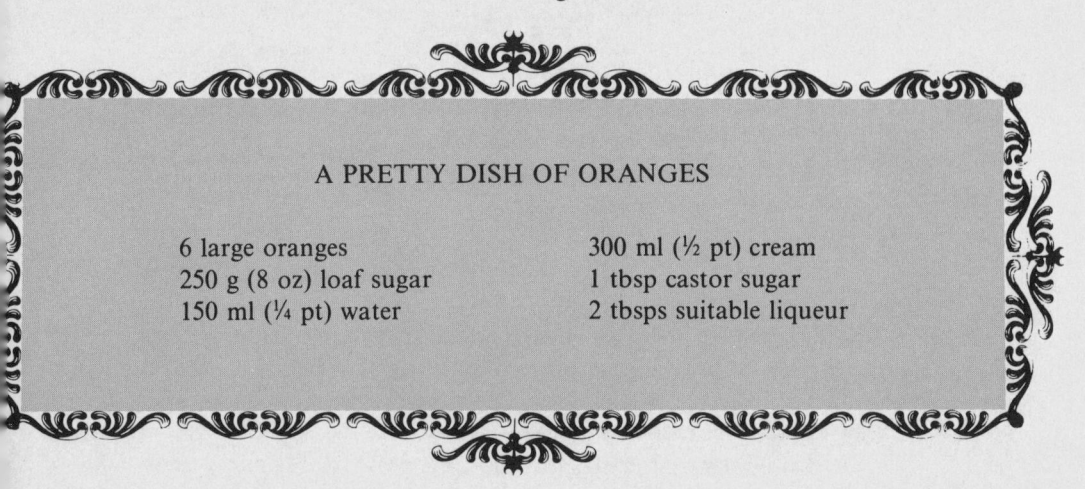

A PRETTY DISH OF ORANGES

6 large oranges
250 g (8 oz) loaf sugar
150 ml (¼ pt) water

300 ml (½ pt) cream
1 tbsp castor sugar
2 tbsps suitable liqueur

'Put the sugar and the water into a saucepan, and boil them until the sugar becomes brittle, which may be ascertained by taking up a small quantity in a spoon, and dipping it in cold water; if the sugar is sufficiently boiled, it will easily snap. Peel the oranges, remove as much of the white pith as possible, and divide them into nice-sized slices, without breaking the thin white skin which surrounds the juicy pulp. Place the pieces of orange on small skewers, dip them into the hot sugar, and arrange them in layers around a plain mould, which should be well oiled with the purest salad-oil. The sides of the mould only should be lined with the oranges, and the centre left open for the cream. Let the sugar become firm by cooling; turn the oranges carefully out on a dish, and fill the centre with whipped cream, flavoured with any kind of liqueur, and sweetened with pounded sugar. This is an exceedingly ornamental and nice dish for the supper-table.'

A COOLING JELLY

When that was done, the basket which was filled with grapes and other fruit, was unpacked, and all its contents were quietly put away. When that was done, a moment's whisper despatched Maggy to despatch somebody else to fill the basket again; which soon came back replenished with new stores, from which a present provision of cooling drink and jelly, and a prospective supply of roast chicken and wine and water, were the first extracts.

Little Dorrit Ch XXIX

Making jelly—either savoury or sweet—was not a simple matter of opening a pre-prepared packet; it involved the laborious task of making a good, clear jellied stock from calf's feet. The following recipe, for making and clarifying the base stock for any jelly is one that was used for sweetened jellies; further flavouring beyond the addition of sugar was added to make a variety of finished dishes. Elaborate jelly moulds, often castellated, crenellated, domed, and decorated, received layers of jelly interlayered with strawberries, white currants, or raspberries; or plain sugared jelly was coloured and then layered in stripes in the moulds; or sherried jelly was placed in an open-centred mould, the centre to be filled with whipped cream.

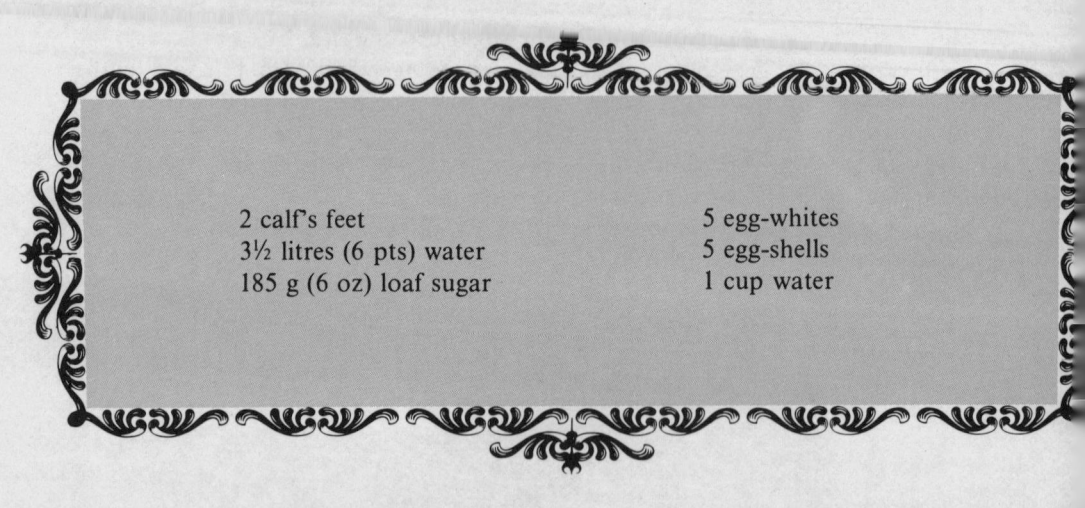

2 calf's feet
3½ litres (6 pts) water
185 g (6 oz) loaf sugar

5 egg-whites
5 egg-shells
1 cup water

'The stock for jellies should always be made the day before it is required for use, as the liquor has time to cool, and the fat can be so much more easily and effectually removed when thoroughly set. Procure 2 nice calf's feet; scald them, to take off the hair, slit them in two, remove the fat from between the claws, and wash the feet well in warm water; put them into a stewpan, with the above proportion of cold water, bring it gradually to boil and remove every particle of scum as it rises. When it is well skimmed, boil it very gently for 6 or 7 hours, or until the liquor is reduced rather more than half; then strain it through a sieve into a basin, and put it in a cool place to set. As the liquor is strained, measure it, to ascertain the proportion for the jelly, allowing something for the sediment and the fat at the top. To clarify it, carefully remove all the fat from the top, pour over a little warm water, to wash away any that may remain, and wipe the jelly with a clean cloth; remove the jelly from the sediment, put it into a saucepan, and, supposing the quantity to be a quart, add to it 6 oz of loaf sugar, the shells and well-whisked whites of 5 eggs, and stir these ingredients together cold; set the saucepan on the fire, but *do not stir the jelly after it begins to warm*. Let it boil about 10 minutes after it rises to a head, then throw in a teacupful of cold water; let it boil 5 minutes longer, then take the saucepan off, cover it closely, and let it remain ½ hour near the fire. Dip the jelly-bag [*a flannel sieve*] into hot water, wring it out quite dry, and fasten it on to a stand or the back of a chair, which must be placed near the fire, to prevent the jelly from setting before it has run through the bag. Place a basin underneath to receive the jelly; then pour it into the bag, and should it not be clear the first time, run it through the bag again. This stock is the foundation of all *really good* jellies, which may be varied in innumerable ways, by colouring and flavouring with liqueurs, and by moulding it with fresh and preserved fruits. To insure the jelly being firm when turned out, ½ oz of isinglass clarified might be added to the above proportion of stock ...'

At Mr John Chivery's tea table

Biscuits, Cakes, etc.

A DISH OF RUSKS

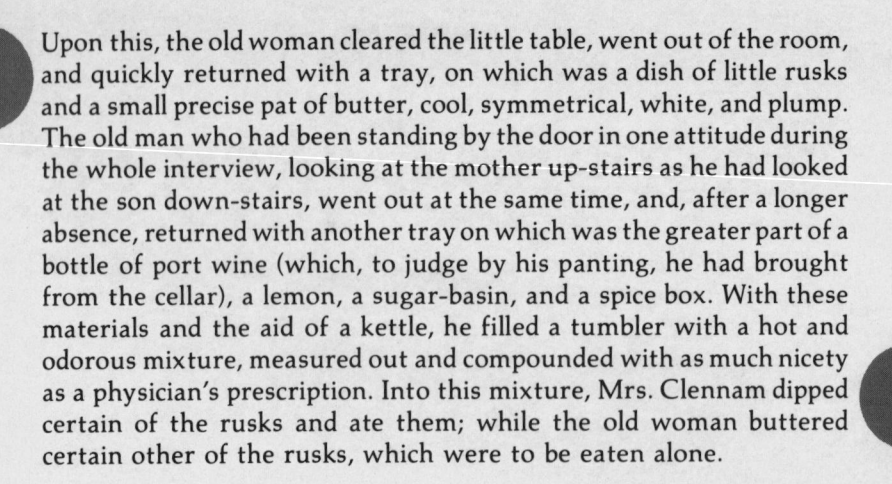

Upon this, the old woman cleared the little table, went out of the room, and quickly returned with a tray, on which was a dish of little rusks and a small precise pat of butter, cool, symmetrical, white, and plump. The old man who had been standing by the door in one attitude during the whole interview, looking at the mother up-stairs as he had looked at the son down-stairs, went out at the same time, and, after a longer absence, returned with another tray on which was the greater part of a bottle of port wine (which, to judge by his panting, he had brought from the cellar), a lemon, a sugar-basin, and a spice box. With these materials and the aid of a kettle, he filled a tumbler with a hot and odorous mixture, measured out and compounded with as much nicety as a physician's prescription. Into this mixture, Mrs. Clennam dipped certain of the rusks and ate them; while the old woman buttered certain other of the rusks, which were to be eaten alone.

Little Dorrit Ch III

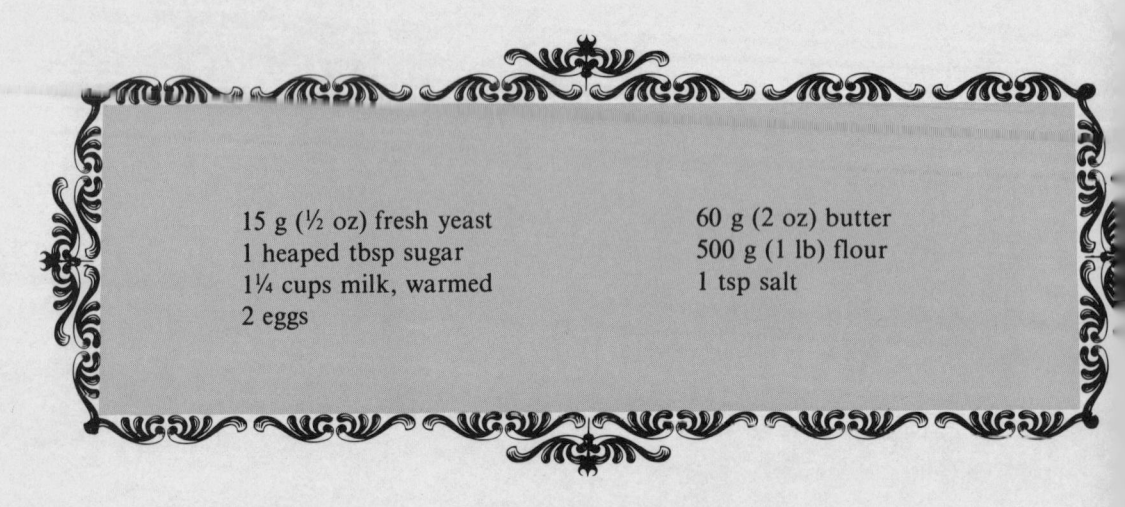

---

15 g (½ oz) fresh yeast
1 heaped tbsp sugar
1¼ cups milk, warmed
2 eggs

60 g (2 oz) butter
500 g (1 lb) flour
1 tsp salt

Work the yeast in a warm container with 1 teaspoon of the sugar until it forms a liquid. Have the warmed milk in a saucepan, add the butter in small pieces, and stir until the butter has melted. Sift the flour and salt into a bowl, and stir in the sugar. Beat the eggs well, and add them to the milk. Stir in the yeast. Make a well in the centre of the flour and pour in the milk mixture. Mix in the flour from the sides of the bowl, cover with a cloth, and leave in a warm place until frothy. Knead it into a firm dough, and then divide it into small cakes the size of an egg. Place the pieces on a greased and floured baking sheet, and leave in a warm place until they have risen—approximately 30 minutes. Bake in a hot oven for 20 minutes, then remove them to a warm place to dry thoroughly. Split the cakes in half, then return them to a slow oven to dry slowly, until golden brown throughout. Store in a well sealed tin.

YORKSHIRE CAKES FOR BREAKFAST

It was a substantial meal; for, over and above the ordinary tea equipage, the board creaked beneath the weight of a jolly round of beef, a ham of the first magnitude, and sundry towers of buttered Yorkshire cake, piled slice upon slice in most alluring order. There was also a goodly jug of well-browned clay, fashioned into the form of an old gentleman, not by any means unlike the locksmith, atop of whose bald head was a fine white froth answering to his wig, indicative, beyond dispute, of sparkling home-brewed ale. But, better far than fair home-brewed, or Yorkshire cake, or ham, or beef, or anything to eat or drink that earth or air or water can supply, there sat, presiding over all, the locksmith's rosy daughter, before whose dark eyes even beef grew insignificant, and malt became as nothing.

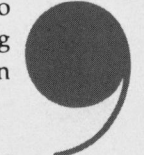

Barnaby Rudge Ch IV

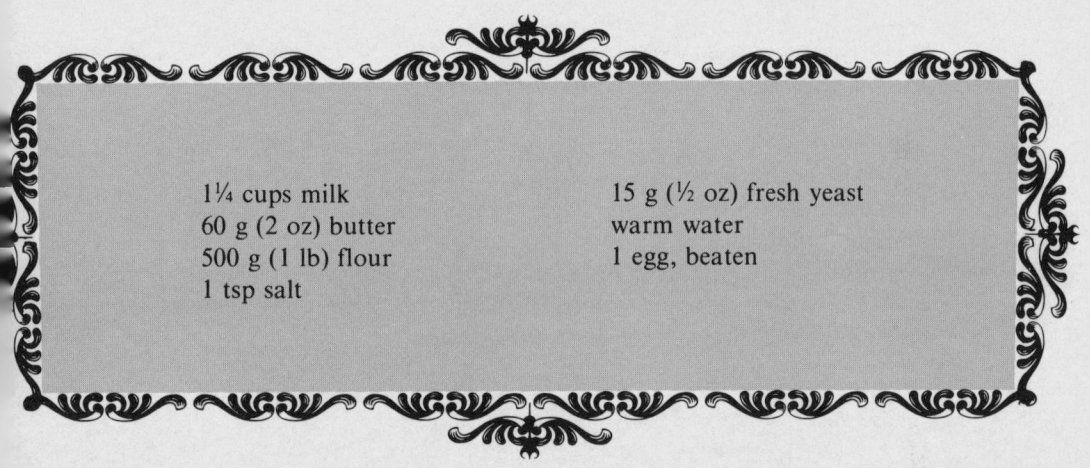

1¼ cups milk
60 g (2 oz) butter
500 g (1 lb) flour
1 tsp salt

15 g (½ oz) fresh yeast
warm water
1 egg, beaten

Warm the milk, remove from the heat, and stir in the butter until it dissolves. Allow to return to no hotter than blood temperature. Dissolve the yeast in a little warm water. Sift the flour and the salt into a warm bowl, add the yeast to the milk, and pour the liquid into the centre of the flour. Add the beaten egg. Mix together to form a soft dough and knead until smooth and elastic. Cover with a cloth, and leave to rise in a warm place for 1½ hours. Knead the dough on a floured board, and make it into 6-8 cakes. Place the cakes on a floured baking sheet, and leave to rise. Cook at 220°C (425°F) for 5 minutes, then lower the heat to 200°C (400°F) and cook for approximately a further 10 minutes. Serve hot with butter.

MR VENUS'S MUFFINS

'My tea is drawing, and my muffin is on the hob, Mr. Wegg; will you partake?'
It being one of Mr. Wegg's guiding rules in life always to partake, he says he will. But, the little shop is so excessively dark, is stuck so full of black shelves and brackets and nooks and corners, that he sees Mr. Venus's cup and saucer only because it is close under the candle, and does not see from what mysterious recess Mr. Venus produces another for himself, until it is under his nose. Concurrently, Wegg perceives a pretty little dead bird lying on the counter, with its head drooping on one side against the rim of Mr. Venus's saucer, and a long stiff wire piercing its breast. As if it were Cock Robin, the hero of the Ballad, and Mr. Venus were the sparrow with his bow and arrow, and Mr. Wegg were the fly with his little eye.
Mr. Venus dives, and produces another muffin, yet untoasted; taking the arrow out of the breast of Cock Robin, he proceeds to toast it on the end of that cruel instrument. When it is brown, he dives again and produces butter, with which he completes his work.

Our Mutual Friend Bk 1 Ch VII

'Edward, my father had a son, who being a fool like you, and, like you, entertaining low and disobedient sentiments, he disinherited and cursed one morning after breakfast. The circumstance occurs to me with a singular clearness of recollection this evening. I remember eating muffins at the time, with marmalade ...'

Barnaby Rudge Ch XXXII

Muffins, when cooked at home rather than bought—and buying is usually the most convenient—are traditionally baked on a girdle, but a stout and heavy cast-iron frying pan will serve. As well, special rings are sold in which to cook the muffins; failing these, use small cans, such as tuna is sold in, measuring approximately 10 cm across, having the top and bottom removed and the edges smoothed.

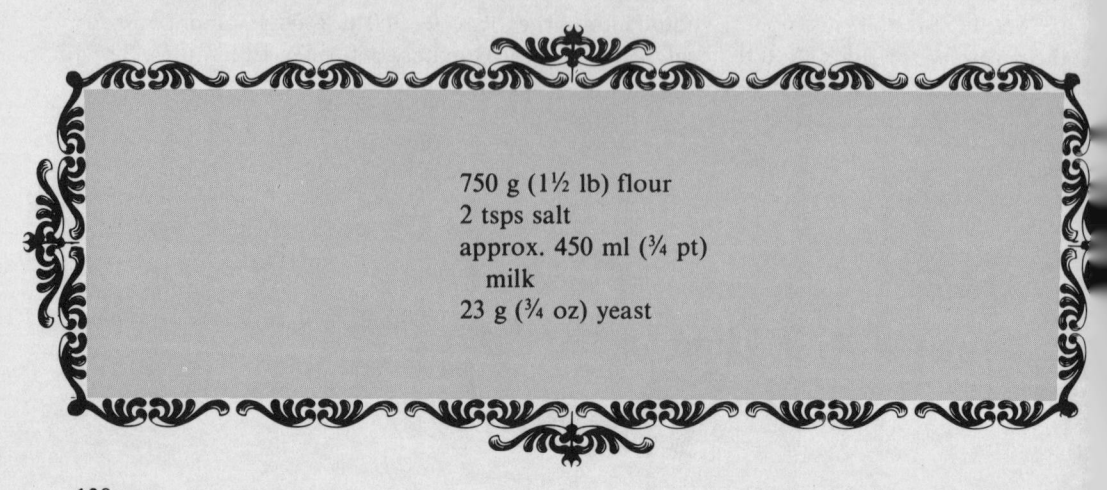

750 g (1½ lb) flour
2 tsps salt
approx. 450 ml (¾ pt) milk
23 g (¾ oz) yeast

Sift the flour and the salt into a bowl, and place it in an oven that has been set at the lowest temperature. Allow the flour and the bowl to become warm. Place the milk in a saucepan, heat it to blood temperature, and dissolve the yeast in it. Allow the yeast to prove. Blend together the yeast mixture and the flour, adding a little more flour if the dough is sticky. Knead to a soft dough. Cover, and leave in a warm, draught-free place until the dough is well risen. Divide the dough into pieces, and pat them into the correct size—to fit the rings—with floured hands. Have the insides of the rings buttered, and place a piece of dough inside each ring. Leave for 10 minutes. Place the girdle on a moderate heat, place the muffins in the rings in the girdle, and cook to a light brown on one side. Remove the rings, turn the muffins over, and brown on the other side.

To toast muffins:
'Divide the edge of the muffin all round, by pulling it open to the depth of about an inch, with the fingers. Put it on a toasting-fork, and hold it before a very clear fire until one side is nicely browned, but not burnt; turn, and toast it on the other. Do not toast them too quickly, as, if this be done, the middle of the muffin will not be warmed through. When done, divide them by pulling them open; butter them slightly on both sides, put them together again, and cut them into halves; when sufficient are toasted and buttered, pile them on a very hot dish, and send them very quickly to the table.'

SOFT, SEEDY BISCUITS

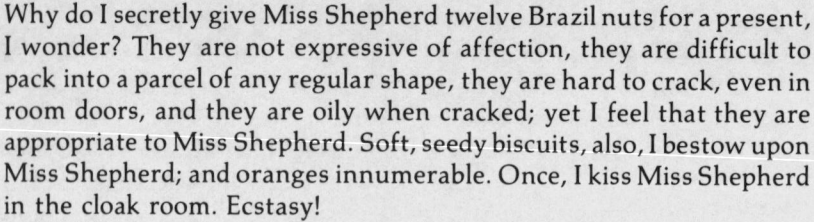

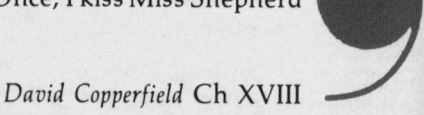

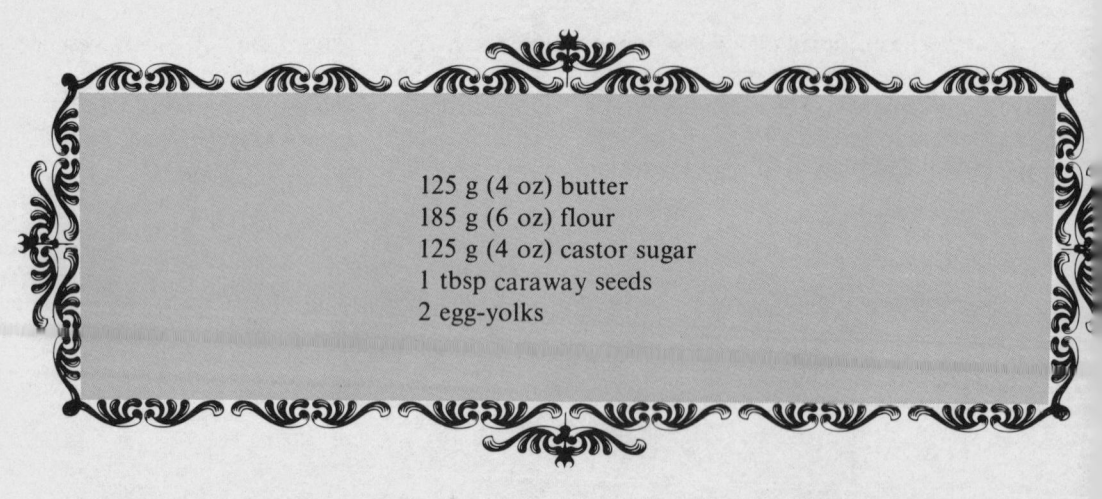

Why do I secretly give Miss Shepherd twelve Brazil nuts for a present, I wonder? They are not expressive of affection, they are difficult to pack into a parcel of any regular shape, they are hard to crack, even in room doors, and they are oily when cracked; yet I feel that they are appropriate to Miss Shepherd. Soft, seedy biscuits, also, I bestow upon Miss Shepherd; and oranges innumerable. Once, I kiss Miss Shepherd in the cloak room. Ecstasy!

David Copperfield Ch XVIII

125 g (4 oz) butter
185 g (6 oz) flour
125 g (4 oz) castor sugar
1 tbsp caraway seeds
2 egg-yolks

Place the butter in a warmed basin, and beat it to a cream. Sift the flour and gradually beat it into the butter. Stir in the sugar and the caraway seeds. Beat the egg-yolks, then beat them into the contents of the bowl. Place a sheet of buttered greaseproof paper on a baking tray. Drop the mixture on to the tray from a teaspoon, allowing for the biscuits to spread. Bake at 160°C (325°F) for 12-18 minutes. The biscuits should retain a lightness of colour.

LADIES' FINGERS TO DIP IN WINE

It was a most wonderful closet ... The upper slide on being pulled down (leaving the lower a double mystery), revealed deep shelves of pickle-jars, jam-pots, tin canisters, spice-boxes, and agreeably outlandish vessels of blue and white, the luscious lodgings of preserved tamarinds and ginger. Every benevolent inhabitant of this retreat had his name inscribed upon his stomach. The pickles, in a uniform of rich brown double-breasted buttoned coat, and yellow or sombre drab continuations, announced their portly forms as Walnut, Gherkin, Onion, Cabbage, Cauliflower, Mixed, and other members of that noble family. The jams, as being of a less masculine temperament, and as wearing curl-papers, announced themselves in feminine calligraphy, like a soft whisper, to be Raspberry, Gooseberry, Apricot, Plum, Damson, Apple, and Peach. The scene closing on these charmers, and the lower slide ascending, oranges were revealed, attended by a mighty jappaned sugar-box, to temper their acerbity if unripe. Home-made biscuits waited at the Court of these Powers, accompanied by a goodly fragment of plum-cake, and various slender ladies' fingers, to be dipped in sweet wine and kissed.

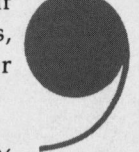

The Mystery of Edwin Drood Ch X

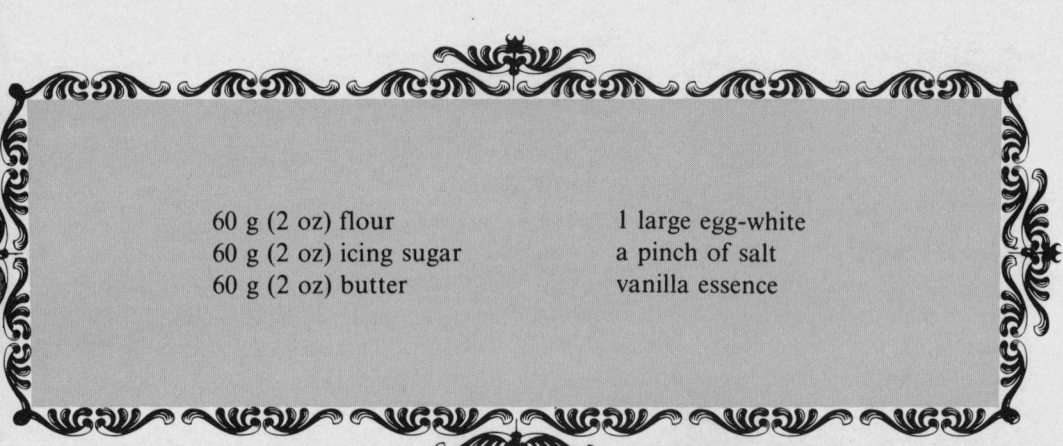

60 g (2 oz) flour
60 g (2 oz) icing sugar
60 g (2 oz) butter

1 large egg-white
a pinch of salt
vanilla essence

Place the butter and sugar in a bowl, and cream them together. Sift together the flour and the salt. Beat the egg-white. Add the egg-white to the butter mixture, beating well, then stir in the flour. Add a few drops of vanilla essence. Fill an icing syringe with the mixture, using the plain flat tube. Grease a baking tray, and squeeze out lengths of about 5 cm (2 in.) each of the mixture. Bake at 190°C (375°F) for approximately 10 minutes.

A SHILLING IN ALMOND CAKES

'Perhaps you'd like to spend a couple of shillings or so, in a bottle of currant wine by-and-by, up in the bedroom?' said Steerforth. 'You belong to my bedroom, I find?'

It certainly had not occurred to me before, but I said, Yes, I should like that.

'Very good,' said Steerforth. 'You'll be glad to spend another shilling or so, in almond cakes, I dare say?'

I said, Yes, I should like that, too.

'And another shilling or so in biscuits, and another in fruit, eh?' said Steerforth. 'I say, young Copperfield, you're going it!'

David Copperfield Ch VI

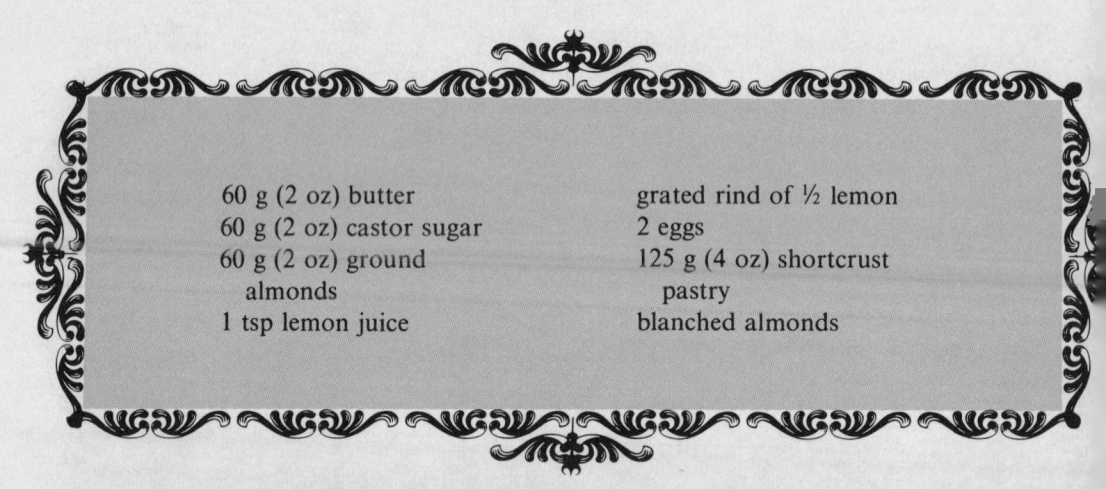

---

60 g (2 oz) butter
60 g (2 oz) castor sugar
60 g (2 oz) ground almonds
1 tsp lemon juice
grated rind of ½ lemon
2 eggs
125 g (4 oz) shortcrust pastry
blanched almonds

Melt the butter and place it in a bowl. Add the sugar, ground almonds, lemon juice and rind. Separate the eggs, and add the yolks to the mixture in the bowl, beating them in well. Whip the whites well, and carefully stir them into the mixture. Roll the pastry out on a floured board, and cut it into circles to fit patty tins. Line the patty tins with the pastry, and fill each with the almond mixture. Decorate the top of each cake with a few blanched almonds. Bake at 230°C (450°F) for 10-15 minutes.

A PARTIALITY FOR GINGERBREAD

Mr. Dick was very partial to gingerbread. To render his visits the more agreeable, my aunt had instructed me to open a credit for him at the cake-shop, which was hampered with the stipulation that he should not be served with more than one shilling's-worth in the course of any one day. This, and the reference of all his little bills at the county inn where he slept, to my aunt, before they were paid, induced me to suspect that he was only allowed to rattle his money, and not to spend it.

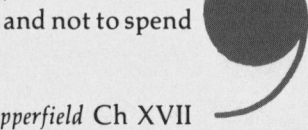

David Copperfield Ch XVII

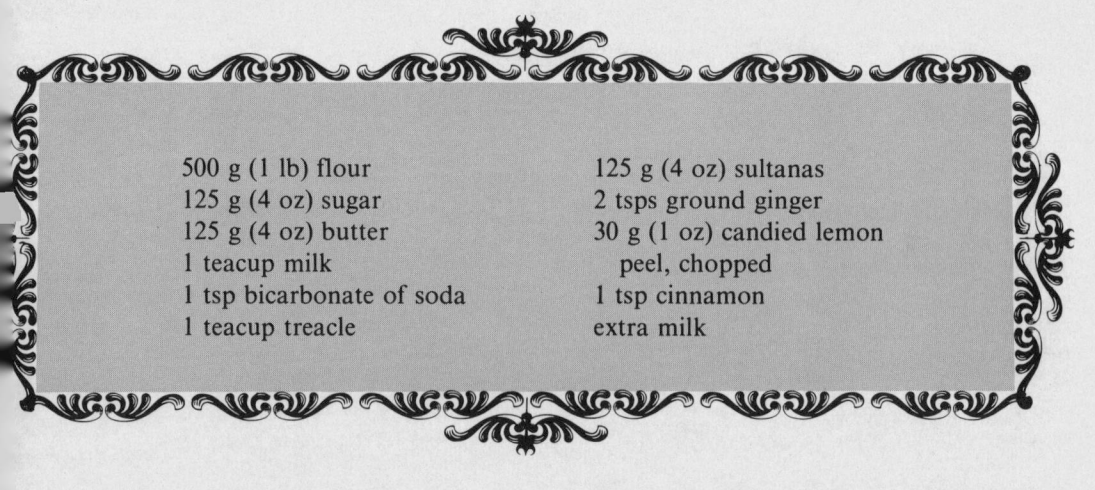

500 g (1 lb) flour
125 g (4 oz) sugar
125 g (4 oz) butter
1 teacup milk
1 tsp bicarbonate of soda
1 teacup treacle
125 g (4 oz) sultanas
2 tsps ground ginger
30 g (1 oz) candied lemon peel, chopped
1 tsp cinnamon
extra milk

Sift the flour, cinnamon and ginger into a bowl. Place the milk and treacle in a saucepan, and warm until the treacle is dissolved. Rub the butter into the flour, add the sugar, sultanas, and candied peel, and mix well. Dissolve the bicarbonate of soda in a little extra milk, and at the last moment before using the warm milk and treacle, pour in the soda. Mix well, and pour into the flour mixture. Beat well together, and turn quickly into a greased, deep, square tin. Bake in a moderately slow oven for 1 hour.

A HOMEMADE PLUM-CAKE

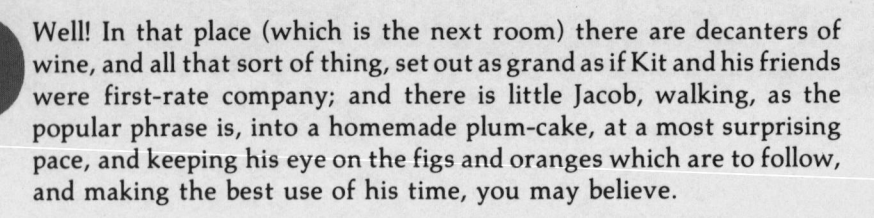

Well! In that place (which is the next room) there are decanters of wine, and all that sort of thing, set out as grand as if Kit and his friends were first-rate company; and there is little Jacob, walking, as the popular phrase is, into a homemade plum-cake, at a most surprising pace, and keeping his eye on the figs and oranges which are to follow, and making the best use of his time, you may believe.

The Old Curiosity Shop Ch LXVIII

Mr. Swiveller replied by taking from his pocket a small and very greasy parcel, slowly unfolding it, and displaying a little slab of plum-cake, extremely indigestible in appearance, and bordered with a paste of white sugar an inch and a half deep.

The Old Curiosity Shop Ch L

---

250 g (8 oz) raisins
250 g (8 oz) currants and sultanas
125 g (4 oz) mixed peel
185 g (6 oz) butter
185 g (6 oz) brown sugar

1 tbsp treacle
4 eggs
375 g (12 oz) plain flour
salt
¾ tsp bicarbonate of soda
milk

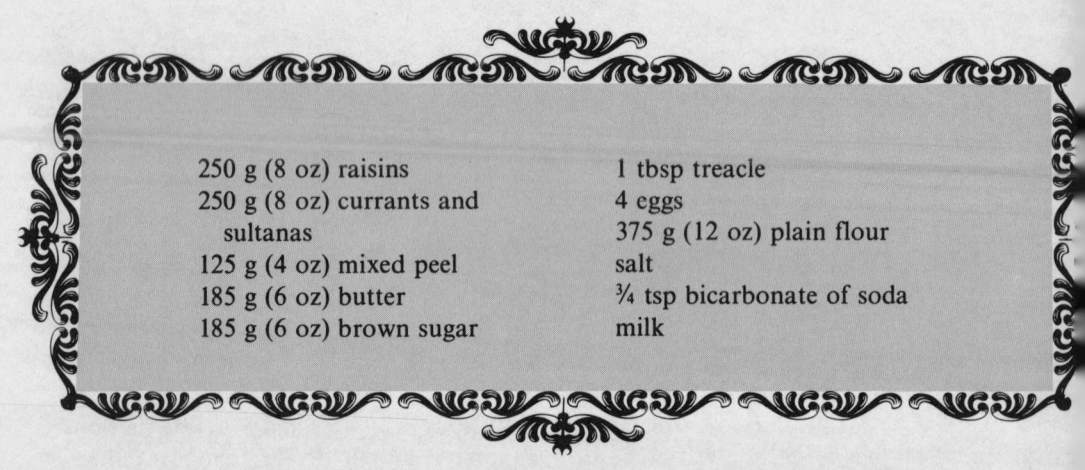

Take a cake tin measuring 23 cm x 9 cm (9 in. x 3½ in.) deep. Line the tin with greased paper. Chop the mixed fruit and mixed peel into fairly small pieces. Cream together the butter and sugar in a bowl and stir in the treacle. Beat in the eggs well, adding one at a time. Sift the flour and salt, and stir in the creamed mixture. Stir in the mixed fruit and mixed peel, and blend all together well. Dissolve the bicarbonate of soda in a little milk and add it to the cake mixture. Pour the mixture into the cake tin, and bake at 180°C (350°F) for 1½ to 2 hours, or until the cake is firm to the touch and a cake tester emerges clean. Turn out on to a wire rack, remove the paper, and leave to cool. Store in an airtight container; this way it will keep for a considerable time.

TWELFTH CAKE

> Christmas ... Lavish profusion is in the shops: particularly in the articles of currants, raisins, spices, candied peel and moist sugar. An unusual air of gallantry and dissipation is abroad: evinced in an immense bunch of mistletoe hanging in the greengrocer's shop doorway, and a poor little Twelfth Cake, culminating in the figure of a Harlequin—such a very poor little Twelfth Cake, that one would rather call it a Twenty-fourth Cake or a Forty-eighth Cake—to be raffled for at the pastrycook's, terms one shilling per member.
>
> *The Mystery of Edwin Drood* Ch XIV

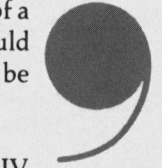

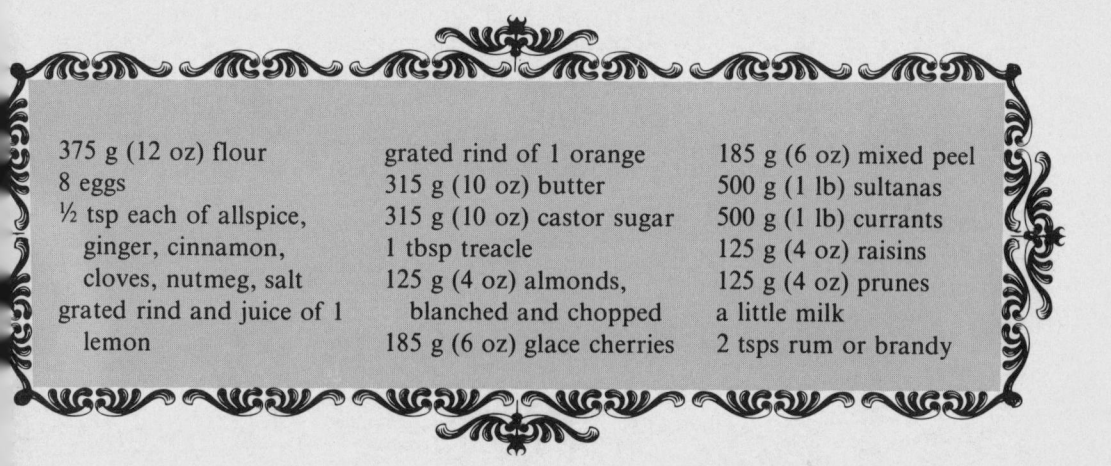

375 g (12 oz) flour	grated rind of 1 orange	185 g (6 oz) mixed peel
8 eggs	315 g (10 oz) butter	500 g (1 lb) sultanas
½ tsp each of allspice, ginger, cinnamon, cloves, nutmeg, salt	315 g (10 oz) castor sugar	500 g (1 lb) currants
	1 tbsp treacle	125 g (4 oz) raisins
	125 g (4 oz) almonds, blanched and chopped	125 g (4 oz) prunes
grated rind and juice of 1 lemon		a little milk
	185 g (6 oz) glace cherries	2 tsps rum or brandy

Wash and dry the cherries, and chop them. Soak the prunes in cold water, stone and chop them. Chop the raisins. Cream together the butter, sugar and treacle. Sift 90 g (3 oz) of the flour, and stir it into the butter mixture. Add the eggs, one at a time, beating well after each addition. Sift the rest of the flour, the spices and the salt into a bowl, and stir in the orange and lemon rind, almonds, cherries, mixed peel, sultanas, currants, raisins and prunes. Add the fruit and the flour mixture to the butter mixture, with the lemon juice, blending well but lightly. Add a little milk if necessary to make it all of a stiff dropping consistency. Turn the mixture into a deep 23-cm (9-in.) tin that has been lined with 3 layers of greaseproof paper, with the paper extending above the top of the tin by about 5 cm (2 in.). Dip fingers in warm water and smooth the top of the cake very lightly, making a slight hollow in the centre. A round of corrugated paper can be tied around the outside of the tin also, if preferred, to prevent the cake becoming too hard. Bake at 180°C (350°F) for 2 hours, lower the temperature to 150°C (300°F) and bake for a further 2-2½ hours. Allow the cake to cool in the tin; wrapping a rug around the tin is of assistance, as it allows the cake to cool very slowly. When the cake is cold, pour 2 tsps of rum or brandy over the base. The cake can be further moistened a couple of times over the following weeks. Store, wrapped in foil or greaseproof paper, in an airtight container. Before use, decorate ornamentally with icing.

Note: Originally, rich cakes such as this were baked in a hoop, on about 12 layers of paper, on a baking tray.

SWEET SEED CAKE

Miss Lavinia and Miss Clarissa partook, in their way, of my joy. It was the pleasantest tea-table in the world. Miss Clarissa presided. I cut and handed the sweet seed-cake—the little sisters had a bird-like fondness for picking up seeds and pecking at sugar; Miss Lavinia looked on with benignant patronage, as if our happy love were all her work; and we were perfectly contented with ourselves and one another.

David Copperfield Ch XLII

'What kind of funeral was it?' says the formal lady, when he returns home. 'Oh!' replies the formal gentleman, 'there never was such a gross and disgusting impropriety; there were no feathers.' 'No feathers!' cries the lady, as if on wings of black feathers dead people fly to Heaven, and, lacking them, they must of necessity go elsewhere. Her husband shakes his head; and further adds, that they had seed-cake instead of plum-cake, and that it was all white wine. 'All white wine!' exclaims his wife. 'Nothing but sherry and madeira,' says the husband. 'What! No port?' 'Not a drop.' No port, no plums, and no feathers!

Sketches of Young Couples

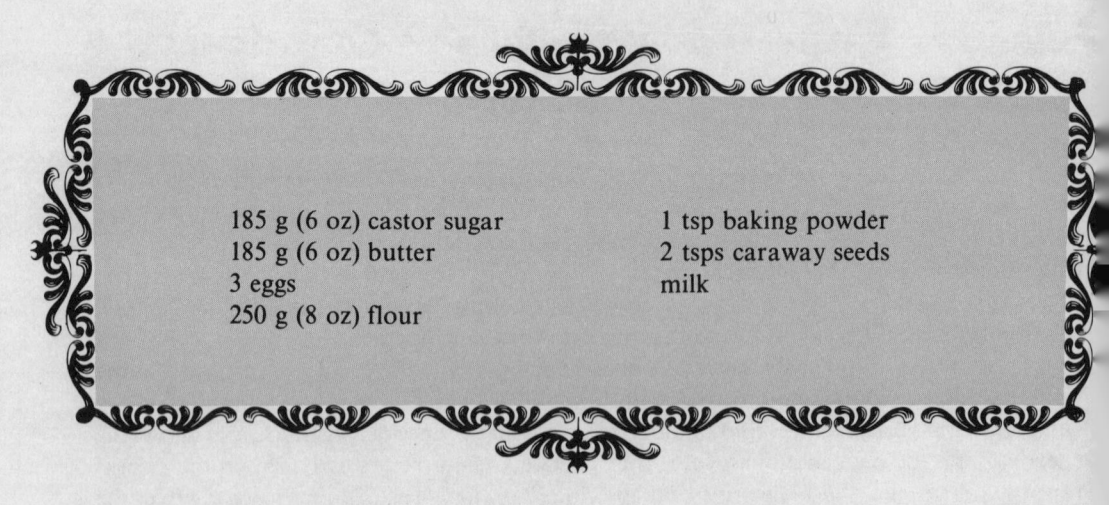

---

185 g (6 oz) castor sugar
185 g (6 oz) butter
3 eggs
250 g (8 oz) flour

1 tsp baking powder
2 tsps caraway seeds
milk

Cream together the sugar and butter until soft and fluffy. Beat the eggs, and add them, one-third at a time, beating in well at each addition. Sift the flour and the baking powder into a bowl, and stir in the caraway seeds. Fold the flour mixture into the creamed butter and sugar. Gradually add a little milk to make a dropping consistency. Have ready a 15-cm (6-in.) cake tin that has been greased and then lined with greaseproof paper. Turn the mixture into the tin and bake at 180°C (350°F) for approximately 1¼ hours.

TARTS TO MAKE THE FLESH SHINE

'Here! You go and buy a tart—Mr. Nickleby's man will show you where—and mind you buy a rich one. Pastry,' added Squeers, closing the door on Master Wackford, 'makes his flesh shine a good deal, and parents thinks that's a healthy sign.'

Nicholas Nickleby Ch XXXIV

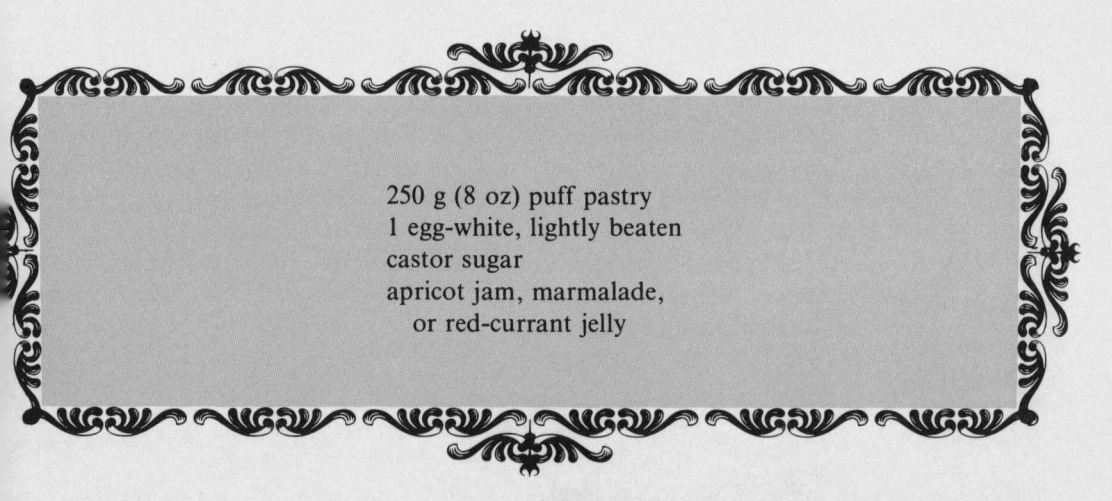

> 250 g (8 oz) puff pastry
> 1 egg-white, lightly beaten
> castor sugar
> apricot jam, marmalade,
>   or red-currant jelly

'Roll some good puff-paste out thin, and cut it into 2½-inch squares; brush each square over with the white of an egg, then fold down the corners so that they all meet in the middle of each piece of paste; slightly press the two pieces together [*the top and the bottom*], brush them over with the egg, sift over sugar, and bake in a nice quick oven [*220°C or 425°F*] for about ¼ hour. When they are done, make a little hole in the middle of the paste, and fill it up with apricot jam, marmalade, or red-currant jelly.'

BIFFINS

'Mrs. Harry Walmers, junior, fatigued, sir?' says Cobbs. 'Yes, she is tired, Cobbs; but she is not used to be away from home, and she has been in low spirits again. Cobbs, do you think you could bring a biffin, please?'
'I ask your pardon, sir,' says Cobbs. 'What was it you—'
'I think a Norfolk biffin would rouse her, Cobbs. She is very fond of them.'

The Holly-tree

Biffins are a form of semi-dried apple, and, for Dickensian characters at least, frequently appeared as dessert, along with oranges and nuts.
'The apples are placed in a cool oven, six or seven times in succession, and flattened each time by gentle pressure, gradually applied, as soon as they are soft enough to bear it; after which they are taken out, and as soon as cold put on clean dishes or glass plates. The sour are the best sort for baking. If the process is well managed the appearance of the prepared fruit is very rich, and the flavour is delicious.'

BRANDY BALLS

Next day the court is alive ... The Sol's Arms does a brisk stroke of business all through the morning. Even children so require sustaining, under the general excitement, that a pieman who has established himself for the occasion at the corner of the court, says his brandy-balls go off like smoke.

Bleak House Ch XI

The following recipe, while an authentic nineteenth century one, is not recommended for use today:
'Boil brown sugar to the crack; work in good peppermint and 1 oz. of ivory black to 7 lbs. sugar; roll them to the proper size and cut them off; then roll round with the hand.'

LUMPS-OF-DELIGHT

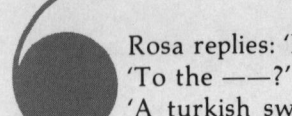

> Rosa replies: 'I want to go to the Lumps-of-Delight shop.'
> 'To the ——?'
> 'A turkish sweetmeat, sir. My gracious me, don't you understand anything? Call yourself an Engineer, and not know *that*?'
>
> *The Mystery of Edwin Drood* Ch III

The true Turkish sweetmeat is somewhat difficult to make at home, as it usually takes up to three hours of continuous stirring; it is best acquired in the old-fashioned way by buying it from a specialist in Turkish sweetmeats. However, the following recipe makes a very pleasant confection, without the arduous labour:

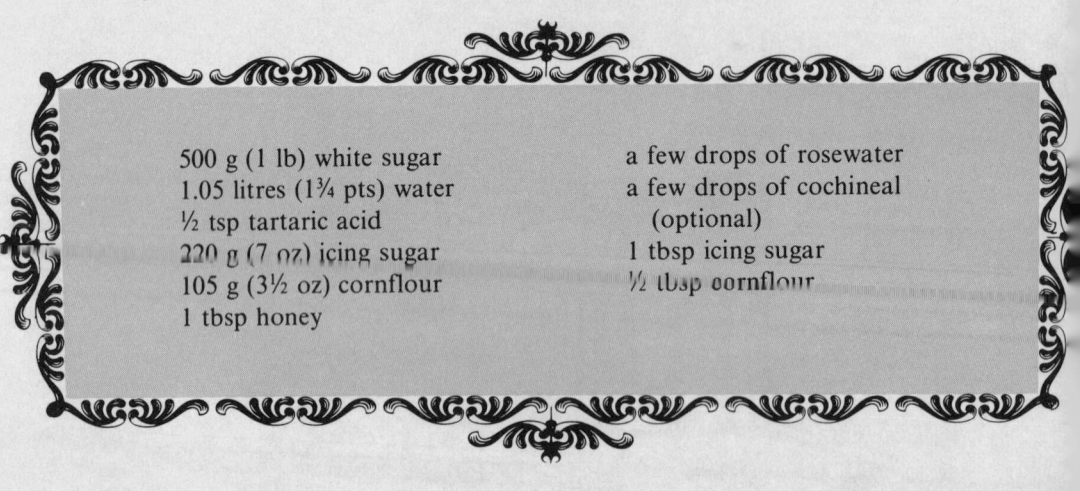

500 g (1 lb) white sugar
1.05 litres (1¾ pts) water
½ tsp tartaric acid
220 g (7 oz) icing sugar
105 g (3½ oz) cornflour
1 tbsp honey
a few drops of rosewater
a few drops of cochineal (optional)
1 tbsp icing sugar
½ tbsp cornflour

Place the white sugar in a solid-based saucepan with 150 ml (¼ pint) of the water, and slowly bring to the boil. Boil steadily for 10 minutes, or until a soft ball is formed when a drop is placed in cold water. Remove from the heat and add the tartaric acid, but do *not* stir. In a bowl, blend together the icing sugar and the cornflour, diluting with a little of the remaining water. In another saucepan place the remaining water, heat until hot, add the sugar and cornflour mixture, and stir until the mixture boils. Cook until thick and clear, then add the syrup mixture. Beat well together and boil for approximately 20 minutes, until it is transparent and of a pale colour. Add the honey and the rosewater (and colour with a little cochineal if desired) and pour the mixture into a lightly greased tin. Leave until firm. Sieve together 1 tablespoon of icing sugar and half a tablespoon of cornflour on to a plate or board. Turn the confectionery out on to the plate, and cut into neat squares with a sharp knife. Coat each square lightly with the icing sugar mixture.

HARDBAKE

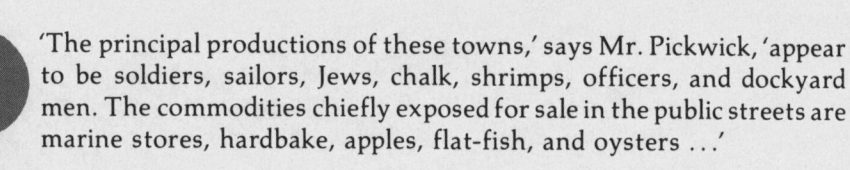

'The principal productions of these towns,' says Mr. Pickwick, 'appear to be soldiers, sailors, Jews, chalk, shrimps, officers, and dockyard men. The commodities chiefly exposed for sale in the public streets are marine stores, hardbake, apples, flat-fish, and oysters ...'

The Pickwick Papers Ch II

Hardbake, or Almond Toffee, was a great favourite, along with Everton Toffee, Russian Toffee, Acid Drops, Butterscotch, Sugar Plums, Candied Fruit and Barley Sugar.

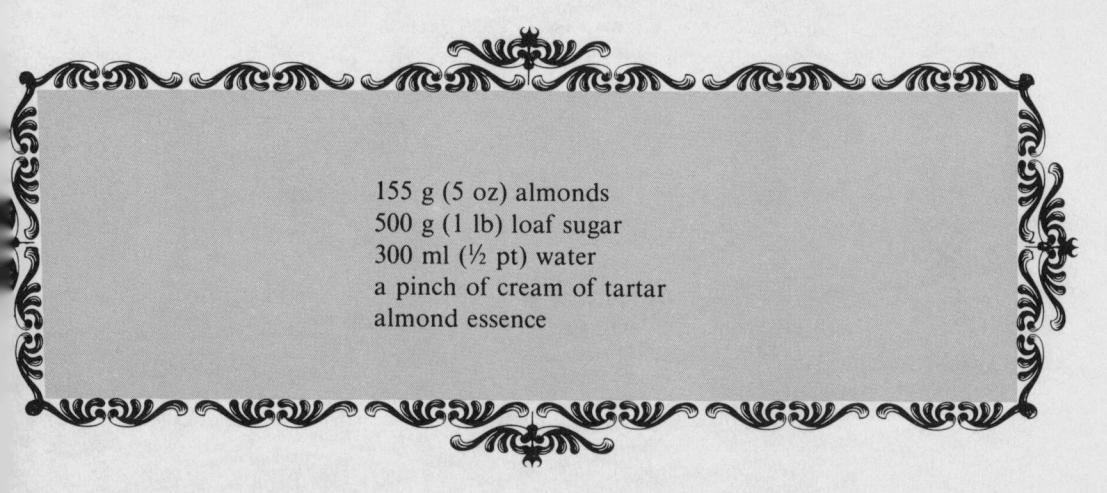

155 g (5 oz) almonds
500 g (1 lb) loaf sugar
300 ml (½ pt) water
a pinch of cream of tartar
almond essence

Have the almonds blanched, skinned, halved, and dried well. In a saucepan, dissolve the sugar in the water, add the cream of tartar, bring to the boil, and continue to cook until the syrup is a deep amber colour. Remove from the heat and stir in the almonds and a few drops of almond essence. Bring to the boil once more, then pour the mixture onto a greased or oiled tin. Leave to set.

The gin shop

Drinks and Beverages

MONSEIGNEUR'S DRINKING CHOCOLATE

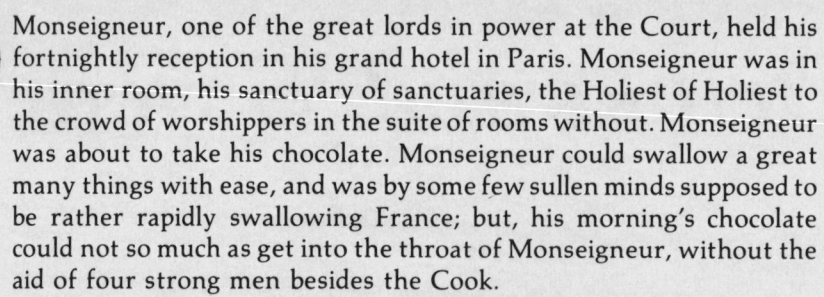

Monseigneur, one of the great lords in power at the Court, held his fortnightly reception in his grand hotel in Paris. Monseigneur was in his inner room, his sanctuary of sanctuaries, the Holiest of Holiest to the crowd of worshippers in the suite of rooms without. Monseigneur was about to take his chocolate. Monseigneur could swallow a great many things with ease, and was by some few sullen minds supposed to be rather rapidly swallowing France; but, his morning's chocolate could not so much as get into the throat of Monseigneur, without the aid of four strong men besides the Cook.

Yes. It took four men all four a-blaze with gorgeous decoration, and the Chief of them unable to exist with fewer than two gold watches in his pocket, emulative of the noble and chaste fashion set by Monseigneur, to conduct the happy chocolate to Monseigneur's lips. One lacquey carried the chocolate-pot into the sacred presence; a second, milled and frothed the chocolate with the little instrument he bore for that function; a third, presented the favoured napkin; a fourth (he of the two gold watches), poured the chocolate out. It was impossible for Monseigneur to dispense with one of these attendants on the chocolate and hold his high place under the admiring Heavens. Deep would have been the blot upon his escutcheon if his chocolate had been ignobly waited on by only three men; he must have died of two.

A Tale of Two Cities Ch VII

Allow 30 grams (1 oz) of dark chocolate to each person. To every 60 grams (2 oz) allow 1¼ cups of water and 1¼ cups of milk. Break the chocolate into a saucepan and add one-third of the water; dissolve the chocolate over a gentle heat. Add another one-third of the water, beat well, and simmer for 5 minutes. Beat well again, add the rest of the water, and simmer a further 5 minutes. Beat yet again. Add the milk, heat through, and beat well. Serve with sugar and, if liked, a teaspoon of lightly beaten cream to each cup.

Note: The process can be simplified, but the end product will not be quite so good.

Monseigneur's man with the 'little instrument' would have used an upright mill with a long handle. It had a perforated bowl which contained scraped chocolate. The mill stood in the chocolate pot, the liquid was poured over the bowl, and the handle of the mill was then twirled between the palms of the hands until the mixture was well beaten and frothy. Chocolate mills can occasionally be bought, but a whisk serves the purpose well.

LEMONADE

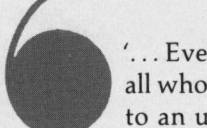

'... Every Tuesday evening there was lemonade and mixed biscuit, for all who chose to partake of those refreshments. And there was science to an unlimited extent.'

Bleak House Ch XVII

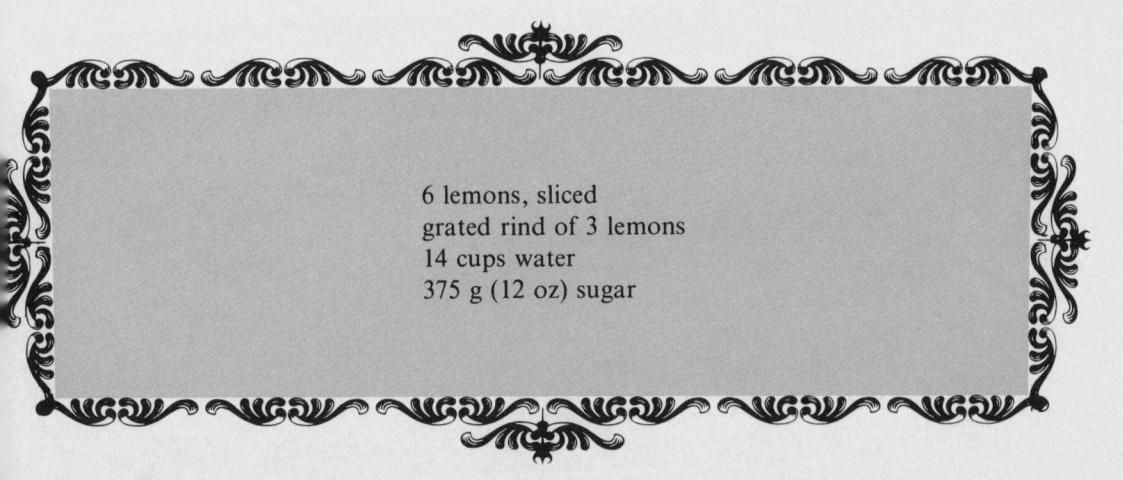

6 lemons, sliced
grated rind of 3 lemons
14 cups water
375 g (12 oz) sugar

Bring the water to the boil, and pour it into a bowl which contains the lemon slices, rind, and sugar. Stir until the sugar has dissolved. Cool, strain, and chill.

Note: A little sherry was frequently added to the beverage.

SHERRY FLIP

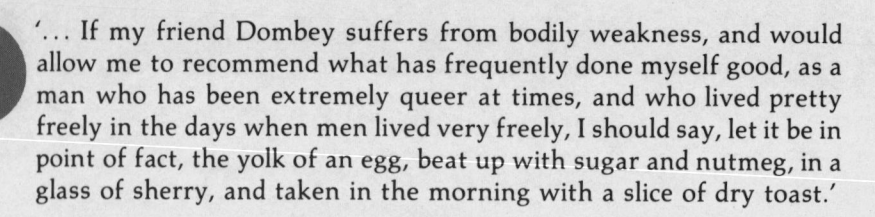

'... If my friend Dombey suffers from bodily weakness, and would allow me to recommend what has frequently done myself good, as a man who has been extremely queer at times, and who lived pretty freely in the days when men lived very freely, I should say, let it be in point of fact, the yolk of an egg, beat up with sugar and nutmeg, in a glass of sherry, and taken in the morning with a slice of dry toast.'

[Cousin Felix allows rum as a substitute on other occasions.]

Dombey and Son Ch LXI

'Bishop said that when he was a young man, and had fallen for a brief space into the habit of writing sermons on Saturdays, a habit which all young sons of the church should sedulously avoid, he had frequently been sensible of a depression, arising as he had supposed from an overtaxed intellect, upon which the yolk of a new-laid egg, beaten up by the good woman in whose house he at that time lodged, with a glass of sound sherry, nutmeg, and powdered sugar, acted like a charm.'

Little Dorrit Ch XXI

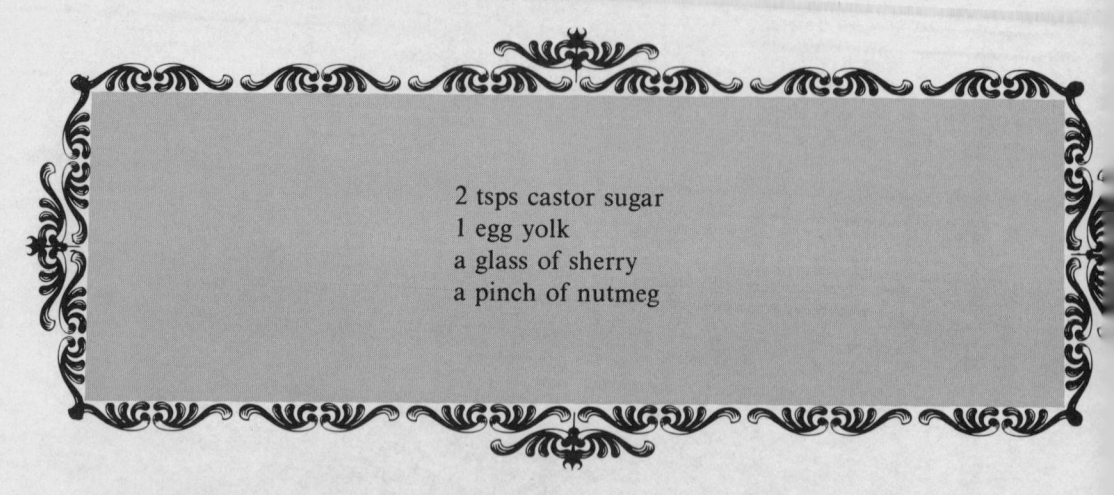

2 tsps castor sugar
1 egg yolk
a glass of sherry
a pinch of nutmeg

Beat all ingredients together. Serve. (One recipe admits the addition of ice shavings.)

SHERRY COBBLER

'Mr. Tapley ... produced a very large tumbler, piled up to the brim with little blocks of clear transparent ice, through which one or two thin slices of lemon, and a golden liquid of delicious appearance, appealed from the still depths below, to the loving eye of the spectator ...
'This wonderful invention, sir,' said Mark, tenderly patting the empty glass, 'is called a cobbler. Sherry cobbler when you name it long; cobbler, when you name it short.'

Martin Chuzzlewit Ch XVII

'Everybody was thirsty, and the Patriarch was drinking. There was a fragrance of limes or lemons about him; and he had made a drink of golden sherry, which shone in a large tumbler, as if he were drinking the evening sunshine.'

Little Dorrit Ch XXXII

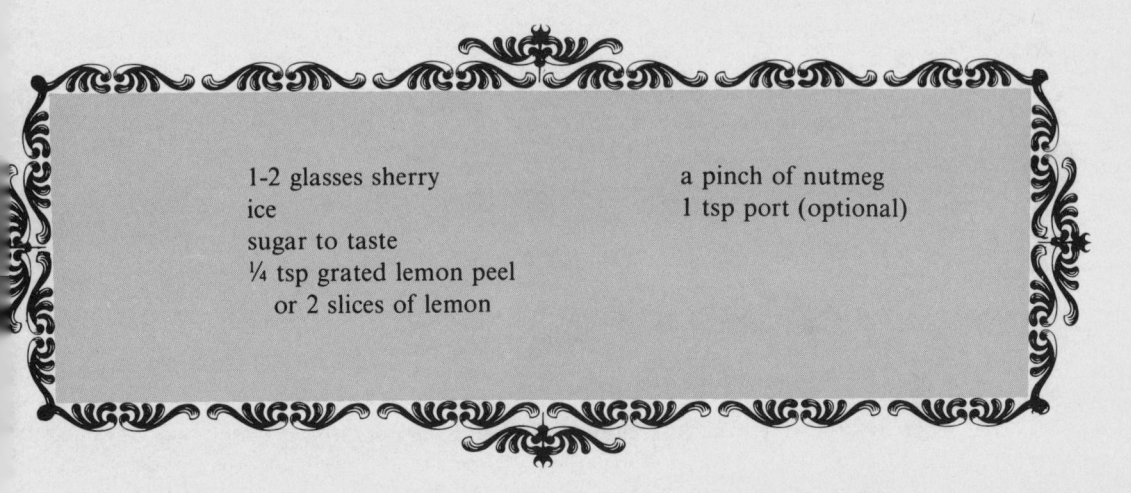

1-2 glasses sherry
ice
sugar to taste
¼ tsp grated lemon peel
  or 2 slices of lemon
a pinch of nutmeg
1 tsp port (optional)

Place the sherry in a tumbler, and stir in sugar to taste. Add the port (optional). Fill the glass with ice cubes, add the lemon peel or slices, and add the nutmeg.

HOT NEGUS

No supper did Miss Potterson take that night, and only half her usual tumbler of hot Port Negus. And the female domestics—two robust sisters with staring black eyes, shining flat red faces, blunt noses, and strong black curls, like dolls—interchanged the sentiment that Missis had had her hair combed the wrong way by someone.

Our Mutual Friend Ch VI

When they were alone again, the Captain insisted on her eating a slice of dry toast, and drinking a glass of spiced negus (which he made to perfection) ...

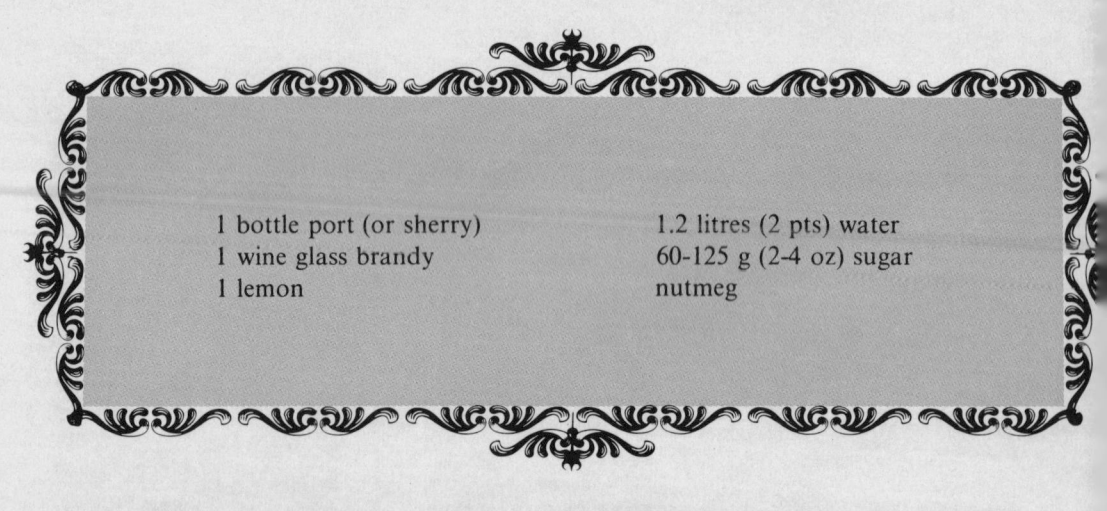

Dombey and Son Ch XLIX

1 bottle port (or sherry)
1 wine glass brandy
1 lemon

1.2 litres (2 pts) water
60-125 g (2-4 oz) sugar
nutmeg

Warm together the port and the brandy. Have ready a warmed jug, and have the water boiling. Slice the lemon, and place it in the jug with the sugar and nutmeg. Pour in the warmed wine, then add the boiling water. Serve very hot.

Note: The quantity of water can, of course, be decreased; the amount used seems to have depended on the alcoholic aptitudes and habits of the drinker. Some recipes omit the brandy.

MULLED PORT

After Mrs. Weller and the red-nosed gentleman ... had vented a variety of pious and holy execrations ... the latter recommended a bottle of port wine, warmed with a little water, spice, and sugar, as being grateful to the stomach, and savouring less of vanity than many other compounds.

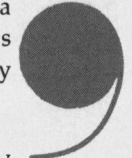

The Pickwick Papers Ch XLV

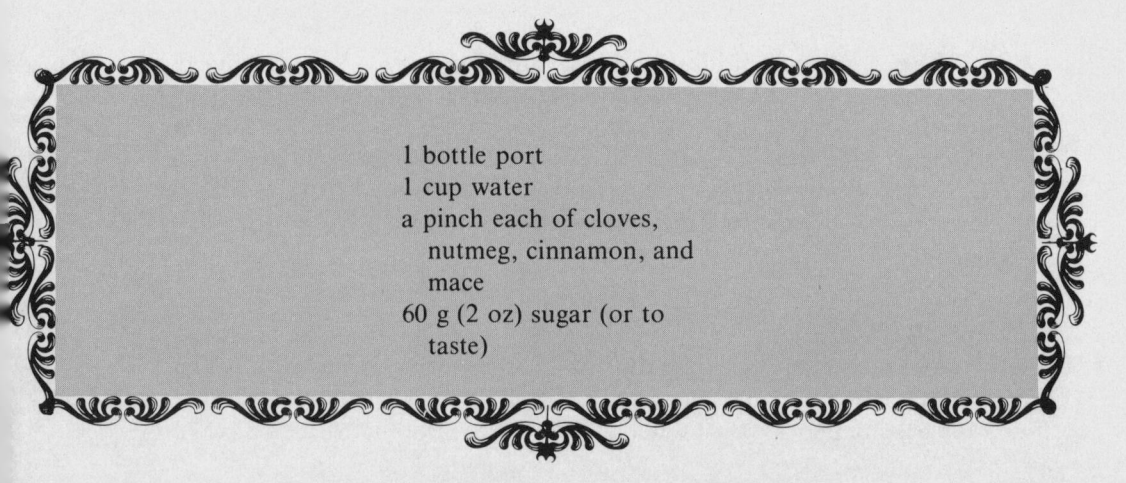

1 bottle port
1 cup water
a pinch each of cloves, nutmeg, cinnamon, and mace
60 g (2 oz) sugar (or to taste)

Boil together the water and spices for 5 minutes, then stir in the sugar. Add the port, heat it very hot, and serve.

Note: The final heating was usually achieved with the aid of the special 'sugar-loaf hat' described in the making of Purl (see recipe).

SHRUB AND WATER

> The shrub, when tasted from a spoon, perfectly harmonising with Miss Jenny's palate, a judicious amount was mixed by Miss Potterson's skilful hands, whereof Riah too partook. After this preliminary, Miss Abbey read the document; and, as often as she raised her eyebrows in so doing, the watchful Miss Jenny accompanied the action with an expressive and emphatic sip of shrub and water.
>
> *Our Mutual Friend* Bk 3 Ch II
>
> The gentleman in blue, and the man in orange, who were the chief exquisites of the party, ordered 'cold shrub and water,' but with the others, gin and water, sweet, appeared to be the favourite beverage. Sam called the greengrocer a 'desp'rate willin,' and ordered a large bowl of punch; two circumstances which seemed to raise him very much in the opinion of the selections.
>
> *The Pickwick Papers* Ch XXXVII

Shrub was usually made by mixing rum with a syrup of lemon juice and water; this was used as a base for punch or had water added to it to form a simple drink. Limes were also used; in fact, shrub is able to be made from many fruit juices.

---

300 ml (½ pt) lemon, lime, or lime and lemon, juice
1.2 litres (2 pts) rum
750 g (1½ lb) sugar

Place all ingredients in a container, seal, and allow to mellow for a few weeks. Dilute with water to serve.

THOSE DELECTABLE DRINKS, PURL, FLIP, AND DOG'S NOSE

'For the rest, both the tap and parlour of the Six Jolly Fellowship-Porters gave upon the river, and had red curtains matching the noses of the regular customers, and were provided with comfortable fireside tin utensils, like models of sugar-loaf hats made in that shape that they might, with their pointed ends, seek out for themselves glowing nooks in the depths of the red coals, when they mulled your ale, or heated for you those delectable drinks, Purl, Flip, and Dog's Nose. The first of these humming compounds was a speciality of the Porters, which, through an inscription on its door-posts, gently appealed to your feelings as 'The Early Purl House'. For it would seem that Purl must always be taken early; though whether for any more distinctly stomachic reason than that, as the early bird catches the worm, so the early purl catches the customer, cannot here be resolved.

Our Mutual Friend Bk 1 Ch VI

Bob's reappearance with a steaming jug broke off the conversation. But although the jug steamed forth a delicious perfume, its contents had not received that last happy touch which the surpassing finish of the Six Jolly Fellowship-Porters imparted on such momentous occasions. Bob carried in his left hand one of those iron models of sugar-loaf hats before mentioned, into which he emptied the jug, and the pointed end of which he thrust deep down into the fire, so leaving it for a few moments while he disappeared and reappeared with three bright drinking-glasses. Placing these on the table and bending over the fire, meritoriously sensible of the trying nature of his duty, he watched the wreaths of steam, until at the special instant of projection he caught up the iron vessel and gave it one delicate twirl, causing it to send forth one gentle hiss. Then he restored the contents to the jug; held over the steam of the jug each of the three bright glasses in succession; finally filled them all, and with a clear conscience waited the applause of his fellow-creatures.'

Our Mutual Friend Bk 1 Ch XIII

PURL

Purl was a simpler drink than Flip (see below), though no doubt it required skill to make it to perfection. It was made originally from ale spiced with wormwood, and then it became warm ale spiced with nutmeg and ginger, and the like, then sweetened with sugar; by the nineteenth century gin was customarily added. *Continued overpage*

FLIP

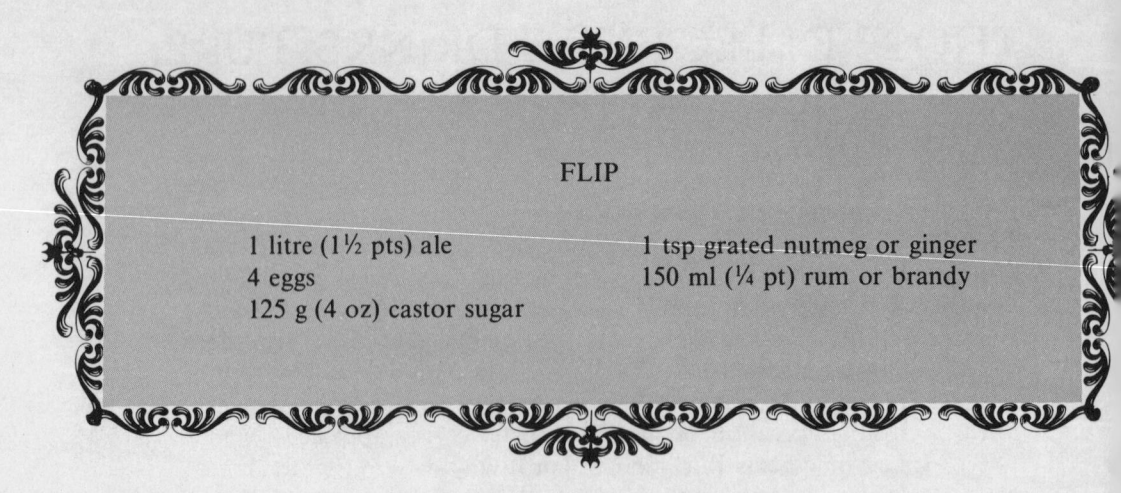

1 litre (1½ pts) ale
4 eggs
125 g (4 oz) castor sugar

1 tsp grated nutmeg or ginger
150 ml (¼ pt) rum or brandy

Failing the possession of 'one of those iron models of sugar-loaf hats' and an open fire, place the ale in a saucepan, and warm it. Beat together the eggs, nutmeg or ginger, and the sugar, then beat in the rum or brandy. Pour the egg mixture into a jug. When the ale is very hot, pour it into another jug. Pour it from one container to another until it is as smooth as cream. This was styled 'One Yard of Flannel'.

Note: The quantities used varied. Another recipe calls for the same amount of eggs and sugar, but mixes them with 2½ litres (4 pt) of ale and 300 ml (½ pt) of gin.

DOG'S NOSE

Warm 300 ml (½ pt) of ale, and to it add wine glass of gin. Add a further 300 ml (½ pt) of cold ale; serve.

A JUG OF EGG-HOT FOR TWO

"We sat before a little fire, with two bricks put within the rusted grate, one on each side, to prevent its burning too many coals; until another debtor, who shared the room with Mr. Micawber, came in from the bake-house with the loin of mutton which was our joint-stock repast. Then I was sent up to Captain Hopkins' in the room overhead, with Mr. Micawber's compliments, and I was his young friend, and would Captain Hopkins lend me a knife and fork ...

There was something gipsy-like and agreeable in the dinner, after all. I took back Captain Hopkins's knife and fork early in the afternoon, and went home to comfort Mrs. Micawber with an account of my visit. She fainted when she saw me return, and made a little jug of egg-hot afterwards to console us while we talked it over."

David Copperfield Ch XI

Beat the eggs with the 2 tablespoons of water. Heat, but do not boil, the cup of water and the sherry. Pour the heated liquid over the eggs, stirring all the time. Sweeten to taste with a little sugar, and add a little nutmeg. Place the mixture in the top of a double saucepan and heat gently. Stir until the mixture thickens. Serve.

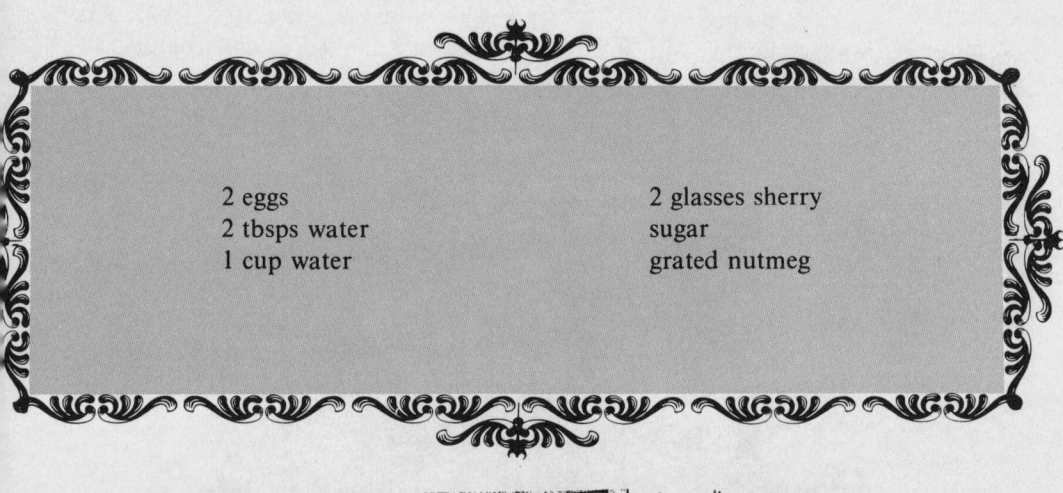

2 eggs
2 tbsps water
1 cup water
2 glasses sherry
sugar
grated nutmeg

A BOWL OF BISHOP

> At half-past ten—late hours for the square—there appeared a little tray of sandwiches and a bowl of bishop, which bishop coming on the top of the double-diamond, and other excitements, had such an effect upon Tim Linkinwater, that he drew Nicholas aside, and gave him to understand, confidentially, that it was quite true about the uncommonly handsome spinster, and that she was to the full as good-looking as she had been described ...

Nicholas Nickleby Ch XXXVII

'Take three best oranges, and grill them to a pale brown colour over a clear fire. Place them in a small punch bowl, and pour over them half a pint of claret, in which a pound and a quarter of loaf sugar is dissolved, and cover it. When served, cut the oranges into pieces, and place in a jug containing the remainder of the bottle of claret, made hot. Some use Lisbon wine instead of claret.

"Fine oranges
Well roasted with sugar, and wine in a cup,
They'll a sweet bishop make when gentle-folks sup."
—Swift.'

A more modern approach is to grill two good, thin-skinned oranges under a low heat, until they are a pale brown colour. Pierce each orange several times with a knife, place them in a bowl, and add 125 g (4 oz) sugar. Add the contents of a bottle of red wine, cover, and leave to stand for a day and a night. Serve warmed or cold.

CHARLES DICKENS'S OWN PUNCH

'To divert his thoughts from this melancholy subject, I informed Mr. Micawber that I relied upon him for a bowl of punch, and led him to the lemons. His recent despondency, not to say despair, was gone in a moment. I never saw a man so thoroughly enjoy himself amid the fragrance of lemon-peel and sugar, the odour of burning rum, and the steam of boiling water, as Mr. Micawber did that afternoon. It was wonderful to see his face shining at us out of a thin cloud of these delicate fumes, as he stirred, and mixed, and tasted, and looked as if he were making, instead of punch, a fortune for his family down to the latest posterity.'

David Copperfield Ch XXVIII

No doubt it is of the punch which he himself made that Dickens is thinking in this description of the intricate rites involved in making the brew. In a letter which Dickens wrote in 1847, he gave his own recipe for making punch, and the extract is below. Dickens's instructions should not be followed completely today: the punch should be left to warm on top of the stove, not in it; it possibly could alight in a modern oven.

'Peel into a very common basin (which may be broken in case of accident, without damage to the owner's peace or pocket) the rinds of three lemons, cut very thin and with as little as possible of the white coating between the peel and the fruit, attached. Add a double handful of lump sugar (good measure), a pint of good old rum, and a large wine-glass of good old brandy—if it be not a large claret glass, say two. Set this on fire, by filling a warm silver spoon with the spirit, lighting the contents at a wax taper, and pouring them gently in. Let it burn three or four minutes at least, stirring it from time to time. Then extinguish it by covering the basin with a tray, which will immediately put out the flame. Then squeeze in the juice of the three lemons, and add a quart of *boiling* water. Stir the whole well, cover it up for five minutes, and stir again.

At this crisis (having skimmed off the lemon pips with a spoon) you may taste. If not sweet enough, add sugar to your liking, but observe that it will be a *little* sweeter presently. Pour the whole into a jug, tie a leather or coarse cloth over the top, so as to exclude the air completely, and stand it in a hot oven ten minutes, or on a hot stove one quarter of an hour. Keep it until it comes to table in a warm place near the fire, but not too hot. If it be intended to stand three or four hours, take half the lemon peel out, or it will acquire a bitter taste. The same punch allowed to grow cool by degrees, and then iced, is delicious.'

A MIGHTY BOWL OF WASSAIL

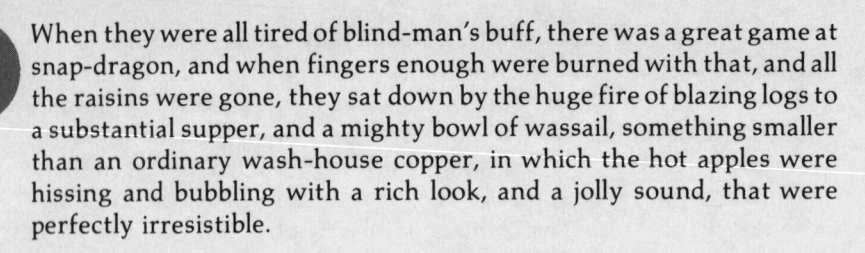

When they were all tired of blind-man's buff, there was a great game at snap-dragon, and when fingers enough were burned with that, and all the raisins were gone, they sat down by the huge fire of blazing logs to a substantial supper, and a mighty bowl of wassail, something smaller than an ordinary wash-house copper, in which the hot apples were hissing and bubbling with a rich look, and a jolly sound, that were perfectly irresistible.

The Pickwick Papers Ch XXVIII

I urged ... that I was possessed by the desire to treat the travellers to a supper and a temperate glass of hot wassail; that the voice of fame had been heard in that land, declaring my ability to make hot wassail ... In the end I prevailed, to my great joy. It was settled that at nine o'clock that night a turkey and a piece of roast-beef should smoke upon the board ...

The Seven Poor Travellers

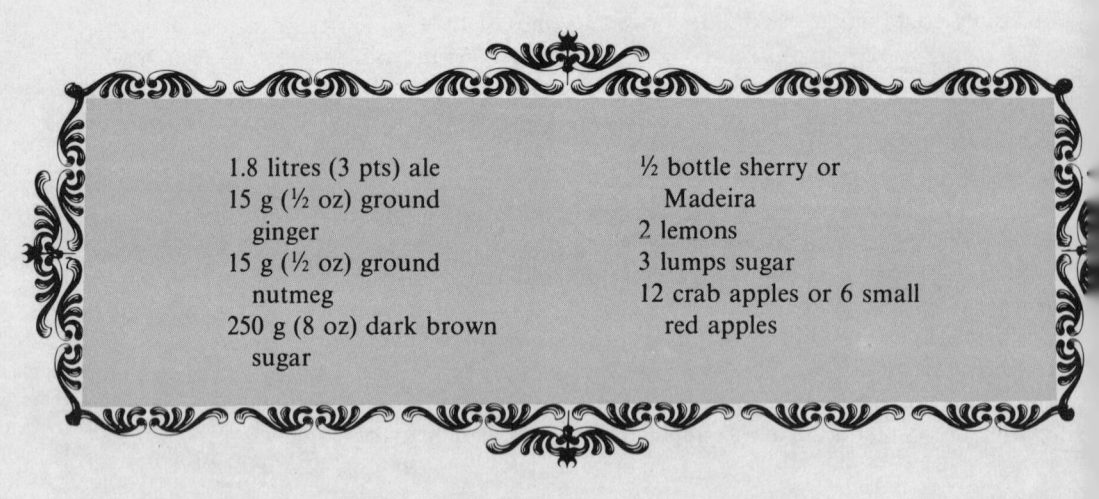

1.8 litres (3 pts) ale
15 g (½ oz) ground ginger
15 g (½ oz) ground nutmeg
250 g (8 oz) dark brown sugar
½ bottle sherry or Madeira
2 lemons
3 lumps sugar
12 crab apples or 6 small red apples

Place 2½ cups of the ale in a saucepan, add the ginger, nutmeg, and the brown sugar, and bring to the boil. Rub the lumps of sugar on the outside of one of the lemons, to remove all the zest. Thinly slice the other lemon. Add the sugar lumps, the sherry or Madeira, and the rest of the ale, to the saucepan, and make it very hot, but do not boil. Place the lemon slices in a large bowl, and pour the hot liquid over them. Add the sizzling roasted apples. To roast the apples: Slit the skin for easier cooking, and bake the apples in a moderate oven until their texture looks soft and mashable. During cooking, baste with a little ale if they appear to be becoming too dry.

Miscellaneous

THE DEMNITION EGG

'It's very easy to talk,' said Mrs. Mantalini.
'Not so easy when one is eating a demnition egg,' replied Mr. Mantalini; 'for the yolk runs down the waistcoat, and yolk of egg does not match any waistcoat but a yellow waistcoat, demmit.'

Nicholas Nickleby Ch XVII

To boil an egg: 'Put the eggs into boiling water, and let them take about three minutes. They are said to be good for clearing the voice.'

To poach an egg: 'Break it into boiling water and dip some of the water, with a spoon, upon it, or them, as the case may be, until cooked to suit; then lift with a skimmer, upon a plate, or upon slices of buttered toast, or into egg cups, in which a bit of butter has just been put, and let each, otherwise, season to suit themselves.'

To make mirror eggs: 'Spread a piece of butter upon a dish that can be set on the fire, break the eggs over it, adding salt, pepper and two spoon-fuls milk; place it on a slow fire, with a red-hot shovel over it, and serve when the eggs are set.'

A WILD EXTENT OF NEW CHEESES

Many and many a pleasant stroll they had in Covent Garden Market; snuffing up the perfume of the fruits and flowers, wondering at the magnificence of the pine-apples and melons; catching glimpses down side avenues, of rows and rows of old women, seated on inverted baskets shelling peas; looking unutterable things at the fat bundles of asparagus with which the dainty shops were fortified as with a breastwork; and, at the herbalists' doors, gratefully inhaling scents as of veal-stuffing yet uncooked, dreamily mixed up with capsicums, brown-paper, seeds: even with hints of lusty snails and fine young curly leeches. Many and many a pleasant stroll they had among the poultry markets, where ducks and fowls, with necks unnaturally long, lay stretched out in pairs, ready for cooking: where there were speckled eggs in mossy baskets, white country sausages beyond impeachment by surviving cat or dog, or horse or donkey, new cheeses to any wild extent, live birds in coops and cages, looking much too big to be natural, in consequence of those receptacles being much too little; rabbits, alive and dead, innumerable. Many a pleasant stroll they had among the cool, refreshing, silvery fish-stalls, with a kind of moonlight effect about their stock-in-trade, excepting always for the ruddy lobsters.

Martin Chuzzlewit Ch XL

Homemade cheese was a readily procured product; it could come from an established home industry, or it could be made occasionally as supplies of milk allowed. When the night's milk came in, it would be strained into large pans and left where it would keep sweet and cool throughout the night. In the morning, the cream would be dipped off, and the milk emptied into a tub. The morning's milk would be slightly warmed and added to that which had been kept the previous night. The cream was then returned to the milk by washing it through a strainer with some of the warmed milk. Rennet was added, the tub covered, and all was left until it had completely turned.

The cheese hoop, covered with a cheese cloth, was then placed above another tub, and with a skimmer the curd was placed in it. The curd was pressed down with the hands, and more was added until it sank or settled to the bottom of the cloth. The newly forming cheese was placed in a clean hoop, salt was added, and it was pressed by a weighted board for two to three hours. A new cloth, a longer pressing in the hoop, then the cheese was re-salted and pressed again. No whey was to remain in the cheese, as this produced a bad flavour.

Beautiful cheese from buttermilk would also be made:

'The buttermilk, after being boiled and allowed to stand until cool, is placed in a cheese-form or heavy linen bag until the whey is drained off, when it is salted, not too heavily, and spiced according to taste, and thoroughly mixed. About a spoonful of alcohol is then added for each pound, and the mass is thoroughly kneaded, and formed into cheeses of any desired size or form, which are dried in the air, and then wrapped in clean linen cloths that have previously been moistened with hot whey, and packed in a well-covered cask, and stowed in a warm place. Four days suffice to render them fit for use, but they improve by age.' If the small cheeses became too dry, they were often wrapped in horseradish leaves, and packed in a cask, to restore them.

The most charming little cheeses could be made by anyone from small quantities of cream. Small wooden moulds could be bought, and homemade mats of common rushes were placed at the bottom of them. The mould was placed on a dish, the mat placed in the bottom, then a fine piece of muslin dipped in brine. Then the sweetest of cream was added. More muslin, another rush mat, and then a block of wood to add pressure. This was placed in a cool place for three days, after which it would be ready for eating.

HOT BUTTERED TOAST

' The fire was blazing brightly under the influence of the bellows, and the kettle was singing gaily under the influence of both. A small tray of tea-things was arranged on the table, a plate of hot buttered toast was gently simmering before the fire, and the red-nosed man himself was busily engaged in converting a large slice of bread into the same agreeable edible, through the instrumentality of a long brass toasting-fork. Beside him stood a glass of reeking hot pine-apple rum and water, with a slice of lemon in it; and every time the red-nosed man stopped to bring the round of toast to his eye, with the view of ascertaining how it got on, he imbibed a drop or two of the hot pine-apple rum and water, and smiled upon the rather stout lady, as she blew the fire.

The Pickwick Papers Ch XXVII

The responsible duty of making the toast was delegated to the Aged, and that excellent old gentleman was so intent upon it that he seemed to me in some danger of melting his eyes. It was no nominal meal that we were going to make, but a vigorous reality. The Aged prepared such a haystack of buttered toast, that I could scarcely see him over it as it simmered on an iron stand hooked on to the top bar; while Miss Skiffins brewed such a jorum of tea, that the pig in the back premises became strongly excited, and repeatedly expressed his desire to participate in the entertainment ... We ate the whole of the toast, and drank tea in proportion, and it was delightful to see how warm and greasy we all got after it. The Aged especially, might have passed for some clean old chief of a savage tribe, just oiled.

Great Expectations Ch XXXVII *'*

There is something quite specially relaxing about making toast in front of the fire; it allows anticipation to combine with a simple watchful cooking process that needs no beating or scraping or stirring or spattering—merely the pleasure of being seated before good coals. To make toast in the old-fashioned way, as many nice even slices as are needed should be cut, each about 7 mm (¼ in) thick; the fire should be of good bright coals. The bread should be impaled on a toasting fork, being toasted first on one side and then on another, until it is a good colour, never burnt. For delicacy, trim off the crust; for plain eating, leave it on. Good butter should be used, and each slice should be cut as soon as it is buttered (there are those who advocate buttering it on both sides); the slices should be piled lightly on a dish on which they are to be served. Keep them warm by the fire. It is inadvisable to cut through four or five slices at a time, as all the butter is squeezed from the top ones, while the bottom one swims in liquid. Serve with tea, or, perchance, pineapple rum.

THE DELICACY OF ANCHOVY TOAST

'Arthur ... repaired to his mother's room, where Mr. Casby and Flora had been taking tea, anchovy paste, and hot buttered toast. The relics of those delicacies were not yet removed, either from the table, or from the scorched countenance of Affery, who, with the kitchen toasting-fork still in her hand, looked like a sort of allegorical personage; except that she had a considerable advantage over the general run of such personages, in point of significant emblematical purpose.'

Little Dorrit Ch XXIII

In Dickens's day, the anchovies were usually acquired whole, to be filleted by the cook. Anchovy butter, anchovy paste, and potted anchovies are very similar—often, indeed, the same. Differences usually come from the strength of the anchovy flavour in proportion to the amount of butter and seasonings that the pounded anchovy flesh is mixed with. Potted anchovies, for instance, required the fillets from two dozen anchovies to be pounded with 250 g (8 oz) butter, while anchovy butter had the proportion of the fillets of six anchovies to 500 g (1 lb) butter. Where the mixture was a strong one, the toast would first be buttered; where not, the butter in the mixture served. Anchovy butter was often made into small pats, which were piled on to a plate and served as a breakfast accompaniment. Now we usually buy anchovies already filleted and in a tin; it is a simple matter to make them into anchovy butter.

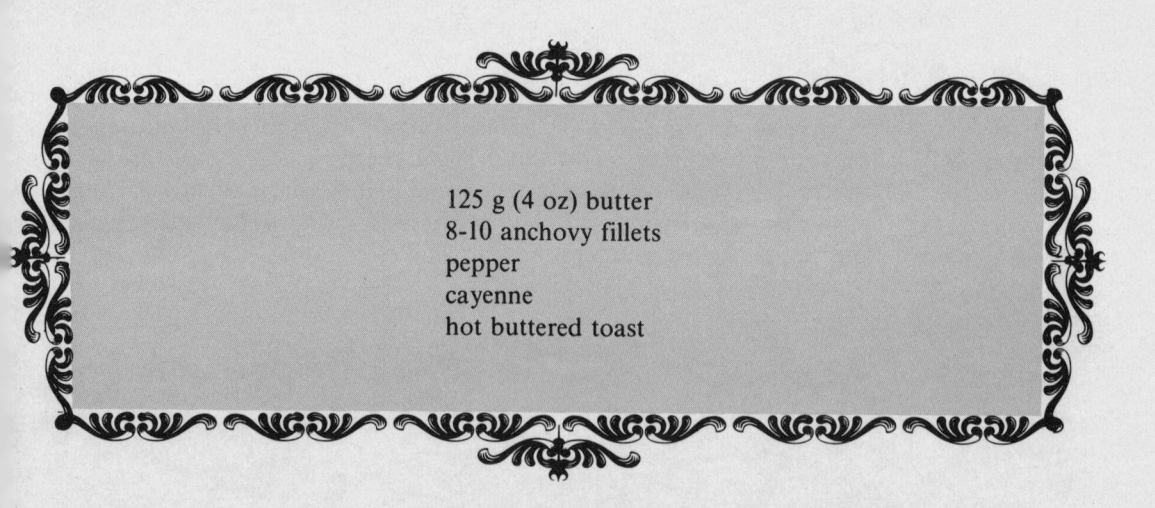

---

125 g (4 oz) butter
8-10 anchovy fillets
pepper
cayenne
hot buttered toast

Pound the anchovies to form a paste. Soften the butter in a bowl (do not allow it to liquefy) and add the anchovy flesh. Blend both well together. Mix in well a good sprinkling of pepper and cayenne. Cool. Form into one large, or several small, pats, or place the mixture in a small compact pot. Serve with hot buttered toast.

Note: A small quantity of made mustard and mace or nutmeg can also be added to the anchovy mixture.

Another pleasant way of eating anchovy toast is to spread the toast with anchovy butter, lattice the top of the toast with anchovy fillets, and place under a hot grill to heat through.

AN ALTERNATIVE TO MRS PRIG'S SALAD DRESSING

' Mrs. Prig, looking steadfastly at her friend, put her hand in her pocket, and with an air of surly triumph drew forth either the oldest of lettuces or the youngest of cabbages, but at any rate, a green vegetable of expansive nature, and of such magnificent proportions that she was obliged to shut it up like an umbrella before she could pull it out. She also produced a handful of mustard and cress, a trifle of the herb called dandelion, three bunches of radishes, an onion rather larger than an average turnip, three substantial slices of beetroot, and a short prong or antler of celery: the whole of this garden stuff having been publicly exhibited, but a short time before, as a twopenny salad, and purchased by Mrs. Prig on condition that the vendor could get it all into her pocket. Which had been happily accomplished, in High Holborn, to the breathless interest of a hackney-coach stand. And she laid so little stress on this surprising forethought, that she did not even smile, but returning her pocket into its accustomed sphere, merely recommended that these productions of nature should be sliced up, for immediate consumption, in plenty of vinegar.
'And don't go a-droppin' none of your snuff in it,' said Mrs. Prig. 'In gruel, barley-water, apple-tea, mutton-broth, and that, it don't signify. It stimulates a patient. But I don't relish it myself.'

Martin Chuzzlewit Ch XLIX

Those who would wish to demur against vinegar as a salad dressing, but desire to keep to the tone of the times, might try this possibility (perhaps upon a selection of fresh, washed and dried salad greens, garnished afterwards with 'hard-boiled eggs, cut in slices, sliced cucumbers, nasturtiums, cut vegetable-flowers, and many other things that taste will always suggest to make a pretty and elegant dish'):

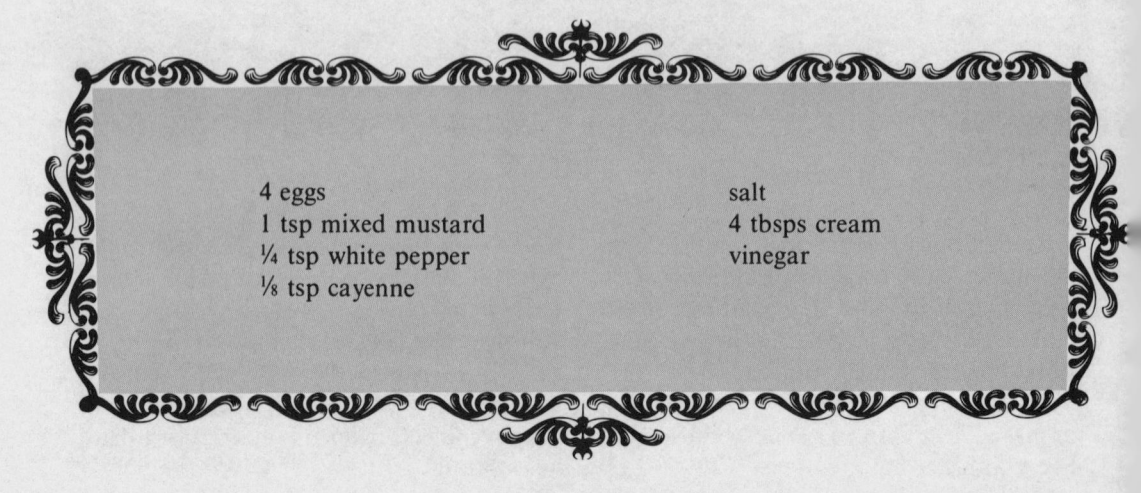

4 eggs
1 tsp mixed mustard
¼ tsp white pepper
⅛ tsp cayenne

salt
4 tbsps cream
vinegar

'Boil the eggs until hard, which will be in about ¼ hour or 20 minutes; put them into cold water, take off the shells, and pound the yolks in a mortar to a smooth paste. Then add all the other ingredients, except the vinegar, and stir them well until the whole are thoroughly incorporated one with the other. Pour in sufficient vinegar to make it of the consistency of cream, taking care to add but little at a time. The mixture will then be ready for use ... The whites of the eggs, cut into rings, will serve very well as a garnishing to the salad.'

STIR-ABOUT

> At one o'clock, the boys, having previously had their appetites thoroughly taken away by stir-about and potatoes, sat down in the kitchen to some hard salt beef, of which Nicholas was graciously permitted to take his portion to his own solitary desk, to eat it there in peace.
>
> *Nicholas Nickleby* Ch VIII

Stir-about was one of the innumerable dishes devised for the sending of oatmeal to the table; it is a dish which can be immensely agreeable when presented as a porridge in combination with cream, honey, and brown sugar, but one that is hardly delectable when it basically consists of water. Stir-about 'is made by very gradually shaking over and stirring into water boiling over the fire, as much oatmeal as will bring it to the thickness required'. The nineteenth-century writer considered this not such an economical dish as that made by the process of soaking the oatmeal overnight, and then boiling it; given that opinion, it would seem odd that Mrs Squeers produced it the way she did; but no doubt her pence-saving was achieved by the ambiguity of 'to the thickness required'.

Another similar dish, 'brose', was made by pouring boiling water on oatmeal, then stirring it until it became thick and smooth; 'fat brose' was made by proceeding in the same manner, but adding soup skimmings to the dish.

While The Chimes were yet in operation out of doors ...

Index

Almond cakes, a shilling in 142
Anchovy toast, the delicacy of 171
Apple parsties 129
Apple pudding, baked 112
Apple sauce 56
Arrowroot gruel 11

Baked apple pudding 112
Baked cherry batter pudding 114
Baked currant batter pudding 113
Baked puddings, the little apparition's 115
Bakewell tart 128
Balls, brandy 149
Barley water 11
Barnaby Rudge 32, 46, 58, 76, 82, 137, 138
Batter pudding, baked cherry 114
Batter pudding, baked currant 113
Batter pudding, plain baked 114
Batter pudding, the waiter's favourite 113
Beef, a dish of stewed 50
Beef, cold boiled, and beer, the grateful influence of 46
Beefsteak and kidney pie 68
Beefsteak and mushroom pie 70
Beefsteak pudding 44
Beef-tea, a basin of 10
Biffins 148
Biscuits, soft, seedy 140
Bishop, a bowl of 164
Bleak House 40, 57, 60, 70, 92, 120, 149, 155
Bloaters, Yarmouth, a savoury meal of 21
Boiled leg of mutton with caper sauce 26
Boiled chicken and parsley butter, a very Lord Mayor's feast of 62
Boiled turbot—a noble dish of fish 21
Bones, marrow 101
Brawn 95
Bread-and-butter pudding, Mrs Walmer's 118
Breaded lamb chops and warm ale 32
Broth, mutton, with a chop 8
Butter, parsley 63

Cake, plum-, homemade 144
Cake, sweet seed 146
Cake, twelfth 145
Cakes, almond, a shilling in 142
Cakes, Yorkshire, for breakfast 137
Calf's head pie 39
Calf's-foot jelly, a delicate restorative 98
Caper sauce 27
Caudle 10
Charles Dickens's own punch 165
Cheese, pork 97
Cheese, toasted, pettitoes and 87

Cheeses, new, a wild extent of 168
Chicken, boiled, a very Lord Mayor's feast of 62
Chicken, roast, with shrimp stuffing and forcemeat balls 60
Chimes, The 80
Chocolate, Monseigneur's drinking 154
Chops, breaded lamb, and warm ale 32
Chops, grilled mutton 33
Christmas Carol, A 46, 95, 122
Christmas mince pie, Mrs Joe's 124
Christmas plum pudding, a speckled cannon-ball of a 122
Cobbler, sherry 157
Cod and oyster pie 18
Cricket on the Hearth, The 101

Damson pudding 121
David Copperfield 22, 28, 32, 35, 50, 56, 70, 100, 107, 113, 115, 117, 129, 140, 142, 143, 146, 163, 165
Devilled grill and kidneys, a 85
Devilled sauce (1) 85
Devilled sauce (2) 86
Dog's nose 162
Dombey and Son 14, 16, 33, 38, 85, 88, 90, 94, 102, 106, 130, 156, 158
Dressed tongue carved with a pair of scissors 92
Dumplings, suet 47

Egg sauce and sausages 102
Egg, the demnition 168
Egg, to boil 168
Egg, to poach 168
Egg-hot for two, a jug of 163
Eggs, mirror, to make 168

Fig pudding 119
Fingers, ladies', to dip in wine 141
Flip 162
Flip, sherry 156
Forcemeat balls, roast chicken with shrimp stuffing and 60
Fry, a little, for supper 88

Gingerbread, a partiality for 143
Goose, roast, Mrs Chirrup's 64
Goose stuffing 65
Goose stuffing, or sage and onion, sauce 65
Gravy soup, a judicious 9
Gravy, the passion for 52
Great Expectations 34, 49, 56, 60, 62, 74, 124, 130, 170
Grilled kidneys to serve with devilled sauce 86
Grilled mutton chops 33
Gruel, arrowroot 11
Gruel, oatmeal 11
Gruel, water 11

Haggis, a lamb's head and a 99
Ham, broiled, rashers of, done to a turn 58
Hardbake 151
Hashed mutton 30
Holly-tree, The 118, 148
Hot buttered toast 170
Hot negus 158
Hot pot 33

Irish stew, a nice 35

Jam roly-poly pudding 120
Jelly, a cooling 132
Jelly, calf's foot, a delicate restorative 98

Ketchup, mushroom 28
Kidneys, a devilled grill and 85
Kidneys, grilled, to serve with devilled sauce 86
Kidneys, stewed, a supper of 84

Ladies' fingers to dip in wine 141
Lamb chops, breaded, and warm ale 32
Lamb's head and a haggis 99
Lemonade 155
Little Dorrit 23, 26, 43, 52, 68, 108, 118, 132, 136, 156, 157, 171
Lobster salad 14
Lumps-of-delight 150

Marrow bones 101
Martin Chuzzlewit 10, 16, 20, 30, 44, 48, 52, 58, 84, 96, 126, 127, 157, 168, 172, 150, 185, 199, 205
Meat, fried sausage, a beautiful little dinner with 100
Meat patties 39
Meat, Strasburg, potted 96
Meats, some potted 96
Melted butter celery sauce at Christmas 66
Melted butter sauce 66
Mincemeat for preserving 125
Monseigneur's drinking chocolate 154
Mr Barley's lamb and split pea stew 34
Mr Micawber's devilled mutton 29
Mr Pinch's steak 48
Mr Venus's muffins 138
Mrs Bagnet's boiled pork 57
Mrs Chirrup's roast goose 64
Mrs Crummles's onion sauce 36
Mrs Joe's Christmas mince pie 124
Mrs Micawber's loin of pork and apple sauce 56
Mrs Prig's salad dressing, an alternative to 172
Mrs Walmer's bread-and-butter pudding 118
Muffins, Mr Venus's 138
Mulled port 159

Mushroom ketchup 28
Mutton, boiled leg of, with caper sauce 26
Mutton broth with a chop 8
Mutton chops, grilled 33
Mutton, hashed 30
Mutton, Mr Micawber's devilled 29
Mutual Friend, Our 8, 15, 42, 68, 72, 119, 138, 158, 160, 161
Mystery of Edwin Drood, The 66, 90, 92, 141, 145, 150

Negus, hot 158
Nicholas Nickleby 36, 44, 54, 92, 112, 147, 164, 168, 173

Oatmeal gruel 11
Old Curiosity Shop, The 17, 21, 82, 98, 106, 144
Oliver Twist 77
Onion sauce, Mrs Crummles's 36
Onions, tripe and 83
Oranges, a pretty dish of 131
Oranges steeped in wine 130
Oyster pie, cod and 18
Oysters, pickled 16
Oysters, stewed 16

Parsley butter 63
Parsties, apple 129
Patties, meat 39
Pennywinkles 16
Periwinkles (*see Pennywinkles*)
Pettitoes and toasted cheese 87
Pickled oysters 16
Pickled salmon, a little bit of 20
Pickwick Papers, The 18, 22, 26, 46, 72, 78, 87, 99, 128, 151, 159, 160, 166, 170
Pie, a round compact raised pork 74
Pie, a very mellering veal and ham 72
Pie, beefsteak and kidney 68
Pie, beefsteak and mushroom 70
Pie, calf's head 39
Pie, Christmas mince, Mrs Joe's 124
Pie, cod and oyster 18
Pie, pigeon 78
Pie, rabbit, sitch a 77
Pie, venison 76
Pig, roast sucking 54
Pigeon pie 78
Plain baked batter pudding 114
Plum-cake, homemade 144
Pork cheese 97
Pork, Mrs Bagnet's boiled 57
Pork, Mrs Micawber's loin of, and apple sauce 56
Pork pie, a round compact raised 74
Port, mulled 159
Potato stew, tripe and 80
Potato, the carbuncular 106
Potatoes in a pudding dish 107
Potatoes, mashed 107
Potatoes, roast 109
Potted meat, Strasburg 96
Potted meats, some 96

Pressed tongues of sheep in curl-paper 94
Pudding, baked apple 112
Pudding, baked cherry batter 114
Pudding, baked currant batter 113
Pudding, batter, the waiter's favourite 113
Pudding, beafsteak 44
Pudding, Christmas plum, a speckled cannon-ball of a 122
Pudding, damson 121
Pudding, fig 119
Pudding, jam roly-poly 120
Pudding, Mrs Walmers's bread-and-butter 118
Pudding, plain baked batter 114
Pudding, treacle 117
Pudding, Yorkshire 108
Puddings, the little apparition's baked 115
Punch, Charles Dickens's own 165
Purl 161

Rabbit pie, sitch a 77
Rashers of broiled ham, done to a turn 58
Raspberry jam tart, the precious 127
Report of the First Meeting of the Mudfog Association 11
Report of the Second Meeting of the Mudfog Association 9
Roast chicken with shrimp stuffing and forcemeat balls 60
Roast potatoes 109
Roast sucking pig 54
Roly-poly pudding, jam 120
Rusks, a dish of 136

Sage and onion, or goose stuffing sauce 65
Salad dressing, Mrs Prig's, an alternative to 172
Salad, lobster 14
Salmon, pickled, a little bit of 20
Sauce, apple 56
Sauce, caper 27
Sauce, devilled (1) 85
Sauce, devilled (2) 86
Sauce, egg, and sausages 102
Sauce, melted butter 66
Sauce, melted butter celery, at Christmas 66
Sauce, Mrs Crummles's onion 36
Sauce, sage and onion, or goose stuffing 65
Sauce, shrimp, to promote quiet digestion 23
Sausage meat, fried, a beautiful little dinner with 100
Sausages, egg sauce and 102
Sausages, various homemade 102
Seed cake, sweet 146
Seven poor Travellers, The 122, 166
Sherry cobbler 157
Sherry flip 156

Shrimp sauce to promote quiet digestion 23
Shrimp stuffing, with roast chicken and forcemeat balls 60
Shrub and water 160
Sketches of Young Couples 14, 64, 121, 146
Soft, seedy biscuits 140
Soles, a pair of 22
Soup, gravy, a judicious 9
Soyer's goose stuffing 65
Steak, Mr Pinch's 48
Steak, stewed, Wemmick's 49
Stew, a nice Irish 35
Stew, Mr Barley's, lamb and split pea 34
Stew of tripe, a savoury 82
Stew, tripe and potato 80
Stewed kidneys, a supper of 84
Stewed oysters 16
Stir-about 173
Strasburg potted meat 96
Stuffed fillet of veal 38
Stuffed roast of veal 41
Stuffing, goose 65
Stuffing, Soyer's goose 65
Suet dumplings 47
Sweet seed cake 146
Sweetbreads, the soporific agency of 90

Tale of Two Cities, A 134
Tart, bakewell 128
Tart, raspberry jam, the precious 127
Tart, treacle 126
Tarts to make the flesh shine 147
Toast, anchovy, the delicacy of 17
Toast, hot buttered 170
Tongue, dressed, carved with a pair of scissors 92
Tongues of sheep, pressed, in curl-paper 94
Treacle pudding 117
Treacle tart 126
Tripe, a savoury stew of 82
Tripe and onions 83
Tripe and potato stew 80
Turbot, boiled, a noble dish of fish 21
Twelfth cake 145

Veal and ham pie, a very mellering
Veal cutlet, the relative merits of 4
Veal in savoury jelly 43
Veal, stuffed fillet of 38
Veal, stuffed roast of 41
Venison pie 76

Wassail, a mighty bowl of 166
Water, barley 11
Water gruel 11
Wemmick's stewed steak 49
Whitebait at Greenwich 15

Yarmouth bloaters, a savoury meal of 21
Yorkshire cakes for breakfast 137
Yorkshire pudding 108